Jonathan Romney is deputy film ᴄ̶ᴜ̶ᴄ̶ of the *Guardian*, where he writes the Framespotting column. He has also written on film for the *New Statesman*, *Time Out*, *Sight and Sound* and *City Limits*, and on music for *The Wire*. He is co-editor of *Celluloid Jukebox: Popular Music and the Movies since the 50s* (BFI Publishing, 1995).

Other titles in this series:

Gary Indiana
Let It Bleed

Steven Shaviro
Doom Patrols

Kathy Acker
Bodies of Work

Lynne Tillman
The Broad Picture

Short

Orders

film writing

Jonathan Romney

First published in 1997 by
Serpent's Tail, 4 Blackstock Mews, London N4

Library of Congress Catalog Card Number: 97-066229

A catalogue record for this book is available from the British Library on request

The following articles first appeared in *New Statesman and Society*: 'Blade Runner – The Director's Cut'; 'Reservoir Dogs • Man Bites Dog (C'est arrivé près de chez vous)'; 'The Public Eye • Damage'; 'Shadows and Fog'; 'Bad Lieutenant • Mean Streets'; 'Orlando'; 'Candyman • Trespass'; 'The Quince Tree Sun (El Sol de Membrillo)'; 'Groundhog Day'; 'Indecent Proposal'; 'Les Nuits fauves (Savage Nights)'; 'Jurassic Park'; 'Last Action Hero'; 'Sliver • Benny's Video'; 'Blue'; 'The Tale of the Fox (Le Roman de Renard) • The Secret Adventures of Tom Thumb'; 'Heaven & Earth'; 'The Age of Innocence'; 'The Conformist (Il Conformista)'; 'Schindler's List'; 'Short Cuts'; 'The Scent of Green Papaya (L'Odeur de la papaye verte)'; 'Germinal'; 'Priit Pärn – Selected Films'; 'Kika'; 'Wolf'; 'The Lion King'; 'Three Colours: Red (Trois Couleurs: Rouge)'; 'Dear Diary (Caro Diario)'; 'Junior'; 'Wes Craven's New Nightmare'; 'Natural Born Killers • Bandit Queen'; 'The Silences of the Palace (Les Silences du palais)'; 'Eyes Without a Face (Les Yeux sans visage)'; 'Outbreak'; 'Clerks'; 'Jefferson in Paris • Bad Boys'; 'Batman Forever • Casper'; 'The Big Sleep'; 'Apollo 13'; 'The Neon Bible'; 'Crimson Tide'; 'La Haine'. 'Dick Tracy and the Aesthetics of Prosthetics' first appeared in *City Limits*, and 'The Museum at Night: The Brothers Quay' first appeared in *World Art*.

Set in Sabon by Avon Dataset, Bidford-on-Avon
Printed in Great Britain by Mackays of Chatham

Contents

Acknowledgements

For encouragement, support and quality rasping, I'd like to thank Paul Julian Smith, Lizzie Francke, Nick James, Chris Darke, Louise Grey, Glyn Brown and Judith Williamson, a pioneer and role model; Marina Benjamin, Boyd Tonkin and Terri Natale who all processed my work at the *New Statesman*; Sarah Bayliss at *World Art*; Malcolm Imrie at Verso; everyone at the *Guardian* for their continuing support; the BFI Library and *Sight and Sound*; my agent Tony Peake; at Serpent's Tail, Pete Ayrton and Laurence O'Toole for suggesting this collection in the first place, and patience and encouragement thereafter; Emma Waghorn, for ruthless scrutiny of the text; Petra Fried, for helping with the selection and for support throughout; and Lauren Fried, whose eye for metaphor is unerring.

Jonathan Romney

Introduction

Let's pretend, just to get warmed up, that the pieces collected here were written in the white heat of critical passion. The critic goes to see a film he or she knows nothing about, is faced, in the darkness of the screening theatre, with a wholly unpredictable revelation of one kind or another – a vision of the grandeur, misery or sheer indifference of cinema – and then goes home to slam out a review before the morning deadline, fired by the need for immediacy of response.

It's true that a few of these pieces, most of them straightforward reviews, were written overnight, but that may be less to do with deadline pressure than with erratic time-management and a residual addiction to the romance of fatigue and stale coffee. But in most cases I'd seen the films in question weeks, even months, before writing about them, and had already had time to assimilate, consciously or not, other critics' responses to a particular film – even if all I'd had to go on was the grumbling of a dejected Monday lunchtime crowd as they shuffled out after the screening.

For the moment, though, let's pretend that the critic sits alone and unarmed in front of the screen and simply volleys back at it his or her unmediated, pristinely independent reactions. That appealing myth would justify the title I've chosen for this collection: *Short Orders*, to imply that these pieces were written at little or no notice, by a critical hired gun always 'on', always up for the dynamic response. So much for the slow, sub-surface germination and grudging drudgery of much of the watching-and-writing process.

So much too for all those factors that, whether you acknowledge them or not, invariably come between the critic and the first viewing of a film. There is always a host of subliminal expectations that you carry with you: you may already feel you know a film inside out, having read exhaustive pre-publicity, location reports, reviews in *Variety* or the *New Yorker* or *Cahiers du cinéma*. A film may already have hovered for a suspiciously long time on some distributor's release list, so that, however good it turns out to be, it already bears the taint of old news. Or perhaps the screening was arranged by that publicist you don't quite trust, who never returns calls, whose invitations come on nasty turquoise photocopy paper. Perhaps you also suspect that, however curious *you* might be about a particular film, it's unlikely to be the sort of thing that either the public or your editor will find remotely sexy; you only half watch, knowing there's no copy in it. The critic is never untrammelled and impartial; the battlefield is littered with a thousand corpses even before we step onto it; better to acknowledge them and write accordingly.

Short Orders also implies the idea of the critic as short-order chef – the hired hand in the fast-food chain, efficiently shunting pre-packaged burgers. It's widely believed that film criticism is essentially culinary, in the most derogatory sense – that a critic's job is to see a film, digest and then regurgitate it in palatable bite-size (or sound-bite-size) form for readers who may or may not choose to see the film themselves. It should be clear by now that I'm using the term 'film critic' largely to refer to people who review films weekly or monthly for newspapers, listing magazines, trade journals. Technically, you'd have to call them 'reviewers', to distinguish this camp from academic writers on film, people who might regard themselves as film theorists, cultural analysts or historians. But the distinction would be invidious: to call a critic a 'reviewer' is to suggest that film reviewing need not, should not, entail any analysis – cultural, ideological, aesthetic or otherwise. Many working critics seem to accept this assumption. I was recently in the audience for an onstage discussion of 'The Role of the Critic', at which the existence of academic criticism was never invoked; the consensus among the participants was that the critic's role was fundamentally to tell the public whether a particular film was or wasn't worth the price of admission. Someone suggested that, perhaps, if you had the space, you might do a little more – but that something more was simply to say with informed judgement whether Sharon Stone was better in her latest film than in the one before.

Seen in this light, criticism becomes a hermetic activity, in which value judgements themselves become meaningless, because based purely on comparisons between products that are considered to be essentially of the same kind. Such an undertaking entirely sidelines discussion of the possible meanings and functions of cinema, let alone of the – often unreasonable – passions that cinema incites. Contrast Judith Williamson's view, proffered while working as weekly critic on the *New Statesman*, that to ask a film critic which films are worth going to is 'as inappropriate as asking a geographer or geologist why they don't tell you where to go for your holiday: my job ... isn't to provide a brochure of favourite beauty spots but to map out the ground and try to understand its construction'.[1] But in practical terms, in a culture in which cinema-going is largely seen as a holiday activity, most film reviewers are obliged to observe the consumer-service imperative one way or another; space and editorial demands dictate that there may be only so much you can say about how a film operates in the wider cultural context.

This is one reason why film reviews tend to be so heavily descriptive, so laden with plot synopsis; the review becomes a bluffer's guide for people who have no intention of seeing the film, but know they're likely to end up talking about it at dinner parties (fair enough: for years I got away with carping about Merchant-Ivory on as little first-hand knowledge as I could manage). In a culture that privileges the literary over the visual, it's generally held that to describe a film in terms of its narrative is to describe it effectively: to say what it's 'about' is the same as saying what it's 'like'. Seen in this light, a film's plot is its programme, its statement

[1] *Deadline at Dawn* (Marion Boyars, London, 1993), p. 32.

of intent (just as, at pre-production stage, a good script is held to be reliable promise of a good film); whether or not a film works is evaluated in terms of how well it tells its story.

But the recounting of plot also serves a further purpose in the relay between film and viewer, mediated by the critic. It means that viewers will only rarely manage to enter a cinema with little or no idea of what they're going to see. Film-going is very rarely a matter of stepping out in search of the unknown – it's more often a case of having your expectations confirmed, whether that means going to see a Jane Austen adaptation, a flying-glass action movie, the latest Eric Rohmer, or a collection of 'difficult' video shorts. People tend to know what they want, and like critics to point them in the right direction. So rather than viewing a film, cinema-goers more often end up *re*-viewing it: living out for themselves the experience they have already had vicariously from reading the review. To see the film is partly to check out how accurately the film fulfils its programme as described by the critic, largely in the form of a plot synopsis. In fact, critics often get letters complaining that a film hasn't conformed to the description: 'The film I saw was not the film you reviewed.' By this criterion, a good review is one that achieves an adequate, verifiable fit with the film – and a good film will similarly conform to the review. The viewer rarely gets to visit places not already mapped out by the critical Baedeker, and those places have largely been mapped out in advance for the critic too, by the film's pre-publicity, its attendant aura, its buzz.

In terms of the well-regulated marketplace, this is all as it should be. The critic appraises the film accurately and passes on that information: that is, correctly identifies and celebrates those films that are, according to wisdom within the industry, destined to be hits, and sifts out or simply ignores the dross and anything considered to be strictly of minority interest. The critic plays an important part in the smooth functioning of the network, becoming a sort of information shuttle ensuring the correct transmission of messages. Caught up in the industry protocol of attending screenings, of observing press embargoes, of a thousand small civilities, the critic is considered not to be outside the industry but an essential, if mistrusted, part of it. Distributors often feel that a bad review of a film destined for success is doing them a disservice, because it breaks the chain of information; it's as discourteous as breaking a chain letter, or committing industrial sabotage. Distributors and publicists often call a bad review a 'negative' one, as if the critic were simply being refractory, refusing to play the game.

But with cinema culture increasingly dominated by monolithic received wisdom (this film will be big, this director will never again be interesting, this type of film-making is not even worth addressing), one of the critic's most valuable functions is to disturb the institutional flow of opinion. The late Serge Daney – a former editor of *Cahiers du cinéma*, and columnist in the daily newspaper *Libération* – proposed another agenda entirely: the critic's work, he argued, should be a '*carnet de route*', a sort of traveller's diary, recording chance encounters, rather than simply the obligatory ones imposed by the contingencies of release schedules and the demands of prevailing good sense. The best encounters, he argued, cannot be pre-programmed, cannot be inscribed into a system of messages successfully transmitted and received, of films that 'work', that find their correct audience, that perform to expectation. The system shouldn't be able to count on the dutiful complicity of critics.

In place of the message 'correctly' received, Daney argues that a dynamic film culture thrives on misreading, 'successful misunder- standing'.[2] What's proposed is a sort of cultural promiscuity and perversity, a commitment to pleasures that aren't programmed or legislated. This is more easily realisable, perhaps, in the film culture of Paris, where it's still possible to immerse yourself in an atmosphere of possibility, of diversity, of the less expected. Chance discoveries are still possible at the various *cinémathèques* and at retrospectives on the repertory circuit, while two monthly journals, *Cahiers* and *Positif*, still devote much of their space to cinema history. In Britain, however, such promiscuity is increasingly

[2] *Devant la recrudescence des vols de sac à main: Cinéma, télévision, information (1988–1991)* (Aléas, Lyon, 1991), pp. 111–12.

unattainable. Fewer non-American films than ever are being released, and if released are barely being seen, as the independent repertory network continues to crumble. Discoveries of unfamiliar terrain, usually under the marginalising category of 'cult' cinema – whether it's Kieślowski, Almodóvar or Japanese *anime* – tend to look somewhat regimented, born as much from marketing as from critical initiatives, and largely at the expense of other material worthy of exposure. It's increasingly hard to justify writing about films that few British audiences will ever see. The critic is obliged to operate in the climate of the date-tied and available. In weeks when – and this is not unknown – the only new film released is the latest Schwarzenegger vehicle, then Daneyesque ideals of chance and openness tend to look a little quixotic. Such is the cultural divide: the British critic obliged to advise, 'If you only go and see one film this week …', and the Parisian *cinéphile* recoiling in horror: 'But how can you *possibly* see only one film a week?'

Meanwhile, there's clearly a need to evolve more flexible strategies for writing about new cinema. In the 1970s and 1980s, mainstream cinema as a field of popular culture gained recognition as a legitimate object of study, first in academia and then in the popular print media, through magazines such as *City Limits*, the style magazines of the 1980s and, briefly, the *Modern Review* – by which time, pop-cultural analysis had become something of an orthodoxy. It's long been common to read the latest film releases as if they were not simply products of the zeitgeist but transparent indicators of it – as if, by virtue of its commercial predominance, any Hollywood success unfailingly had a message to impart about the way we live and signify today.

It has become apparent, though, that mainstream cinema has taken this sort of reading to heart, and that the most apparently straightforward narrative productions are now very much packaged as bundles of subtext, that children's films (*Casper*, *Jumanji*) are increasingly *about* the culture of therapy and the fragmented family, that horror films (*Candyman*, Francis Coppola's *Bram Stoker's Dracula*) increasingly and explicitly foreground debates about sexual identity, the Other, fear of contagion ... Movies, in other words, are increasingly pitched at the cultural analysts, at the makers of smart think-pieces, as if Hollywood had latched on to the sign-chasing intelligentsia as the missing part of the demographic jigsaw, a further target audience to be corralled. It's increasingly rare now to find a major Hollywood film that still requires critical intervention to make it 'interesting', that doesn't come ready-loaded with themes for analysis. What was once below the surface is now stitched into it, and no-one misses out, not even the cultural dissenter.

One response to this rather arid state of affairs would be for the critic to adopt the stance of an intransigent high-art militant – to refuse to write about anything other than the most recondite avant-gardism (yes, but try and make a living out of that). The more viable, indeed more pressing, alternative is to remain open to unreasonable enthusiasms, to wilful perversity, and let these shape the criticism. Yield sometimes to mirages; of course, few of us can get away with devoting more column inches to a Hungarian small-town comedy than to *Jurassic Park*, but what if you wrote about *Jurassic Park* as if it were a Hungarian small-town comedy, and vice versa? It sounds like a great precept, and I only regret it's occurred to me in hindsight, or who knows how some of the following pieces might have turned out. I'm only sure that, increasingly, analytical lucidity is going to need non-lucidity as a back-up, as a source of rhetorical energies. That's where the short deadline, the overnight writing panic, can come in useful, forcing you to write from the unconscious – and, after all, film criticism *is* always an activity undertaken on emerging from a dark room. (As Pauline Kael put it in the preface to one of her collections, 'I don't fully know what I think until I've said it'[3] – which seems to me to sum up the whole point of the enterprise.)

Most of the pieces in this book were written during my three-year stint as weekly reviewer for the *New Statesman and Society*, during which I was fortunate enough to write at length about one

[3] *For Keeps* (Dutton, New York, 1994), p. xxii.

film a week, without being obliged to make value judgements when there were other things about a film that nagged me. It was possible, in other words, to cultivate a degree of the perversity that Daney recommends, and I've tried to continue in that vein more recently in my weekly Framespotting column in the *Guardian*. It meant I could write about films that might not otherwise get much of a look in – although it has turned out that most of the pieces in this book are about mainstream, indeed Hollywood cinema. That's partly because these happened to be the pieces I liked most, partly because it's in these pieces that the ongoing, insistent themes have tended to develop.

I haven't organised the pieces into any thematic order; I gave that idea up after consistently running aground on the arbitrariness of the distinctions I was tempted to try. Instead, the pieces run chronologically, which allows certain arguments to develop narratively from piece to piece; this also means, inevitably, that there are certain repetitions and redundancies. I've book-ended the reviews with two longer pieces – one on the film *Dick Tracy* and the art of prosthetics, the other on the British-based animators the Brothers Quay. The two, I hope, mirror each other's concerns in their contrasting discussions of two different sorts of illusionism, as well as of the body, the screen image and the eye of the viewer, themes that underwrite many of these essays. The final piece, 'Million-Dollar Graffiti', was written specially for this book; it's a note towards an end-of-millennium appraisal of the state of screen illusion, as digital imagery promises to change radically the stakes of cinematic representation. Given the pace at which digital technology is developing, this article was certainly out of date the day after I wrote it.

I've mainly left the articles as they were when published, except in the odd case where I couldn't help cringing at a turn of phrase, or where I've restored the odd aside that was originally subbed out; the footnotes were all added retrospectively. Any other doctoring is largely cosmetic, but in an age when a Hollywood actor can have his bald patch digitally painted in during post-production, I make no apologies.

Dick Tracy and the Aesthetics of Prosthetics

'Prosthesis: That part of surgery which consists of supplementing deficiencies, as by artificial limbs, teeth, etc.' – *Shorter Oxford English Dictionary*

The blockbuster film of the year – as the first weekend's US box-office takings of $22½ million suggest – is Warren Beatty's *Dick Tracy*. The film's main selling point is the fact that it features actors transformed by prosthetic make-up effects, luridly imagined by John Caglione and Doug Drexler, into grotesque caricatures of the human form: living, three-dimensional equivalents of the two-dimensional stylised gargoyles originally drawn by the comic strip's creator Chester Gould.

The use of prosthetics not only to recreate cartoon figures but to create the look of an entire cartoon world is nothing new in the cinema, but it's taken until now for it to seem perfectly natural. When, in 1980, Robert Altman announced his intention of making a live-action *Popeye*, it seemed an inconceivable prospect, and sure enough the film was a box office flop. There was reason enough for that: partly the film's general lack of coherence (and the fact that you couldn't make out a word Robin Williams was muttering under his plastic jaw), partly because there was something genuinely disturbing, not to say alienating, about these deformed figures touting false forearms and chins, inhabiting a stylised, dislocated shanty-shack world, and parodying the human shape. Altman had promised to make a kids' movie, and effectively succeeded in creating an image of Hell.

If, ten years later, the cartoon universe of *Dick Tracy* seems a perfectly acceptable proposition, it's because enough happened in the 1980s to make Hollywood Unrealism common currency. As both the action and horror genres gravitate ever closer to comic-book logic, there's no longer any clear divide between the two- and three-dimensional worlds (although it took *Who Framed Roger Rabbit* to drive the point home). From Pee Wee Herman, through *Beetlejuice*, to *Batman*, director Tim Burton's commercial rise has helped make Comic Unrealism *the* ascendant mainstream form. In the horror realm, Freddy Krueger of *A Nightmare on Elm Street* has presided over the transformations of physical logic and the metamorphoses – stretching, melting, mimicking, imploding – of that once unassailable common denominator, the human body. Body transformations in horror were once possible only through patent camera trickery – the metamorphic dissolves of successive Doctors Jekyll, or of Cocteau's Beast. That changed in the 1980s with the bone-crunching, skin-splitting transmutations of Joe Dante's werewolf movie *The Howling* and Paul Schrader's *Cat People*. Horror's traditional stakes were reversed: the enemy outside was replaced by the enemy in the body; the so-called 'body horror' cycle became the dominant screen scare discourse of the decade; and the human body no longer held good as immutable, reliable measure of the world.

All this makes *Dick Tracy* an appealing but in no way disturbing or particularly anomalous commercial proposition in 1990. What makes the film altogether reassuring, in fact, is that it *does* reaffirm the human body as a measure of the norm, of sanity, of beauty. For at the centre of its world of physical and moral corruption is the shining yellow-raincoated knight played by

Warren Beatty, a figure set apart from the dark world he inhabits, in a way that makes him the diametrical opposite of last year's Batman-as-Dark-Knight, the shadow-dweller at one with Gotham City.

In 1990, the role of prosthetics has changed. It's acceptable and no longer necessarily horrific – a far cry from the days of Boris Karloff's forehead in *Frankenstein* (1931), when the very fact of a plastic outcrop was itself nightmarish. In fact, the practice has become an essential part of a mainstream aesthetic dominated by 'false bodies' like Arnold Schwarzenegger's. A recurrent fetish of post-modernism is the image of the body invaded or supplanted by prosthetic 'foreign bodies', as in the writing of Angela Carter, Thomas Pynchon and Juan Goytisolo, or the photography of Joel Peter Witkin.

In this light, *Dick Tracy* is not particularly odd, or new, but it *is* very representative – a kind of culminating, triumphal moment, a festival of prosthesis. For one thing, as a preordained block-buster, a film for which massive commercial success is a foregone – that is, pre-sold – conclusion, it has one thing in common with other prosthetic spectacles like *Batman* and the *Star Wars* cycle. The merchandising campaign that surrounds these films – the logos, the posters, the videos, the spin-off dolls/Batmasks/two-way wrist radios – is itself a prosthetic addition to the body of the film. If an incapacitated body needs a spare limb or two to help it work, then the film supplemented by a few thousand extra mercantile tentacles – to help it reach into the hearts and pockets of the punters – is by nature admitting its own inadequacy as a functional body. You can never quite escape the feeling, when you go and see a blockbuster, that there's nothing really there – partly because, before you even buy your popcorn, you've 'really' seen the film already. And by a perverse knock-on effect, no matter how good the film is, you're already convinced in advance that it's hollow – simply a support mechanism for its own extraneous limbs, which are the real business at hand (just as the actors are simply support mechanisms for their own make-up).

In *Dick Tracy*, however, we're not dealing with the slap-happy addition of a few thousand latex ghoulies liberally squandered à la *Star Wars*. What makes Beatty's film interesting is that it has a whole graduated prosthetic system – if you like, a prosthetic 'palette', by analogy with the film's colour scheme, meticulously elaborated by cinematographer Vittorio Storaro. This system places bodies on an ascending scale from grotesque to normal. At the bottom – significantly, the film doesn't save these for last, but sets a whole stack up for display in the first five minutes – are the truly impossible grotesques (the Brow, Little Face, the Rodent, Flat Top, Steve the Tramp), monsters out of Bosch, more latex than flesh, and played by largely unknown actors (Neil Summers, Chuck Hicks) or the sort of dependable character players you can put a name but rarely a face to (William Forsythe, R.G. Armstrong, Henry Silva).

On the next rung, and in a category of their own, are two highly stylised, but slightly more human gargoyles – Al Pacino and Dustin Hoffman, warped and gnarled as mobster Big Boy Caprice and his henchman Mumbles. The fact that they're still recognisable beneath the make-up is crucial, because they're effectively playing themselves – this category makes explicit reference to the two actors' reputation for being infinitely transformable, the Lon Chaneys of Method Acting.

Next up are the part-grotesques, whose human form remains intact, but with the addition of a single denormalising tweak (a false nose for hood Itchy, a beefsteak kisser for Paul Sorvino's lips), and a few bit players (the odd unnamed thug or policeman).

One more step closer to the norm are the minor parts, whose semi-famous cameo status demands they should be recognisable, and who don't quite attain the rank of gargoyles – Dick Van Dyke (with a little padding on his chin), Michael J. Pollard (with outsize ears). Then come the mass of bit players, discreetly stylised through clothes or make-up, but essentially unremarkable, like most of the film's cops, who simply look like film cops.

At the top of the ladder come the three leads, all inhabiting unequivocally, reassuringly human form: good girl Tess True-heart (Glenne Headly); bad girl Breathless Mahoney (Madonna);

and finally, resplendent in yellow coat and fedora, Beatty's hero, King of the City, to whom all roads finally lead.

These several stages of humanness work in slightly different ways. The pure grotesques establish the terms of reference of the film, but perversely take its logic further from, rather than closer to, the world of Chester Gould's original comic strip. For Gould, caricature worked to create a heightened, distorted effect of realism, rather than a copy of the real. On paper, a Gould grotesque like Prune Face is simply a stylised impression of a figure with a shrivelled face, not a literal depiction of monstrosity. Gould was drawing attention not to a physical deformity but to his own style as a cartoonist. But by recreating Prune Face in literal terms as a mummified creation of weeping latex, the film's make-up wizards miss the point entirely. The latex certainly draws attention to the style of the film – and indirectly to the budget – but it also creates jarring abnormalities of a type not present in the strip.

This nevertheless works to Beatty's own advantage. To portray abnormality is to invoke normality by contrast – the normality of Tracy himself. In the strip, Tracy's features are every bit as stylised as the villains', and originally, it seems, Beatty experimented with appropriate make-up. But in the event, the effect of the uglies is to draw attention to Beatty's features as *excessively* normal, the very measure of beauty. Even the film's logo presses this point, the familiar Tracy cartoon jaw being supplanted by a shadowy but recognisable Beatty profile. Beatty's ordinary profile becomes extraordinary, even mythical, by association with Tracy's legendary hatchet face.

Pacino and Hoffman are a different case. Theirs is the Method Body, still recognisable, but physically, facially, vocally contorted out of shape. This, after all, is their stock in trade as actors. Excessive acting and disguise (self-transformation, even at the cost of some physical pain) has always been a keynote of method acting, so even their transformation here allows them to 'be themselves' – albeit to excess. Because Hoffman and Pacino are essentially parodying their usual act, they can get away with it.

They belong in a lineage of 'transformative' acting in which prosthetics are part of performance and performance is essentially prosthetic: from Chaney, through Olivier's Richard III, to Brando's Godfather with his jawful of orange peel, or Meryl Streep's wig in *A Cry In The Dark*. In *Dick Tracy*, Hoffman and Pacino are recognisably themselves, yet markedly other – a trick Hoffman has always favoured, usually to excess, from his wizened *Little Big Man* to *Tootsie* – a transformation itself almost as much documented as *Dick Tracy*.[1]

All these grotesques emphasise the presence of the three perfectly formed leads. But between Tess, Breathless and Tracy there are major differences. Tess, played by the still little-known Headly, is a cipher of a Regular Gal, whose sensible, monotone wardrobe and neutral make-up style give her a zero degree of beauty that functions mainly to offset the film's real romantic duo. With Breathless Mahoney, what's important is that Madonna brings her own image to the part – Breathless isn't so much a character as simply the latest incarnation of the Ciccone image. If Breathless is a flat, dimensionless vamp, it's because Madonna has always existed as a two-dimensional figure, an unusually fleshless sex symbol. Basing herself on a catalogue of screen goddesses (here, primarily Jean Harlow), she has always used borrowed images to prosthetic effect, as supplements to her body, to her acting style, to her repertory. Madonna's whole-hearted adoption of the roles she plays makes her as much a Method player as Hoffman and Pacino, if not more so. Where their role-playing supposedly hides a substance – pure 'will to act' – Madonna's power to transform makes her into pure surface, a blank screen. Here, she *is* a silver screen, backlit in a succession of blonde-platinum-blue-grey images to be as imperishable and unreal as the screen goddesses who provide her body.

Madonna's costume changes make Breathless less a character

[1] *Dick Tracy* was not the first film to play the 'stars-behind-masks' card. John Huston used this device as a novelty attraction in his 1963 thriller *The List of Adrian Messenger*, which concluded with Tony Curtis, Burt Lancaster *et al* whipping off their disguises to reveal their true identities.

than a succession of stills. That distinguishes her from the final, unchanging image of normality, Beatty's Tracy. Beatty plays the mildly embarrassed cop as a man about whom there is nothing to say, and who has nothing to say either (except his mantra, 'I'm on my way'), and nothing much to do but be the soul of integrity. He always looks the same – yellow coat, yellow hat, like a walking incarnation of the gold standard – and always *is* the same. That's all that distinguishes him, and all that needs to distinguish him. By virtue purely of his difference from the ugliness and the changefulness that surround him (the disguises, the plasticity themselves signs of moral deceit), Tracy is the universal measure of solidity, stability, beauty. And the fact that he's the director, the star and the producer means that, by analogy, Warren Beatty is all these things too.

In short, the entire structure of the film is set up to reinforce this basic point that Warren Beatty is a god in human form, without his actually having to act or be very interesting. But why use so much latex to do it? The answer lies in the more usual role of prosthetic make-up in the movies. The technique is most commonly associated with horror, particularly body horror – the cycle of films that graphically articulate contemporary fears about the body and the self. A common theory identifies body horror with fears about disease, particularly cancer and AIDS, and more generally with images of fragmentation and decay. In this sub-genre, prosthetics, a science of addition, is turned on its head to become a science of subtraction – most notably in David Cronenberg's *The Fly*, in which Jeff Goldblum's body sprouts excrescences only as a prelude to falling to pieces. A film such as John Carpenter's 1982 remake of *The Thing* dramatises an anxiety about the fragmentation of the self – what theorists call the Death of the Subject. Prosthetic addition assumes the existence of something within, an essential body that's there to be supplemented, but body horror suggests that perhaps there's nothing there, except more decay – a *deficiency*, as the dictionary says, a void. And it's notable that the ultimate villain in *Dick Tracy* is the faceless shadow figure known as the Blank, as inseparable a counterpart to Beatty's Tracy as the Joker was to Batman.

It's this sense of void that Beatty is trying to fill. For all the film's spurious status as public event, *Dick Tracy* is ultimately a very private film about one man's self-anxiety – a last-ditch attempt to immortalise himself as Wellesian visionary director, as square-jawed matinee idol, as imperishable icon. Made by a man aware of his advancing years and fading juvenile-lead looks, *Dick Tracy* is not a film about ageing gracefully. It is, in all its ramifications, a prosthesis for Warren Beatty's ego.

5 July 1990

Blade Runner – The Director's Cut

Much has been made of the fact that Ridley Scott's 1982 film *Blade Runner* was first released within two weeks of *E.T. The Extra-Terrestrial*. Steven Spielberg's winsome alien, whose luminous index once hailed every passer-by like some imperious galactic Kitchener, has now been largely forgotten as a folk imp, while a film that seemed fated to be consigned to the trash can of sci-fi ephemera has established itself as a canonical text of '80s popular culture.

The American critic J. Hoberman recently called *Blade Runner* the 'evil twin' to *E.T.*, but what sets the two films apart is not simply that one deals with darkness and decay while the other carries a message of eternal sunshine breakfasts for the nuclear family. Here's another difference. In a famous case of product placement, *E.T.* highlighted a brand of candy called Reese's Pieces, the popularity of which boomed after its appearance in the film. *Blade Runner*, however, seems to have carried a mercantile curse; of the corporations whose neon logos litter the skies of Los Angeles AD 2019, a remarkable number have suffered spectacular falls – Atari, Cuisinart, Bell Telephone, Pan Am ... It goes to show that every speculative projection of the future carries the seeds of its own obsolescence, is inevitably hostage to the vagaries of time.

In fact, the fallibility of *Blade Runner*'s predictions is most appropriate, for obsolescence and evanescence are the film's key themes. It was only right that Reese's Pieces should flourish, having been blessed by the hand of the ugly alien. In keeping with Spielberg's pantheistic philosophy of objects, all things that come into contact with E.T. are called to participate in his destiny, and thereby to attain their own eternal essence. E.T. redeems all he touches – not just in the religious sense but in the pawnbroker's as well. He calls things out of storage, animates them, beatifies them.

In the most un-beatific *Blade Runner*, animate things are caught in the flux of a post-industrial cityscape and returned to inanimation, losing their identity and undergoing a material process of transfiguration, in the irreligious sense of recycling: retrieval rather than redemption. In *E.T.*, things last forever; in *Blade Runner*, they slide inexorably towards their own meltdown.

The film itself is prone to this play of crumbling identity – a peculiar state of affairs that becomes evident with *Blade Runner – The Director's Cut*, billed as the definitive version of a film originally botched by insensitive distributors. After preview audiences declared themselves baffled, Ridley Scott reluctantly added an obtrusive voice-over by Harrison Ford (as the android-hunter hero Deckard) and an upbeat ending. The 'imperfect' 1982 film and the 'corrected' 1992 version thus book-ended a decade in which *Blade Runner* became not just a movie but a Text. Originally frowned on commercially and critically, *Blade Runner* is now seen as the watershed in a whole movement of dystopian sci-fi, its effects visible in films like Terry Gilliam's *Brazil*, Paul Verhoeven's *RoboCop* and *Total Recall*, and the recent *Tetsuo* films by Japanese director Shinya Tsukamoto. All of these touch on questions of recycling and instability in relation to the external world, to culture, to the self, and to an increasingly technologised human body. These films are about trash culture, in the sense that they present a world in which debris has become the only constant in culture. They mark a zeitgeist in which confidence about the possibility of endless cultural and material recycling is matched by an equal scepticism about the stability of things, about concepts of essence and identity.

That zeitgeist is roughly what we now call post-modernism. Among cultural theorists, *Blade Runner* enjoys a special status as a post-modernist primer, for several reasons. First, it is the most thoroughgoing rethink yet of a cinematic archetype of the City, a more fluid recasting of Fritz Lang's dualistic *Metropolis*, with its Overworld and Underworld. Ridley Scott and his 'Visual Futurist' Syd Mead created a labyrinthine world of horizontals and verticals, indeterminately structured in terms of both space and culture. At once futuristic and archaic (hi-tech gizmos *and* roll-top desks), *Blade Runner* presents a universal souk culture, the City as an extreme of the 'melting-pot' model of urbanism – part medina, part downtown Tokyo, wholly pastiche, populated by Hare Krishnas and Hasidim, Goths and Gold Rush greybeards.

Second, *Blade Runner* fitted neatly into a nexus of cultural and technological speculations that followed or were already coming into currency: notably, the 'cyberpunk' wave of science fiction headed by William Gibson; the developing field of Virtual Reality, with its problematising of two- and three-dimensional notions of representation; and the area of theory that addressed such notions, particularly Baudrillard's concepts of simulation and simulacra. Map all this back onto the movie ten years on, and it's easy to imagine that all 1980s thought started with *Blade Runner*.

Rather, it is the other way round: those ideas make the film newly readable in retrospect. To watch *The Director's Cut* against vague memories of the earlier *Blade Runner* is to enter into an appropriately confusing play of perception in which ideas of the 'original' and the 'definitive version' become irrevocably blurred. For a start, the revised film comes to us in the wake of several 'special edition' films (*Aliens, Betty Blue, Dances with Wolves*) presented as improved versions with added footage that in most cases should really have stayed deleted. These de luxe expansions rely on the authority of the films they supplement, but paradoxically undermine them by making them seem inadequate in comparison. *Blade Runner* is another case entirely: seventeen seconds shorter than the first version, it has changed considerably in tone, with the removal of the voice-over in spurious Chandlerese, while a darker ending casts an ambivalent light on the whole. But again, it can only be read in its difference; despite its claim to be definitive (i.e. unique), it is impossible to read it as if the first version never existed. In fact, *The Director's Cut* looks primarily like an object salvaged from the past. Its ragged feel in places adds to the sense of something imperfectly retrieved. Its immediacy is actually enhanced by the feeling that it is an alien artefact, and by our awareness that its 'definitive' status is really the result of retouching.

The new cut offers three principal changes: the removal of the voice-over in which Deckard narrates his mission to track down a group of renegade 'replicants' (androids) headed by the fallen-Satan figure Roy Batty (Rutger Hauer); the removal of the upbeat ending in which Deckard and his replicant lover Rachael (Sean Young) fly into a wide green yonder; and the insertion of Deckard's dream of a unicorn. To take the ending first: the film loses both the spurious optimism of the escape ending and the schematic duality of the city–nature opposition. In *Blade Runner*, there is no longer any welcoming Outside, except the Off-World colony advertised on flying video hoardings, which seem as fictional a construct as the Martian holiday world that Earthbound drones plug into in *Total Recall*.

The import of the unicorn becomes clear with the revised ending, which raises new doubts about Deckard's own identity. [1] The removal of the voice-over affects him similarly: no longer the authoritative narrator, he is now just a player. First seen crouched under an array of neon, he is simply a piece of dormant trash waiting to be retrieved for a new game. What the new Deckard lacks is an identity any more verifiable than that of his quarry. Batty, his counterpart, is investigating his own nature, in the hope

[1] It suggests, in fact, that he too is a replicant. See Philip Strick's persuasive argument in *Sight and Sound*, December 1992.

of outliving his allotted four-year life span. Little wonder, in a film about representations and replicas, that Deckard's task is also an investigation into his self – even into *the* Self.

This comes to light when Batty tells Deckard of his horrific memories, which will die with him. 'I've seen things you people wouldn't believe,' he says, and indeed we *don't* get to see them.[2] What finally lingers in this most spectacular film is the unshown, the forgotten (which may, perversely, be what makes the film so memorable). And what worries us in the end is not the uncertain future of Deckard and Rachael, but their uncertain pasts. Her identity is founded on the fake memory programmed into her; we fear that Deckard's memory may be equally false, but we measure it also against the real horrors that Batty has known, now erased for ever.

The brilliance of *Blade Runner* is in the way it ties questions of identity to the question of spectacle – of the seen and the unseen, what we know we've seen and what we only think we've seen. *Blade Runner* keeps showing us more than we can easily take in – neon, video, androids who look human, humans who look like androids, detail upon detail in the crammed screen – and then highlights the equation between *trompe-l'œil* and fooling the *inner* eye. It plays on the ephemerality of memory and identity, and suggests that the one thing that can't be recycled is memory itself. Not that it suggests there is anything transcendental about memory; rather, by constantly positing its chimeric nature (nothing could be more chimeric than that special-effects unicorn: you can actually see the horse trying to shake the ice-cream cone off its head) it suggests that identity itself can decompose into just more debris in an endlessly plural, endlessly self-parodic culture.

Are these themes actually 'programmed' into the film, or is *Blade Runner* simply a Big Dumb Movie that knows more than it thinks it does (unlike the replicants, who know *less* than they

[2] It's unimaginable that a 1990s Hollywood film would refuse such a flashback. A cautionary example is Peter Weir's *Fearless* (1993), about the aftermath of a plane crash; the film is fatally compromised by its climactic flashback to the crash, which until then has only been talked about.

think)? It might be excessive to cast what is after all a consummately beautiful future-shock epic as the wellspring of all 1980s theory. But science fiction is 'naturally' the province of all speculation on the 'unnatural', and in *Blade Runner* these latter concepts are as blurred as they've ever been. In an increasingly amnesiac culture, it's a film we can stand to be reminded of.

27 November 1992

Reservoir Dogs · Man Bites Dog (C'est arrivé près de chez vous)

Who says the devil doesn't have all the best tunes? In 1971, *A Clockwork Orange* shocked everyone rigid because its droog anti-hero Alex liked to choreograph his ultraviolence to a Beethoven soundtrack. Twenty years on, things are a little more flip. In Quentin Tarantino's *Reservoir Dogs*, Michael Madsen's psycho gangster Mr Blonde tortures a policeman to Stealer's Wheel singing 'Stuck In The Middle With You'.

It's a deeply unsettling scene to watch, not just for the violence itself, but also for Madsen's jokey, debonnaire little dance – a gruesome flirtation with the victim, and with the audience. It works horribly well. I saw the film at a late-night public preview and the general atmosphere was nervy, to say the least; there were uneasy titters throughout, but the weirdest thing was the way one man shouted out 'Sexy!' when Mr Blonde produced his can of gasoline with obvious, ominous intent.

What's scary is that you really want to see him use it – you realise this as the scene develops, and catch yourself doing an anxious double take. *Reservoir Dogs*, the debut by a young director whose *noir* literacy is evident in every detail, is about the glamour of violence, but it's not quite sure whether to analyse it or relish it. A gang of hoods retreat after a failed heist: as one member (Tim Roth) lies copiously bleeding, another (the superb Steve Buscemi) goes supernova pernickety, and a third (Harvey Keitel, authoritative but uncharacteristically muted) tries to hold the whole thing together. That the characters are all casual killers is a given fact. The drama starts from that ground, working your reactions in a way it never could if killing were presented as some antisocial anomaly; here, it's the very basis of society.

Reservoir Dogs is a thoroughgoing example of Theatre of Cruelty, in a quite literal sense. It's more like stage drama than most filmed versions of stage plays; where the latter try to hide their origins by 'opening out', Tarantino makes his film stagey by closing in. If an all-male repertory company were doing *Titus Andronicus* and Pinter's *The Dumb Waiter* on consecutive nights, this is what they'd be playing on the third. The stage is an abandoned warehouse in which characters are carefully positioned to face the audience, as well as for maximum bodily interaction; long takes emphasise the rhythm of words and gestures, and foreground acting skills, to a remarkable degree.

The film's point is that the life of crime is entirely about acting. The chief hood (bulb-headed veteran Lawrence Tierney) allots names – Mr Pink, Mr Orange, Mr White – to the gang members, who first quibble over their parts, then get into them like Method trainees, erasing their own identities. Play a part well enough, the film seems to say, and action becomes an act, and morality simply what's beyond the proscenium arch. The problem is, the same applies for the audience as well. The film's ambivalent achievement is that it makes violence more alive, and therefore more seductive, than any other film I can remember. It reinvents violence as spectacle, and effectively as *live* spectacle, something practically unthinkable in cinema. Tarantino uses a startling array of distancing techniques – voice-overs, flashbacks, repetitive fractured chronology, jovially naff seventies soundtrack, and discreet trickery such as the moment in the torture scene where a shaky camera suddenly cuts away and steadies itself, staring in rigid shock at a corner of the room. But all these ways of highlighting the violence as a funky guignol shtick allow you to dig it all the more.

Reservoir Dogs demystifies, as well as glamorises, but it's hard to say which it does more. Maybe that can only be determined empirically by audience reactions, by whether or not people are moved to shout 'Sexy!'. The film does, however, undercut the most obvious expectation of exploitation movies, by having an all-male cast: significantly, the only woman I can recall in it appears just briefly, to fire the shot that starts the action off.[1]

It's an odd film, involving while it's on, but not leaving any real traces once you leave the cinema. The opposite is true of another new killer-thriller: with *Man Bites Dog*, you might go home feeling you need a shower. It's a pitch-black comedy from Belgium, and its original title, *C'est arrivé près de chez vous* (which translates more like '*It Happened In Your Neighbourhood*'), better conveys its curious mix of banality and sensationalism. This is the serial killer's *Spinal Tap* – a pseudo-documentary in which a group of film-makers (including two of the directors, Rémy Belvaux and André Bonzel) record the daily rounds of an excessively motivated hitman (the third, Benoît Poelvoorde).

Man Bites Dog is not about murderous psychopathology in the way that John McNaughton's rigorously de-glamourising *Henry: Portrait of a Serial Killer* was. It's more an allegory of charismatic fascism, and a moral warning of film's seductiveness for film-makers and audience alike. As a film about film, it may be narcissistic, but it's also masochistically unflattering about the film-makers themselves. The fictional documentarists are spineless hippie wets, cowed by the awful Ben into following him around, hanging on his every word and gunshot, and then indulging in self-congratulatory weeping to camera every time one of their crew gets wasted.

The documentarists are just as monstrous as the more

[1] Watching the film again, I realise there are in fact two women featured, both expendable passers-by in cars.

demonstratively repellent Ben. He may not be as sexy as Tarantino's Blues Brothers lookalikes, but he certainly commands attention – a posturing barroom bore who can hold forth with equal bombast and pedantry on Frank Lloyd Wright and the correct way to kill postmen. One minute he's sentimentalising about family, the next demonstrating a gruesome cocktail inspired by a notorious child murder. The film-makers watch with horror and fascination, as we do; their damnation begins with an invitation to eat oysters (what could be more reassuringly Belgian?) and culminates in a horrifying Christmas celebration that brings to the fore the nasty question of the audience's voyeuristic complicity.

Man Bites Dog is a deeply moral film, but fatally caught up in its own strategies. It uses Ben's anti-charm to corner us into assenting to its gruesome glee in the comedy of inhumanity; once we assent, we're trapped, but then there's nowhere left to go, except into further play on the mechanics of film-making. Ben becomes his own director, with Rémy and André as lamblike minions, but the returns on that situation run out, and the film ends up in skittish farce as the team tangle with a rival killer and crew. In some ways, the film's inquiry into the murderous image goes further than *Henry*, but *Henry* achieved a more lucid view of its subject by having such an unappealing couch potato for a protagonist. In *Man Bites Dog*, the obnoxiously lippy Poelvoorde is too much of a comic *tour de force* to fit the supposed documentary genre. Bursting the limits of the mockumentary illusion, he makes the film marginally easier viewing, an experience that it's possible to read as absurdist gross-out without for the most part letting yourself really be fingered by it. However you react to it, though, you probably won't feel like visiting Belgium in a hurry. On the other hand, I don't believe Stealer's Wheel were ever big there.

8 January 1993

The Public Eye · Damage

A recurrent theme in the continuing paranoia about home video – every living-room a lazar-pit of Sadeian depravity – concerns the malign effects of the pause button. Thanks to this, the argument goes, viewers can freeze-frame particularly horrific images and turn them into their own customised atrocity pin-ups.

It's hard to see why a still picture of violence would necessarily be more powerful or corrupting than a moving one. But one basis of that argument is the privilege traditionally accorded to photography over cinema. This is the assumption that a single photo can magically capture the essential nature of an event, whereas in film any truth is bound to be either faked, an effect of deceitful staging or montage, or simply missed, lost to the eye in the rush of frames. If truth is in there somewhere, the argument goes, the only way to find it is by slowing the film down, tracking down the single frame that shows it all.

Hence the enduring power of stills, which present themselves as a film's platonic perfect moments. Stills, however banal, always seem rich in a promise that no film can ever quite live up to. Hence also the recourse of certain films to the freeze-frame as a corrective to the supposed imperfections of the moving picture. Legislators may worry about its corrupting power, but the freeze-frame's effect is nearly always to defuse an image's power to glamorise – this is the very sobering use it is put to in John McNaughton's *Henry: Portrait of a Serial Killer*. The freeze-frame has the ability to stop the eye in its tracks, to give pause for thought, not least about film itself. To freeze a medium that is ostensibly about motion is to counteract cinema's fundamental illusion, and to remind you forcibly that what you're really watching is still image after still image.

Cinema's traditional inferiority complex with regard to still photography underlies two otherwise unconnected (and otherwise uninteresting) new releases: Louis Malle's *Damage* and *The Public Eye*, a thinly veiled bio-fiction based on the legendary news photographer Weegee. *The Public Eye* is chock-full of photos, *Damage* has only one, but, in both, the still photo marks an attempt to get to the essence of the thing.

The essence of *Damage*, a leaden adaptation of Josephine Hart's pompous melo-novel, is sex; you learn all you need to know about the film (or all its publicists need you to know) from the poster, which has Juliette Binoche and Jeremy Irons entwined in a nude shot that knowingly echoes the poster for *Last Tango in Paris*. The more telling image, though, comes at the end of the film. Irons's Tory MP has had his star-crossed pash with Binoche, his son's fiancée, and sits alone pondering a huge blow-up photo of the three of them – boy and girl looking into the camera, father glaring sullenly at them. There you have the whole film in short-hand – simply the exchange of looks that says: triangle, unspoken passion.

That it is the film's only powerful image shows how misjudged *Damage* is: why end on a picture that tells you no more than you already know? A really powerful freeze ending shows you something that can't be reduced to a formula, or it turns what you've just seen on its head, or freezes a set of ideas so suggestively that you want to live it through again. The most famous end freeze is Truffaut's in *Les Quatre Cents Coups*, because it does so much at once – it turns the young Jean-Pierre Léaud into an icon, it quizzes the viewer, it speaks of possibilities yet to come in this urchin on the verge of a weird, wild life. My own favourite is in Stanley Kubrick's *The Shining*, in which Jack Nicholson is imprisoned inside a photo in the creepy Overlook Hotel – a chilling image, not only because it is inexplicable but because it evokes the potent mythology of photography as a stealer of souls.

The Public Eye takes on a more equivocal challenge – it wants to stop time in its tracks, but it also wants to animate the still photo, to free up all the drama that Weegee conveyed in each shot. The film is about the attempts of press photographer Bernzy (an unusually weary Joe Pesci) to capture the heightened sleaze of 1940s New York for posterity, in photos that he hopes will one day be recognised as great art (as Weegee's were). This is tremendous hindsight on the film's part – just like those biopics where people say, 'One day you'll be a famous composer, Ludwig' – but also a typical example of a mainstream film worried sick that it might not be Art. If this sad bulb-popping nocturnal animal can produce immortal images, the film asks, why can't a movie that minutely recreates the atmosphere in which those photos were taken?

But it answers that question by remaining in awe-struck subservience to photography throughout. Bernzy's business is to keep constantly on the move in order to catch those still moments; he even part-fabricates them, moving a stiff's hat to get the right effect (the film is indifferent towards the ethical implications of this, content to regard it as a perfectionist tic). But where Bernzy hustles, the film stays stock still, bogged down in a standard conspiracy plot with the photographer playing Marlowe to Barbara Hershey's lazily drawn *femme fatale*.

This ponderous narrative slows the images down, mires them in the minutiae of set design and period flavour, whereas Bernzy's photos themselves (a mix of Weegee, other 1940s shots, and artful pastiches) speed time up by catching moments on the hoof. Director Howard Franklin finds another very peculiar medium between film and photography, one that suggests that for an image to be larger than life it has to be slower than life: he stages Bernzy's privileged moments (a crowd scene, a shootout) as slowed-down, deformed stretches of monochrome, as if the film were about to decompose into its constituent frames without actually freezing. It's as though the film were looking for the 'truth' it wants somewhere between photograph and moving picture – actually between the frames, where it can't get to it (because there's literally nothing there but black celluloid).

These sequences, though, are not self-conscious in a way that's intended to make you 'see' the celluloid. Rather, you're supposed to see the world through Bernzy's eyes, but those eyes only work because they're revved up to shutter speed. You can't catch truth by stopping images dead (that's the lesson of Antonioni's great phenomenological thriller *Blow-Up*), but only by speeding them up. It's only when you can't see it that you can see it, and that's the glory of cinema, if you want to be Zen about it. Which is why the best image in *The Public Eye* is a still of Bernzy sitting at the boot of his car, which serves as his developing lab. It's a perfect pregnant moment, because it shows him simply waiting for the next photo. And by a neat twist, it's about the only still from the film that looks as if it could have been taken by Weegee himself.

5 February 1993

Shadows and Fog

Woody Allen's *Shadows and Fog* had its press screening so long ago that I can barely remember seeing it, and it doesn't help that I've since lost my notes. Or maybe it does; conceived as a sort of waking nightmare, the film functions even better as such if you think you dreamed it in the first place. It would have been released last year if the director's own domestic horror story hadn't put it in the shade and made its follow-up, *Husbands and Wives*, more fertile hunting ground for detectors of coded scandal.

Released with little warning and a minimum of media fuss, *Shadows and Fog* now comes across as a sort of furtive after-thought, which is again appropriate, since furtiveness is what the film is about. It's what you might call Allen's *film maudit* – which is *Cahiers du cinéma* for 'the one they don't talk about'. Quite a few directors have such a thing in their catalogue, and they usually come about when someone decides to pay tribute to German Expressionism. Prime examples are Lars von Trier's loopy *Europa*, last year's most underrated piece of pure-cinema bravado; Ingmar Bergman's misbegotten co-production curio *The Serpent's Egg* (1977), set in 1920s Berlin; and, recently, wunderkind Steven

Soderbergh's *Kafka*, which for a long time in Britain languished in pre-release purgatory.

Tributes to the dark gods of Weimar cinema are probably doomed because Murnau, Lang and their generation were the directors whose visions first gave their successors enduring nightmares – not the nightmares you get from mere monster flicks, but the ones caused by film itself and its sheer engulfing accumulation of murky shadow. How can a director possibly pastiche something so primally creepy? You can tell that this stuff still gets under Allen's skin – his antihero Kleinman (*sic*, I'm afraid) wanders around a too-big nocturnal labyrinth (shot by Carlo di Palma, designed by Santo Loquasto), cracking gags that this time are utterly ineffectual against the terrors of night, sex and malevolent fate. Allen, of course, has to go one better, so you get not just the spirits of *M* and Joseph K but also Fellini's circus iconography, and a titular nod to Alain Resnais's documentary about the Holocaust, *Night and Fog*, which suggests a rather weightier load to the innocence-and-persecution theme than the film is able to justify.

The story is essentially a frame for a series of talkative diversions that keep the night from drawing in and swallowing up the action entirely – characters wander in and out of the dark, taking shelter in bars, brothels and conversation (no Allen film has made it so clear that for him intellect is a refuge from animal anxieties). Allen's wizened schlemiel (uncomplimentary self-parody taken to the point of narcissism) is roused from his lonely room one night by a posse of vigilante burghers who want his help in tracking down a mysterious killer; soon, he's himself mistaken for the killer, while the real monster (the chillingly dour Michael Kirby) hangs close at hand.

Not surprisingly, the script is interested less in the search for the killer than the search for meaning – of art (exemplified in John Malkovich's egotistical circus clown), of philosophy (in John Cusack's dissolute student), of sex and love (Mia Farrow as a waifish runaway, and a round table of whores including a dryly witty Jodie Foster). But the central theme is guilt, transferred in high Kafka style to Allen's blundering innocent. The joke – which aspires to the inscrutable neatness of a Kafka parable – is that everyone thinks Kleinman is guilty although he's not, yet because he assumes (correctly) that everyone *will* think he's guilty, he *is*, in some obscure way.

As such, that fits in with the droll 'Why me? Why *not* me?' shtick that Allen has been peddling since his stand-up days. But there's something unsettling here, because the apparently blameless Kleinman really does have an indelible blot upon his life, having once scandalously wronged his ex-fiancée (he was caught in a cupboard with her sister). But we only find that out in passing, when the reference to his quite appalling mistreatment of her is tossed aside as a mildly surreal self-hate gag, with the flipness that Allen usually reserves for his wanking jokes. Yet it's a leadenly ugly moment – a confession all the more alarming because it slips out so casually, as though someone about to be acquitted of shoplifting absent-mindedly asked for ten murders to be taken into account. It's a remarkable indicator of the way that guilt functions as a constant in Allen's work – as a shield for more guilt. Now that *is* Kafkaesque.

Shadows and Fog is a brave but half-formed stab at that risky undertaking, the totally personal film that flies in the face of box-office wisdom – a venture often doomed to hermetic self-regard, although Allen has had memorable stabs before. But it never lets you beyond its surface. Here, the effect of the ensemble cast is different to what we're used to. Usually, we recognise the stars but appreciate the way they sink discreetly into character parts; here they stick out like sore thumbs, quite manifestly stars playing at being in an Allen movie (most brazenly, Foster, acting like a casual chat-show guest, and Madonna, fleeting in a sphinxy Dietrich part). The effect may be Brechtian (there's Weill on the soundtrack), but possibly more Brechtian than Allen bargained for – no-one gets to come alive here, except Donald Pleasence, exuding his dependable ghoulish cool.

Shadows and Fog is a marginal Allen film, but probably central for Woodyologists, because it shows his evasive ambiguities more clearly than usual – the desire to bury himself in a crowd *and* stand out from it, the desire to hide everything and exhibit it at the same time. It's not an Allen film to see for the one-liners – unless Schopenhauer is your idea of a great stand-up – but it's fascinating in a strange half-baked way.

12 February 1993

Bad Lieutenant
· Mean Streets

Seeing Harvey Keitel in the week's two best films, you wonder how it is that a Jewish guy from Brighton Beach cornered the acting market in Catholic guilt. Back in 1973, in Martin Scorsese's *Mean Streets*, Keitel's mobster Charlie declared, 'You don't make up for your sins in church; you do it in the streets.' Nineteen years later in *Bad Lieutenant*, director Abel Ferrara gives that famous opening line a cruel twist by taking Keitel off the streets and putting him in church, where he ends up writhing on his knees, screaming obscenities at a vision of Jesus. Keitel is now the Cain to Charlie's tainted Abel: from being a crook with a heightened sense of good and evil, he's become a cop who seems to be beyond either.

Bad Lieutenant is currently a prime exhibit, along with *Reservoir Dogs* and *Man Bites Dog*, in discussions of the 'New Violence' that's supposedly sweeping the movies (and which really only exists in opposition to Hollywood's witless Old Violence). All three films may use violence unflinchingly as part of their rhetoric of confrontation, but they do it to very different ends. *Reservoir Dogs* is the work of an enthusiastic B-film junkie testing the boundaries between exploitation and entertainment; *Man Bites Dog* makes a slap-happy but traditionally art-film enquiry into cinematic voyeurism. But only *Bad Lieutenant* aspires to be an enquiry into the soul.

That makes it an old-fashioned film in many ways – it's really following paths that Scorsese trod in *Taxi Driver* and *Raging Bull* – but it's an extreme one nonetheless. Of all these recent movies, it's the one that most comes across as a hard case; there's no feeling of distance between us and Keitel's intense, almost exhibitionistic performance, and Ferrara makes no concessions to our pleasure. The film's intensity is like a bad drug, oppressive and barely pleasurable, but addictive. And the film dares what only real hard-case films do: it dares to be boring.

Ferrara, who made his name with *The Driller Killer* and *Ms. 45: Angel of Vengeance*, is hooked on extremity, and here you get it all – drugs, blasphemy, obscenity, violence and shaky camera-work. The title is loaded: the film started life in a reportage rap song written by Ferrara, in which 'bad' means street-tough, as you'd expect, but also literally tainted, soiled rotten, probably beyond redemption (the rap remains in the form of a crunchingly aggressive Schoolly D number, the holocaust in Keitel's head).

The nameless Lieutenant drops his kids off at school, crams his face with coke, then cruises town interspersing bouts of routine homicide work with smack and crack, dousing himself in vodka, stopping to jerk off over two terrified girls in a car – it's all in a day's work in the NYPD. The rest of the time, he pursues his main obsession, which is to get himself suicidally deeper into debt betting on a baseball game that might save his life or end it.

When a nun is brutally raped in church, the local Catholic community offers a reward, and the Lieutenant sees a way out. The money might get him out of hock, but perhaps it's his soul rather than his life that he wants to save. There's a horrendous moment when a ravaged Keitel gets down on his knees to howl vindictively at Jesus: 'Where were you?' It's hardly a conventional moment of grace; the confrontation is undercut both by the department store kitsch of the Jesus figure who materialises before him and by the waking moment that follows. This abjection is more like arrogance, the Lieutenant effectively usurping Christ's place along with his best line, 'Why hast thou forsaken me?' He's forsaken for sure, and even the devil can't help him (unless you care to read him *as* the devil, God's bad lieutenant).

It's a strange moment, so viscerally extreme as to be almost embarrassing – there's a real sense of intrusiveness, not least because you somehow feel that it's going too far to shoot such a scene in a real church (it's amazing how Ferrara can get straight to your feelings of delicacy). Ferrara's theme of violation extends to breaking all the other proprieties of shooting in church – 'FUCK' daubed over a Last Supper, Keitel yelling 'You fuck!' at Jesus, or gazing in prurient wonder at the nun's naked body.

The theme of abjection as a prelude to redemption pervades Christian mythology and the existential literature derived from it, from Dostoevsky to Camus to Paul Auster; but Ferrara subverts the idea by effectively making religion itself the vehicle for obscenity. The rape, for example, is shot in a way entirely at odds with the film's feel of low-budget, long-take realism; it's cut fast and lit luridly, like a nightmare rock video, and spliced with a violently incongruous image of Christ on the cross – a scene that only makes dramatic sense if you rationalise it as the Lieutenant's own fantasy, and then not quite.

The sense of extremity extends to the film's realism – is Keitel really shoving all that stuff up his nose, those needles into his arm? It certainly looks like it, and it's painful to behold. The film also assaults our sensibility by testing our patience: the dialogue in a club scene defies audibility; droning expositions of baseball minutiae demand our attention; and a conventional plot line refuses to emerge.

Bad Lieutenant might come across like an opportunistic trawl through the fantasies of a misogynist auteur suffering from post-communion depression, if not for the predominant sobriety of the direction (sobriety isn't the word; think rather hangover) and for Keitel's performance. He's on screen in practically every shot, and what impresses, apart from his ability to veer from catatonically terse to screeching agonist, is his patience – the ability to push a scene to the limits of the tolerable by milking one line over and over, or simply to do nothing, to hold centre stage by acting like a slab of inert matter while nothing happens around him.

It's a deeply unpleasant film, but a compelling one – there's little so bracing as a season in hell. It's also thoroughly ambivalent. You could see *Bad Lieutenant* as a wallow in the thrill of excess fatigue, or as an excessively moral work – it's hardly an effective advert for a life of slime. Some have seen it as a straight parable about redemption, but, if it were, it would be quite uninteresting – a return ticket to the depths that allows us to gawp and then gives us a let-out. In fact, it makes no sense as such; the apotheosis the Lieutenant contrives for himself is so bathetic, and so derisive of all notions of order (narrative, legal or holy), that there's no catharsis other than the negative kick of sheer frustration. What we're dealing with is nihilistic irony, an impression that the airless, claustrophobic, static feel bears out. It's hard to explain the film's appeal without making it sound like a prurient freak-fest, but imagine a *Crime and Punishment* in which only the cops get punished, endlessly – you'd want to read that, wouldn't you?

Mean Streets seems almost cosy in comparison, its dialogue like florid poetry next to *Bad Lieutenant*'s terseness. Compared to Scorsese's pushy psychos in *GoodFellas*, these hoods are softies, and their brawling – as in the priceless poolroom sequence – like a basketful of puppies tumbling. But it's a more powerful film than *GoodFellas* because Scorsese inveigles us into an exuberant, reassuring world cushioned in the microscopic milieu of Little Italy, and then coolly blows it up at the end, when we realise how easily we've allowed ourselves to be talked over by these wise guys' self-deceptive rhetoric of boyish bonhomie. The film is still riveting, still looks breathlessly paced, still has a bustling humanity that you won't find in a Ferrara film. *Bad Lieutenant* is harder simply because, like its gambler hero, it keeps upping the ante; Scorsese plays his cards close to his chest and deals with peerless flair. Wouldn't you rather be handed your ticket to hell with a quip and a slap on the back?

19 February 1993

Orlando

In cinema, history usually repeats itself as mini-series, but just occasionally it repeats itself as panto. I always feel there's something panto-like about historical films, in any case. But maybe that's just true from a British perspective, because throughout the 1970s anyone who dressed up for the screen in an Elizabethan ruff or a Victorian crinoline would inevitably end up wearing the same gear on a Morecambe and Wise Christmas special.

Then why not make historical films as much like panto as possible? Two new British films do just that, so much so that in Sally Potter's *Orlando* you expect to see Aladdin's genie pop up at any minute – as a knowing allusion to Ingres-style orientalism, of course. Derek Jarman's *Wittgenstein* has all but got Daisy the Cow marching across the screen, eyelids flapping, to illustrate some obscure ontological debate.

The biopic is a particular kind of historical film. It needs to be a bit of a panto because, if it isn't, it becomes desperately reverent, pure hagiography. You couldn't, by any stretch of the imagination, call *Orlando* a biopic in the usual sense, except that Virginia Woolf called her original historical fantasy a 'biography' rather than a novel. In literature, a biography is usually presumed un-problematically to be a record of the life, but film biographies are more usually after-the-event narratives leading up to martyrdoms or tragic apotheoses. It's no accident that so many recent subjects – Jimmy Hoffa, Malcolm X, Bugsy Siegel – end up getting killed (or, in the case of Oliver Stone's absent subject JFK, begin by getting killed). These films are closed books.

But an alternative biography film – a Woolfian one, say – would keep the book open, emphasise the *bio-*, the living process. Instead of taking the life from the vantage point of the death, the anti-biopic takes the death from the vantage point of the living – painting a portrait of the subject complete with his or her mortality built in. That's more or less what Sally Potter's film, very loosely following Woolf's original, attempts to do – following its chimeric hero/ine's inexorable flight towards the future and his/her ever-deferred death.

The book casts light on that living process, unpicking the business of biography-writing by spiking it with all manner of stylistic flourishes and self-conscious digressions in the best *Tristram Shandy* manner. The film similarly sets out to paint Orlando's labyrinthine life of surprises in a visually and narratively baroque style.

Orlando starts out male in one Elizabethan era and ends up female in another. By casting an ageless, androgynous Tilda Swinton throughout, Potter points up the question of identity and its stability through a lifetime of contingent changes. Is Orlando always Orlando whether male or female, got up in flounces and furbelows, Byronic turbans or modern-day biking gear? And is the story the same whatever visual styles it's cast in – whether it's copping visual licks off Eisenstein or Brueghel the Elder, kitting Orlando out like a Reynolds *grande dame* or a Hilliard dandy?

Whatever happens, *Orlando* is always very much a 1990s film, forever undercutting historical illusionism with a campy sense of anachronism, not least in its casting. A lofty, desiccated Quentin Crisp reaches some sort of personal apotheosis as Queen Elizabeth I, Heathcote Williams is a slobbish littérateur, and Ned Sherrin spits out one-liners like grape pips as a scabrous Alexander Pope. Paradoxically, these very specific cultural references in the casting are likely to date the film most, irrevocably fixing it to an early '90s Radio 4 culture (although the above are all really '60s/'70s survivors). And what's really the point of these gags anyway – is the idea that Ned Sherrin is the Pope of our times, or that Pope was the Sherrin of his?

The film never lets you forget that it's *filmed*, constantly dousing you in the lushness of its designs and photography (the latter by Alexei Rodionov). But the opulence can't disguise the fact that *Orlando* never quite inhabits its own ground. It immediately strikes you as having elements of Jarman and Greenaway, and of course you want to kick yourself for making such obvious comparisons about a left-field British art film; you see a three-foot-high powdered wig anywhere and it has to be *The Draughtsman's Contract*, right? But if Potter had really wanted to lay those comparisons to rest, she wouldn't perhaps have used Jarman's regular star Swinton, or his costume designer Sandy Powell; and she wouldn't have had Greenaway's designers Ben Van Os and Jan Roelfs or herself co-written a soundtrack that's a dead ringer for Michael Nyman's wheezy staccato pomp.

The problem is, the visuals really are the film's strength – it's as much a sumptuous ballet as it is a panto, and its most eloquent moments are about movement: a host of ice-skating boyars, and a great sequence in which a pannier-skirted Swinton daintily negotiates a roomful of furniture. But narratively the film is too episodic and directionless, without hitting the book's wonderful heights of diffuseness. The great ambivalence of Woolf's book is that Orlando's sex starts off switching in a fairly stable fashion, then oscillates capriciously and indeterminately between the two.

Potter, though, seems content to stick with straight male–female reversal, and although this duality is cleverly shadowed in other aspects of a film obsessed with doubles – an Eastern potentate surrounded by twins, the use of St Petersburg to literally double for London – on the narrative front, she's stuck with straight binaries. The film never gets round to mobilising its infinite potential for sexual polyvalence. Instead, we get a straightforward parable about a young man who has a rattling good time, then turns into a woman who doesn't. In straight role-reversal terms, the ironies are bland. Orlando's fiancée, abandoned for a Russian beauty, moans about the treachery of men; five minutes later Orlando, rejected in turn, bewails the treachery of women. Orlando the swashbuckling bravo is a particularly appealing figure in the first half – Swinton, an established champion at sardonic gender-play,[1] makes the most of being a woman acting out the Elizabethan ideal of feminised masculinity. But in the second half, where she-Orlando is required to yawn through the epigrammatic misogynies of Addison and Pope, and suffer the iniquities of the property laws, the film collapses into a one-dimensional lament on woman's sorry estate, delivering a weary shrug rather than the relishable subversions it had promised.

Potter finally seems less interested in her subject than in the possibilities of filming it – and wouldn't you know it, 1990s Orlando ends up swapping her quill for a camcorder. What does give the film a real sense of presence, however, is Swinton's performance, as wry and distracted as ever, but making unprecedented exploration of the quizzical double take direct to camera. She rises admirably to the occasion by *not* rising to it, by making a wonderfully blank, sardonic clotheshorse. Eric and Ernie would have been proud to swap repartee with her.

12 March 1992

[1] She gave a notable one-woman/man performance as Max/Ella in Manfred Karge's stage play *Man to Man*, and John Maybury's 1992 video version.

Candyman ∙

Trespass

The late Angela Carter, when giving public readings of her favourite fairy-tales, liked to place special emphasis on one motto, which was the advice given to the inquisitive new bride in Bluebeard's castle: 'Be bold, be bold ... but not *too* bold.' That phrase is the key to most fairy-tales, and to pretty well every horror film ever made. Horror films are invariably about people who are bold enough, or foolish enough, to step over thresholds, and who therefore end up getting what they deserve, or desire.

You can't have horror – just as you arguably can't have any narrative – without a structure of taboo and transgression. Critics have been harping on this for years, but these days practitioners of horror are doing it too; as a result, the genre has become too self-conscious for its own good. Horror films today tend to be either weary juggling with conventions (the convictionless slapstick of the *Nightmare on Elm Street* series, and the ghoulish Freddy's degeneration into a jovial video-game bogeyman), or riddled with pompous knowingness about the genre's own more grandiose aspirations.

You can't expect any genre to exist in an ideal state of unblemished ingenuousness, but it does seem that to programme horror's key notions – the Return of the Repressed *et al.* – explicitly into films is as futile as trying to make up a convincing dream. A popular genre is most effective when striving to articulate something that has not yet been worked out; when it knows it all already, there's nothing left to say. Hence, the enduring effect of '40s and '50s horror, where the genre seemed still tongue-tied enough not to know quite what was on its mind (although that was largely a question of what period decorum allowed it to say). Hence, later, the genuine shock quality of George Romero's zombie cycle,[1] where long-muted anxieties broke through to the surface for the first time, in truly novel and upsetting ways.

Now, however, so much theory seems to be taken for granted that the most intelligent horror films could have been assembled by marketing executives with Freud in one pocket and *Fangoria* magazine in the other. A particularly disappointing new example, *Candyman* is based on a story by British ghoul-guru Clive Barker, whose own efforts as a director (*Hellraiser* and *Nightbreed*) have been explicitly about crossing the border and swooning heartily into the dark embrace of the Other. *Candyman* is the same again, except that director Bernard Rose is more interested in psychological suggestion than in the grand mythic gloss that Barker is prone to.

Candyman's smart opening ploy suggests, only too briefly, that self-consciousness can pay off. In a scenario straight out of *Halloween*, a lecherous teenager, rash enough to utter the word 'Candyman' five times, summons up a legendary hook-handed ghoul and is summarily filleted. But this turns out to be one of many apocryphal anecdotes collected by Helen (Virginia Madsen), an academic researcher. Cut to a lecture theatre, where her creepy husband Trevor is glibly laying urban myth to rest: 'Let's face it, folks, there *are* no alligators in the sewers.' You could hardly have

---

[1] *Night of the Living Dead* (1969), *Dawn of the Dead* (1979), *Day of the Dead* (1985).

a more direct statement of *Candyman*'s theme. For sewers, read the unconscious; for alligators, read slithering, subversive desires.

Just as, in the traditional horror school of dark shadows and suggestion, you see what you want to see, here what you want will come to you, and woe betide you if you're not prepared to believe in it. What gets you into trouble is not desire but repression. Helen wants to believe the myth *and* to dismiss it, but libidinous desire wins out over rational judgement. She's terrified and fascinated by two things. One is her own other side: suspected of a gory murder, she protests, 'I believe that no part of me, however hidden, is capable of that.' The second hidden thing is the repressed of the city itself: its black population.

Helen's act of trespass begins when, as a white bourgeois rationalist, she tries to contain and classify a black proletarian myth about a black ghoul who inhabits black territory – the brutally deprived Chicago housing project Cabrini Green. The black world is literally just the other side of the mirror; by some fluke of urban planning, Helen can take down the mirror in her condo bathroom and look into the darkness of the abandoned housing project on the other side. Like *The Shining* and *Poltergeist*, with their defiled burial grounds, *Candyman* is based on the notion of an unredressed American wrong – a general social wrong in addition to the specific wrong inflicted on the Candyman's mortal previous incarnation (he is the spirit of a black man hounded for having a white mistress).

But all this is shaky ground. The conflation of blackness and female desire is a rare theme in horror, the only previous version I know being Jacques Tourneur's mesmerising *I Walked With a Zombie* (1943). But the relentless focus from Helen's viewpoint makes blackness strictly the correlative of her fantasy (or the audience's). *Candyman* is caught up in a very male idea of what white women's fantasies may be about – Helen's 'other nature' has to be freed up through symbolic ravishment by a priapic (but safely mutilated/castrated) black ghoul.

The equation of blackness with the underneath, the irrational, is itself as old as Webster's Dictionary – in *Candyman*, of course, black people just naturally *know* about the creepy beyond. But *Candyman* pushes this commonplace to an extreme. Helen may desire to see the downside of the city, but in terms of what *we* see (if you take 'we' as a predominantly white film-going audience), the black realm is the very spectacle of what is undesirable. Her visit to Cabrini Green – all decay, graffiti and B-boys skulking with sexual menace – is a descent into Hell.

The horror of black urban existence is something that, arguably, can only be handled from the inside. There's a world of difference between the domestic horror of *Boyz N The Hood* – an everyday story of life in Hell – and *Candyman*'s inescapable, if inadvertent, suggestion that to be black is to be *from* Hell. But this is bound increasingly to be the great tension in American mainstream cinema – the fascination with black culture, coupled with the desire to keep it at arm's length.

Walter Hill's asinine *Trespass* is another example of this. In it, two witless white treasure-hunters stray into a deserted warehouse in East St Louis, where they run foul of those two infinitely glamorous folk demons of rap, Ice T and Ice Cube. There's a nice irony at work here – the original title *Looters* was changed in the wake of the Rodney King riots, but of course the looters, the trespassers, are the white guys. Is this theme of white trespass (cf. *The Bonfire of the Vanities*) a symbolic warding-off of black trespass onto white terrain? Could Hollywood bear to make a film about blacks in Beverly Hills, other than Eddie Murphy?

Trespass is duplicitous work, aimed both at the black audience for gangsta-rap imagery since *New Jack City* and at white urban anxieties. The black hoods may be the smart cookies with the technology *and* the loyalty beneath the ruthlessness, while the white boys are just dumb-ass and venal. But they're also straight from Hell. The film serves as the crudest 'don't mix with these guys' warning; no *Lethal Weapon* interracial buddy-bonding here.

In both *Trespass* and *Candyman*, racial difference itself is the horror – the latter film may try to unpick sexual and social myths of that difference, but of course it perpetuates them in the end. As an old-fashioned exploiter, *Trespass* is too dumb – and too dull –

to know better. *Candyman* only thinks it knows better. It's really not *that* bold, not as brainy as it thinks, and not that scary either.

19 March 1993

The Quince Tree Sun (El Sol de Membrillo)

You can sum up the plot of *The Quince Tree Sun* in three words – man paints tree – but you'd be hard pressed to exhaust this film's complexities. The artist is Madrid painter Antonio López, a jovial, distracted man who hardly has what you'd call star quality; and the tree is no lofty boughed titan but a scrawny sprig barely subsisting in a corner of his back yard. But set López to work, with his poles and pegs and plumb-lines, and wheel on a few cronies to jolly him up, and you have extraordinary food for contemplation.

At 137 minutes, the film – only the third feature by elusive Spanish director Victor Erice, who made *The Spirit of the Beehive* and *El Sur* – is shorter and less demanding in terms of dead time than Jacques Rivette's superficially similar *La Belle Noiseuse*, but in some ways it's more complex. It goes for workaday banalities of painting that reveal their thematic mysteries less readily than Rivette's grand Romantic commonplaces, ambivalent though they were. Instead of Rivette's muscular expressionist painter agonising over his creation (and contorting his female model into Bendy Toy tangles for the purpose), Erice simply shows you the artisan-like López setting up his canvas and doing an unfussy job with unpromising materials, nine to five, rain or shine – or at least while the light holds.

Of course, it's naive to say that Erice 'shows' you this, any more than López 'shows' you the tree. But what's fascinating about the film is neither the painting itself nor any insight into the painter's talent. You don't see much of the painting (one version of it is ditched halfway through and consigned to the cellar), and there's no reverent oohing and aahing at the sight of the master at work – although the man's very tenacity certainly has its mystique.

Much of the fascination, instead, lies in the fact that we're never quite sure what we're watching. We can never be sure why López is so fascinated by this very ordinary tree – is he looking for something in it, or just looking at it? Likewise, we're never quite sure why we're watching López. Is there a narrative here? Is he going to pull something remarkable out of his palette when we least expect it? Or is the whole thing a fictional set-up, a staged performance masquerading as documentary? Can we believe that all these passers-by really were passing by? Or even that all the infelicitous turns of the weather weren't the result of careful timing on Erice's part?

The film certainly looks like a set-up – but what's set up for our contemplation is the business of cinema itself. It's essential that we're kept wondering. The film could be a fiction in which the actor playing a painter – both happen to be called Antonio López – really paints a tree (unlike *La Belle Noiseuse*, where the point was that Michel Piccoli himself manifestly *wasn't* painting). Or it could be a genuine documentary about Antonio López painting a tree, in which case the presence of the camera (which we don't see until the end) itself becomes a cause for concern. How can all these people – López, his family and friends, a crew of visiting Polish workmen who sample a raw quince and find it wanting – go about their business so naturally without tripping over Erice's crew?

These, of course, are questions endemic to all documentary, especially of the supposed fly-on-the-wall variety. But the question of how Erice's camera intrudes into its object is raised in the painter's own relationship with the tree. For one thing, López frames the tree in an elaborate edifice – a canopy to keep the rain off, a dangling plumb-line and a horizontal string to grid it out, and a couple of pegs to keep himself positioned in the same spot. The object he paints (the tree) is always less than the object he sees (the tree *plus* all its impedimenta). And clearly López himself is always surrounded by the unseen apparatus that Erice brings with him – camera, lights, crew.

López also has a bizarre trick of daubing the tree itself with a complicated system of blotches of white paint, which he measures against his grid to see how much the tree shifts position day by day, how much the leaves sway or the fruit droops. He tells one observer that he's making 'a map of the tree', but effectively the tree, flecked and gridded, becomes a map of itself. Is López then obliged to paint the paint as part of the tree? It's as if he had to dose up the world with paint before it could be paintable – a strange sort of visual homeopathy.

Then there's the unavoidable fact of the object changing before his eyes every day. The wind blows, the leaves droop, and there's always the risk that the quinces will ripen and rot before he can capture the perfect moment of their luminosity that he claims to be after. Time and weather will always defeat him, so he cheats, by getting friends to hold up leaves with a little pole.

This problem of the world changing before the paintbrush can get a purchase on it is a long-standing paradox of realist painting, and it's a problem that the faster-moving medium of cinema is well placed to address. Where Dutch Golden Age painters would fastidiously attempt to incorporate the process of decay into a still life, Peter Greenaway's *A Zed and Two Noughts* actually showed us speeded-up decay as applied to a dead zebra. Erice's most powerful image comes when the quinces reach their most baroque state of fruition; captured in close-up, in full velvet mouldiness, they lie among a sea of discarded fag-ends which form another little map of López's daily routine.

Such paradoxical contemplations of the nature of painting may be endlessly fascinating, but are they just abstract mystification? There's a degree to which López's explanations do appear woolly and mystificatory, but then so are the declarations of most visual artists. When he claims, 'I want to catch the fleeting light,' he may sound a touch pie-eyed, but the pragmatic way he goes about it makes him seem more like a research physicist setting himself a problem to solve. Alchemy is a business too. But what we learn about López's work, the little tricks he uses to train both his perceptions *and* the world he perceives, we also learn about the work of watching a film – the cognitive tricks and little perceptive adjustments we perform in front of the screen.

Routine as López's job is, there's still something slightly awe-struck about *The Quince Tree Sun*, but that's because real work is so rarely represented in cinema. People in film fictions may have jobs, may be working girls or cowboys, but they usually have more interesting things on their minds – killing each other or falling in love – than doing a day's work. So when you actually see someone grappling attentively with the tools of their trade, there's always a touch of the sacramental about it. That's why a shot of a watchmaker is rarely just about a watchmaker at work, but invariably about the Craft of the Watchmaker. Cinema is almost always obliged to hide the tools of its trade, lest their appearance on screen burst the bubble of illusion, so its observation of other trades is usually tinged with a childlike envy.

But the wonderment can be profitably ambivalent. Alain Corneau's recent *Tous les matins du monde* – a film about the lives of Baroque musicians – could be read as a Zen treatise on musical transcendence, but it also made the common-sense observation that you don't transcend unless you practise your scales. Several scenes in Erice's film make symbolic play of the apparatus of art-as-spectacle, all the better to demystify it. An early, poised shot of a Venus de Milo and a wooden frame seems the purest evocation of high art's furnishings – but, by comparison, the actual job of painting looks all the more matter-of-fact.

Like *La Belle Noiseuse*, *The Quince Tree Sun* gives you a sense of a real place and a real time, which happen to be contingent on the not-quite-real time and space of film. The world goes on around López as he paints, but we're only half aware of it – a ghostly nocturnal cityscape, with flickering TVs, surrounds the house, and we hear news reports, but only as broadcasts from elsewhere; López, while he's painting, is in the world but not of it. When you're really working, who listens to the news anyway?

There's a wonderful moment at the end when López finally downs tools and takes a deserved rest, stretching out to pose asleep for his wife María Moreno, herself a painter. But Moreno is also the film's producer, and there's suddenly the sense of her taking charge, becoming at once her husband's boss, a mother putting him to bed, and his inventor. As he dozes off, he becomes her creature, her tree on her canvas, providing a corrective to the male notion of 'mastering' the object (creating a masterpiece) that was the theme of *La Belle Noiseuse*. It's a rather elegiac reversal – the only disappointment being that Moreno doesn't paint white lines on her husband to see how *he*'s drooping.

2 April 1993

Groundhog Day

High-concept comedies are two a penny – it's high time we had a heavy-concept one. *Groundhog Day* is built on a premise that sounds the stuff of pure fairy-tale, or pure nightmare, depending how much of a cynic you are: imagine if you could live the same day over and over again. If you were an idealist you'd think of all the new experiences you could have, all the risks you could take, knowing that whatever went wrong you'd always live to get it right next time. But if you were a cynic you'd feel that you were forever fated to live through identical sequels to the same lousy film.

As a supremely cynical fantasy, *Groundhog Day* goes for the latter option. But its cynicism taps into the cynicism of sequel-era Hollywood itself – the cynicism that will one day give us *Home Alone 23* – and goes one better. Imagine if, instead of a string of sequels, a single film were crammed full of all its own possible sequels, so that a one-joke skit became an infinite regress of repeated gags, each folding into the next. *Groundhog Day* tells us early on that we're going to have the same gag thrown at us time and time again, and challenges us to keep finding new ways to laugh at it.

The first time cynical TV weatherman Phil Connors (Bill Murray) wakes up on Groundhog Day in the impossibly congenial hick town of Punxsutawney, Penn., and the radio's playing Sonny and Cher, we laugh: God forbid it should happen to us. The second time it happens, we laugh but this time nervously: God forbid it should happen twice. The third time, we're already breaking out in a cold sweat, anticipating a water-torture effect – we know that director Harold Ramis and co-writer Danny Rubin will feel no compunction about milking this gag *ad infinitum*.

Fresh hell is one thing Phil doesn't get. Every day is Groundhog Day, and every day he stumbles downstairs to be greeted by an indefatigably chirpy hotel keeper, ambushed by the town bore (the peerless Stephen Tobolowsky), and subjected to the awful annual ceremony in which a small rodent emerges to 'forecast' the weather.[1] From then on, he has to make his own amusements – overeating, reckless driving, meticulously planned seductions, the gradual acquisition of godlike powers.

Groundhog Day may be the purest nightmare movie Hollywood has ever produced – potentially endless repetition, just for its own sake – but it's also the most formalist. It's like a dare between Ramis and Rubin to see how many variants they can work on one theme before 101 minutes are up. They go about it with fiendish ingenuity, undercutting our expectations when we least expect it, but also confirming them just when we're getting as weary as Murray is of having them confirmed; they like to make sure that from time to time it feels like hell for us too.

Another ploy of theirs is to divide up the repetitions into series of routines, and series within series – a chapter of seductions, a chapter of good deeds, a chapter of (successful) suicide attempts. Phil ends up living by the same principle that sustains gag-writers – if a routine doesn't work, try again, then, when you've tried till you're heartily sick of it, find a new routine. Then there are all

[1] I'd like belatedly to reply to the reader who wrote in after this review was published, and asked, 'If a groundhog is a small rodent, then show me a large one.' I wish I'd thought of this at the time, but how about a capybara?

the fine gradations of pacing: sometimes the film assaults us with knowing monotony; sometimes the repetition takes on a delirious, speed-spiked rhythm.

Bill Murray is probably the only comic who could last the course in a film like this. Imagine Robin Williams or Tom Hanks in his place, reacting for all they're worth, and trying to milk the situation for its human element. But Murray's transcendent langour makes him perfect casting for a man whose daily hell begins the second he wakes up – he *always* looks as if he's about to roll over with a muttered curse and go straight back to sleep. Murray has always excelled in treating every situation like a bad Budweiser dream; he's a slow-burning somnambulist who reacts with stony disdain as disasters mount up around him (in an earlier life, he'd have been the guy who stands observing with placid civility as Laurel and Hardy dismantle his car). Here, though, he has something new to deal with – *nothing* happens, unless he makes it happen.

The fact that there is absolutely no explanation for Phil's predicament makes *Groundhog Day* unique in contemporary Hollywood, where everything has to be justified, to the point of absurdity. Look how fastidiously the *Home Alone* films set up ways for Macaulay Culkin to be left behind not once but twice. Here, though, the basic premise needs no justification. Why is a man condemned to live February 2nd over and over? Who knows? Why do insurance salesmen turn into beetles?

Actually, that's not quite true. There is a moral justification, if you choose to see it. Early on, Phil snarls, 'I *make* the weather.' Well, he thinks he does, and in this respect, the time-loop is laid on purely for his moral edification – time will be out of joint until he realises that actually it's the weather that makes him. So everything seems to be set up for a dainty little moral homily ending in a grouch's rehabilitation. But Murray's already done that one, not terribly successfully, in *Scrooged*. *Groundhog Day* has a more cynical agenda. Phil is improved, but for all the wrong reasons and in all the wrong ways. He can become the perfect man purely because he has nothing else to do, having exhausted all the day's other possibilities. Given time, he becomes a god, omniscient and omnipresent, and when that's driven him mad, maybe then he'll settle for being a nice guy. But he's only officially a nice guy when the woman he's lusted after all along (Andie MacDowell) recognises him as one. And that's where the film ends up, in a perfect have-your-cake-and-eat-it male fantasy. Yes guys, even a repellent jerk can get off with Andie MacDowell in twenty-four hours flat (although it might take him eternity to do it).

The probable reason for *Groundhog Day*'s US success is that it appeals at once to absolute idealism and to absolute cynicism. It comes packaged as a moral lesson about human perfectibility, but its deep structure allows for total amorality. Phil gets to do horrible things to other people with impunity, because the next day it'll all be undone. That's the principal behind *Tom and Jerry* violence, but *Groundhog Day* is a first in applying that principal to the comedy of manners. And because everything is possible, even Phil's good deeds – his ridiculous Clark Kent-style life-saving – have no moral value. He simply does them because he can, and because there's nothing else to do.

Groundhog Day is so brazenly funny because, instead of spoon-feeding you as Hollywood comedies tend to, it actually tests your endurance, putting you in the same claustrophobic eternal present as its hero, and constantly daring you to rethink your habitual conceptions of film time. Who'd have thought Ramis and Murray, the stars of *Ghostbusters*, would prove the rightful heirs of Alain Resnais?

7 May 1993

Indecent Proposal

Indecent Proposal is the new schlockbuster by Adrian Lyne, who directed *Fatal Attraction*. This one could have been called *Fiscal Attraction*: Demi Moore and Woody Harrelson are a young couple who have it all – looks, love and money – until the recession hits, and their dream home looks like falling foul of the repo man. Then along comes Robert Redford and offers them one million dollars in exchange for one night with Demi. Tag line: 'He liked her so much he bought her company.'

Indecent Proposal is visually and dramatically anaemic, a high-concept film based on a wafer-thin premise, and shot with all the fussy, over-lit Tampax-ad glitz that has made Lyne the last word in the Lifestyle school of cinema. But the film has gone down a storm at the US box office and on chat shows, where its subject has been mulled over as if it had the philosophical gristle that would qualify it for *The Moral Maze*. The argument is aimed fairly and squarely at Mr and Mrs Married America, especially if they deem themselves a bit liberal, a bit adventurous, but responsibly adult with it. Ladies, would *you* sleep with Robert Redford for a million dollars? And guys, how would *you* feel if she did?

Dumb questions. Of course she would. And of course he'd be down at the club bragging to his buddies about it. Now, if they'd given the Redford part to Danny DeVito, the question might have been more interesting, but not that much. A million dollars is a million dollars. The film doesn't go for complex stakes, just the biggest ones it can think of. Even *Fatal Attraction* had some degree of complexity and ambiguity; what's striking about *Indecent Proposal* is that it thinks entirely in absolutes.

Thus, the Murphys are a *blissfully* happy couple, *totally* in love, who have (and therefore stand to lose) *everything*. The Redford character is *absolutely* staggering, a fairy-tale prince who's not just loaded, but *infinitely* loaded. One single act, and the couple can have *everything* back, *immediately*. The trouble is, although everything is charged with absolute value, nothing has any depth; it's a film of flat, unambivalent signs, which mean nothing more than they seem to. The Murphys' domestic bliss might as well be represented by a drawing of a house with a squiggly line to signify smoke. They live in one beautiful home and dream of building another. When they split up, poor Woody sees his architect's model of a dream house lit from inside by a mystical white glow. Marriage isn't a complex of transactions between two people; it's a house, full stop.

Similarly, money doesn't represent any of the things that it gives access to, like power, or the illicit, or security; it simply represents dollar signs. One Million Dollars is the film's bottom line, its absolute self-referring signifier. When the Murphys go to Las Vegas and win the jackpot, Lyne doesn't actually show them swanking around in dressing gowns emblazoned with dollar signs, or have their eyeballs roll around like cash registers, but they do throw sheaves of greenbacks around their bedroom and roll around in it (I'm willing to believe that visitors to Vegas actually do this).

Then enter Redford, surrounded by penthouse apartments, yachts, helicopters, all the badges of infinite wealth that might look ostentatious in an episode of *Dynasty*. He's called John Gage, but he might as well be called Daddy Megabucks. God knows there are more interesting ways to represent powerful money and its trappings. But this drama of comic-book symbols is less about ideas and things that can be charged with meaning than about the mathematics of pure value.

It's significant, though, that a film that spells everything out so blankly refuses to tell us about one thing – the intimate transaction at the film's centre. We're treated to plentiful saccharine sex between the Murphys – endless backlit marital romping between bouts of tidying up. But the secret sex that (apparently) takes place between Diana and Gage on his yacht remains a mystery, and she and David swear never to discuss it. What happens between them is taboo, because it has happened outside the bounds of marriage. It's indecent – to be more accurate, *obscene*, in the sense of taking place offstage.

Read that way, *Indecent Proposal* turns out to be not at all the 'women's picture' it's been sold as – that is, a film appealing to women's fantasies of what it would be like to have a dream lover as a change from boring old hubby. Rather, the film's turning point comes when David no longer knows exactly what's happening in his wife's life – when she becomes unknowable. From this point on, it is effectively a 'men's picture', addressing male anxieties about the unknowable sexuality of the little woman at home.

David may love Diana, but he has no idea what she's *worth* until another, more powerful man tells him. And he finds out exactly what she's worth, in round figures; the film is a *reductio ad absurdum* of the phrase, 'Babe, you look a million dollars.' *Indecent Proposal* doesn't simply tell us that in a marriage the wife is a liquid asset, it tells us in a way that replicates the star system. If David's biggest asset is Diana, the film's is Demi Moore, currently one of Hollywood's hottest properties (*sic*). The film presents Gage's purchase of her as a rich man's whim, but it also tells legions of adoring Demi fans what they already know – how much a night with her must be worth.

In fact, the film is entirely about Moore as a star, an adorable, value-able object of desire. Demi-Diana is the object of negotiation between the fan (her husband) and the system – or, if you like, the agent (the all-powerful, all-knowing dealer who names her price). Some commentators have seen Gage as a JFK figure, but he's really a Mike Ovitz. And it's true that only when a value is placed on a star's head does she become a star. The crucial transformation happens when she becomes fabulously unknowable; thus Diana to David, thus Demi Moore to her audience.

The film is really an allegory of the unstoppable rise to glory of Demi Moore, but at the price of an old-fashioned sentimental fetishisation of marriage. The institution has never emerged from a melodrama as glowingly coated with holy meaning as it does here. At the end, when David gets his property back, as he surely must, that's one hell of a pedestal he's going to put her on.

But the film's style can't help subverting its content. True love, domestic contentment, the simple life, it argues, are beyond money and acquisitiveness. When you lose everything, love is the one thing that can save you. Yet it's only by passing through the system of finance that the Murphys can come together at the end, and it's only finance – as embodied in the film's production values – that gives the marriage, in all its day-to-day ordinariness, its full meaning, its full emotional *valuation*. The real signs of expense in the film are not so much the obvious ones – the clothes, the swanky dinners on the lawn, the little Taj Mahals that Gage leads Diana round – but in the exceptional density of painstaking detail with which Lyne and his design team have created a lifestyle and documented the routine memories that make the Murphys into a marriage. We aren't allowed to take the couple's history for granted; they don't live in a void, but surrounded by an abundance of meticulously forged evidence of their long-standing togetherness – videos, photos, mementoes of seven years' marriage. We can immediately see how much money and hard work has gone into creating this effect, just as money is the first thing we see when the computer-generated android in *Terminator 2* slithers around the screen like mercury. This is money in the service of the reality effect. Even without John Gage's intervention, it's a million-dollar marriage.

21 May 1993

Les Nuits fauves
(Savage Nights)

The English print of *Les Nuits fauves* is prefaced with a sombre announcement that makes you sit up and pay serious attention. It tells you that the film's director and star, Cyril Collard, died of AIDS this year, aged thirty-five, just three days before the film was awarded four of France's prestigious César awards. Collard was quickly canonised as 'France's own James Dean', becoming not only a tragic icon but an icon of 'revolt', a word that has peculiarly literary and philosophical overtones in French pop culture (it evokes Genet and Rimbaud, rather than Axl Rose). There can't be a French culture magazine that hasn't featured Collard on at least one cover this year. He's no longer just a film director and actor; he's a pop star and a saint as well.

All this makes *Les Nuits fauves* remarkably difficult to read. It's difficult enough to begin with, because it presents all the teasing paradoxes of a film that is quite clearly autobiographical but that, because it's a fiction, can't be read strictly as autobiography. Based on Collard's autobiographical novel, it stars the director himself as Jean, who, having discovered he is HIV-positive, embarks on an unsafe-sex relationship with a young woman, Laura; at the same time, he gets involved with a sexy, semi-fascist boy, Samy. Jean also indulges other appetites to the full – making films, taking crazed high-speed drives through Paris by night, taking part in nocturnal orgies with anonymous male lovers by the side of the Seine, golden showers optional. Jean lives life like there's no tomorrow, which indeed there isn't. He's leading a sleepless, charmed life, immune even to car crashes – immune to everything except his physical lack of immunity. But it's as if his life force is all the greater because he's passed his mortality on to others, as he does in a symbolic – and possibly literal – way to Laura.

The film is hard to watch now because all the time the protagonist is proclaiming his own unquenchable life force we know he's already doomed. Or, at least, we know Collard is. Can we say the same about Jean and assume, as most commentators have, that Jean and Collard are one and the same? The film plays quite calculatedly on these paradoxes of identity and impending mortality – as if in the full knowledge that Jean's *cri de coeur* from *within* life (at the end, he declares, '*je suis dans la vie*') would soon be read as Collard's cry from *outside* it.

What has made Collard an icon is not simply the fact of his death, but the sheer appetite that he exudes. There's an immense energy in the acting, particularly in the febrile scenes between Jean and Laura – unbridled psychodramas in the style of Collard's one-time employer, director Maurice Pialat, with Romane Bohringer displaying a rare ferocity. There's a similar verve to the wheeling camerawork, the nervy editing, the soundtrack (from flamenco to the Pogues to Collard's own rather ropy pop songs), and the very shape of the narrative, which skips drunkenly between scenes, sub-plots, sexual encounters. Collard described both himself and his film as 'bulimic', and it's this restless omnivorousness that makes the film so gripping throughout. The whole thing – with all its incidentals – is in the image of Jean's own polysexuality.

For this is a film not about AIDS, but about Collard. He puts himself at the centre of the drama; he's not only the raging desire around which everything revolves, but also the object of desire that everyone tussles over. There's one scene in which Jean is racked by panic at the thought of dying, after a night on the tiles. But otherwise he remains flirtatiously impassive through-out, wearing a smile of confident, wolfish amusement whether he's getting off with a lover or hurtling through space in his car.

The film's not about sex, but about desire – specifically, about Collard's desire to be seen and desired. Collard is interested not in any specific sexuality, hetero-, homo-, or bi-, but in polysexuality in an almost abstract form, as pure hunger. It was inevitable, then, that *Les Nuits fauves* should have been accused of failing to project any sense of a gay identity. It's unsettling that most of its images of gay sex – the tusslings in the Seine catacombs, a bit of fascistic S & M in a rugby-club brothel – are presented under the sign of darkness, clearly labelled 'wild side'. Gay sex is effectively presented as a side order, a dangerous nocturnal flirtation, even aligned with crypto-fascism in Samy's extracurricular encounters. But it's not as dangerous as the transcendental peril of boy–girl love.

There's no doubt that the film privileges heterosexual love, even treating AIDS as if it were specifically an outcropping of a straight tradition of discourse on *amour fou*. The film begins with Jean being told – apparently in a dream – that the virus can teach him how to love. The rest of the film traces his sentimental education. But if he learns to love, and to live, it's at the expense of others, notably Laura. Once he has told her he is HIV-positive, she wil-fully chooses to risk exposure to the virus, to seal their love pact; but once he has gone off with Samy and she becomes uncon-trollably jealous, it seems to be love itself, rather than the virus, that is destroying her. She goes literally mad with love.

Laura is victimised by the narrative in other ways. She's identified from the beginning as a child, rather than a woman – Jean gives her puppies and soft toys, she tells him about sex at thirteen with an older man, and at seventeen she still snuggles up in Mummy's bed in her pyjamas. She represents the part of Jean that's all childlike appetite, but it's the part he has to reject as uncontrollable.

What she has picked up from him is not the virus itself, but love *as* a virus – a contagion that she, as a child, as a woman, can't quite handle in the way he can. It's simply too strong for a little girl. This is French cinema's favourite story, a woman paying for her man's sentimental education – look at Betty Blue going mad and blind, so that her dippy lover can become a great writer. Laura contributes to Jean's (and Collard's) fate in much the same way.

The problem with *Les Nuits fauves* is not so much that it's narcissistic but that it's narcissistic in this peculiarly macho way. Of course Collard is expressly fashioning himself a shiny memorial to the self – a self that, in the final, embarrassingly metaphysical scene, takes on aspects of a Christ-like rebirth. It's no accident that Collard quotes Jean Genet early on. Genet's myth of self is one that depends on consuming others to live; it's a process that may not be cynical but it is certainly merciless.

Part of the film's reception in France has been to do with sentimental reverence – as if Collard's death made his work beyond reproach. And the film indeed goes out of its way to defuse accusations that it glorifies such sentimental woolliness. The person who talks in grandiose terms about rebel destiny is an old hippie, whom Jean accuses of indulging in '70s talk, but you feel the film wants you to subscribe to the notion regardless of Jean's cynical dismissal. Jean is quite clearly presented as an irresponsible figure, incapable of handling Laura's love; yet what you take away from the film is the sense of the absolute imperative of *amour fou* over workaday contingencies like safe sex.

The problem with the film is not that it refuses to wave a sensibly admonishing finger. But it depoliticises AIDS in a more insidious way. What the film is about, finally, is inverting the old metaphor that sees love as a malady – *Les Nuits fauves* takes a specific malady and presents it as love. That's nothing new – that inversion goes back at least as far as *La Dame aux camélias*. But times are too tough to indulge in the old Romantic fantasies, and it is trivial to use such a hugely charged issue as AIDS as a vehicle for such banal mythifying. We're beyond love's sweet sickness now.

25 June 1993

Jurassic Park

One of the most memorable images in Steven Spielberg's *Jurassic Park* comes when a Tyrannosaurus Rex rears up in triumph and a banner flutters down reading, 'When Dinosaurs Ruled the Earth'. It's a nice self-congratulatory touch, reminding us how far saurian cinema has come in sophistication since the 1969 film of that name. But it also points out that *now* is the time when the big scaly ones truly reign supreme. Much of *Jurassic Park* is laden with messages – not so subliminal either – directly concerning the film's own status as an unvanquishable monster. It was a foregone conclusion that the huge marketing industry attached to the film would make *Jurassic Park* and its subject matter a world-wide preoccupation.

So it's tempting to suggest that *Jurassic Park* isn't really about dinosaurs at all. Perhaps the dinosaurs are simply the incarnation of whatever it is that the film is really about – the unthinkable, the sublime, or maybe just the downright bloody huge. It's certainly plausible to see them as the latest manifestation of that transcendental object of awe that keeps appearing in Spielberg films: the shimmering phantoms released at the end of *Raiders of the Lost Ark*, the angelic aliens in *Close Encounters of the Third Kind*, or, more portentously, the Hiroshima mushroom cloud that the young hero of *Empire of the Sun* mistakes for a soul rising up to heaven.

There is indeed a brief transcendental moment in *Jurassic Park*, but it comes towards the beginning, when the scientists visiting the dinosaur theme park run by jolly billionaire John Hammond (Richard Attenborough) gape in awe at a herd of long-necked behemoths grazing in the sun. Their immediate reaction and ours is, 'Can such things be?', and then we think, 'How do they do it?' (a question one character actually asks), and the spell is dissipated. We immediately know we're dealing with a special effects demonstration, and the only question is what other tricks the film will go on to pull (remarkable ones, as it happens, not least a thundering herd of ostrich-like gallomimuses).

But there's no real sense of awe in *Jurassic Park* – nothing is unveiled as it is in Spielberg's other films (remember the excruciating slow build-up of *Close Encounters of the Third Kind?*). There's something oddly casual about the film – like a mountebank revealing the Eighth Wonder of the World, then showing you a bigger, better one. The film has a curious agenda: it knows its job, which is to present breathtaking illusions, but it also wants us to know they're illusions, so that we don't get too impressed and forget the other more serious topics it has on its mind.

Foremost among those topics are questions of the environment and of nature. At heart, *Jurassic Park* is an old-fashioned science-gone-too-far movie, and the role of its scientist heroes (Sam Neill, Laura Dern and chaos theorist Jeff Goldblum) is to wave a warning finger about how you just can't mess with nature. At one point it's discovered that the dinosaurs on Attenborough's island, all cloned from DNA and designed to behave artificially, are spontaneously doing odd things like changing sex, deviating from their programmed behaviour patterns. Horror of horrors, they're turning natural. So Goldblum was right when he fulminated, 'Life will not be contained! Life finds a way!'

In case we're not sure what kind of life the film has in mind, there are plenty of children on hand to remind us. Early on, Neill's character, a confirmed infantophobe, lectures a boy on the horrors of being eaten alive, and cautions him, 'Have some respect.' For the rest of the film, he's obliged to swallow his child-loathing and protect Hammond's cute computer- and fossil-literate grand-children. The film's real story is about his learning to love kids – to stop being a big kid himself and become a daddy, tender, protective and in touch with nature (his own and the primeval world's). Clearly, this is a complex running through Spielberg's films, which always scratch at the itchy problem of boys becoming men – as in his irksome Peter Pan fantasy *Hook*.

Of course, you always knew that Neill would get in touch with the daddy within. You can tell it right from the beginning when he's carping away about how he hates kids, and Laura Dern gives an indulgent little smile, because she – his destined mate – knows him better than he knows himself. Here's a cute touch: he's a palaeontologist, she's a palaeobotanist; he knows bones, she knows flowers. And when the final image of the film is a redemptive flight of storks, you hold your breath waiting for the nappies to be unpacked. (An ornithologist friend points out that they are in fact pelicans. That may be true, but I recognise a symbolic stork when I see one.)

Curiously, though, Neill also confesses to hating computers (which kids, of course, love – it's the techno-whiz granddaughter who saves the day). The film itself hates technology too – it can't wait to jettison the computer graphics and hardware gadgetry that appear early on and get to grips with the thrill of prehistory. Paradoxically, everything that's modish and state-of-the-art is condemned as being old hat, commonplace sci-fi stuff. What makes the film 'new' – hyper-modern – is its embrace of the ancient. There's another similar distinction at work – between the unimaginably huge dinosaurs and the inconceivably small scale on which they're created. These monsters are the product of *microgenics*, cloned out of DNA taken from the blood of pre-historic mosquitoes.

In fact, Spielberg's monsters are created in much the same way. Many of these lumbering titans are actually computer-generated – built out of thousands upon thousands of minuscule pixels, artfully manipulated just as Hammond's scientists manipulate the DNA chain. So the film is supremely conscious of the process of its own making, which it reproduces in its subject matter. But it's also curiously embarrassed about them. Like Neill, the film *hates* computers, although it's obliged to use them. Wouldn't it be better, it's implied, if this all *were* real, if it weren't necessary to simulate? Hammond himself, reminiscing about a flea circus he once ran, says he created Jurassic Park because he wanted to show the world 'something that wasn't an illusion', to which Dern retorts, 'It still *is* a flea circus . . . It's all an illusion.'

Hence the film confesses to its own rather pathetic bad faith. *Jurassic Park* marvels at its own image-making, but hates the means it uses to achieve it; it revels in the act of creation, but despairs at the idea that it's all bread and circuses. Making artificial monsters is no kind of creation, the film suggests; natural reproduction is. Spielberg gives us the time of our lives treating us like impressionable kids, but at heart he feels we should be concerning ourselves with more adult business. His next film is about Auschwitz.

16 July 1994

Last Action Hero

I've recently heard people casually batting around a chilling prognosis for the next millennium: the idea that future generations will have no use for irony. That may be because the current generation has used it all up. If that's so, it's all gone into the latest Arnold Schwarzenegger film *Last Action Hero*. And it may be that the world is already ushering irony to an ignominious grave by greeting the film with unalloyed contempt.

Last Action Hero has so far been almost unanimously panned by critics, who've seen it as a grotesque lapse into bad faith, as misjudged hubris, and as a gesture of out-and-out contempt for its audience. Its crime is to parody a Schwarzenegger movie, under the guise of a Schwarzenegger movie. In the film, Arnie has as many bullets in his ammo belt as ever, but this time they're satiric ones, targeted at his own persona, at the action genre and its conventions, and at the reasons people go to see Arnie movies in the first place. This has been perceived as a graceless exercise in biting the hands that feed you.

The film could arguably be accused of short-changing its public by promising but not providing a proper Arnie film. But if you take a 'proper' Arnie film to be one in which he has an unassailable iron-man persona, a mere handful of monosyllabic lines, and a multimillion-dollar special effects budget, that simply begs the question of how 'proper' the films that fitted that bill were in the first place. As far back as *The Terminator*, Schwarzenegger was already implicitly parodying his persona by taking the idea of tungsten-tough immutability to ludicrous extremes. By the mere fact of including him, any film automatically becomes a part of a very flexible genre called the 'Arnie movie'; the man cuts a figure so totally incommensurate with any notion of the real that his very presence tends to restructure any vehicle he's in. All his films, whether 'serious' like *Total Recall* or 'comic' like *Twins*, are largely about the need to change the normal fictional concept of the real in order to accommodate a body and an accent that have no place in any fiction dealing with the real world. The very fact of casting a man thus accented as a character named 'Doug Quaid' (*Total Recall*) is already to invoke a reality that is as radically other as can be imagined.

Last Action Hero, however, is not a straight self-parodic romp like *Kindergarten Cop*. Instead, it's the closest we may get to 'abstract Arnie' – a meditation on the phenomenology of what it's like to watch a Schwarzenegger movie. As the film begins, we think we're watching the new Arnie film, but it turns out we're watching a segment of a fake Arnie film, *Jack Slater III*, through the eyes of eleven-year-old Danny, sitting in a Times Square fleapit. It turns out that Danny isn't a Schwarzenegger fan – he couldn't give a toss about Schwarzenegger – but a Jack Slater fan. He knows he's fallen into the right dream when he gets to see a sneak preview of *Jack Slater IV* and is magically spirited into the film, where he's able to help Slater out by recourse to the conventions of the genre. He finds he can live life as if he'd read the script.

There's nothing new about this sort of cinematic trick. It goes back to the exhaustively self-reflexive Olsen and Johnson comedy *Hellzapoppin'* (1941) and was last and most spectacularly pulled in the cinema in *Gremlins 2*, in which Joe Dante committed a spectacular act of directorial hara-kiri by debunking all the premises of his earlier hit *Gremlins*. Among his coups was to have his host of sniggering nocturnal ghouls mock their incarnation in the first film – which is essentially the same as Cervantes's ploy in Part Two of *Don Quixote*.

Last Action Hero similarly removes the walls between the real and the fictional, between knowledge of the world and knowledge of the movies. In the process, however, it often gets bogged down in pedantic niggling about conventions. The boy Danny is a real pain in this respect, a genre die-hard who thinks he's outsmarted reality, but just wants everything to conform to a fictional template. The joke's good when it refers to other films – he's able to warn Slater that the character played by F. Murray Abraham is a bad guy, because he killed Mozart in *Amadeus*. But it gets irritating when Danny thinks the conventions out loud. During a death-defying stunt, he reasons, 'I'm a good guy, it's going to work,' but then realises, 'I'm a comedy sidekick, it's not going to work!' Danny, you can tell, will grow up to be a seen-everything, liked-nothing trainspotter critic, one of those that can never forgive a loose plot thread or a cheap special effect.

These critics, of course, will loathe *Last Action Hero* because it's *all* loose strands, because the logic of its paradoxical Russian-doll structure just isn't consistent. But it doesn't have to be. Once you've removed the fourth wall of illusion, you might as well start demolishing the entire cinema. *Last Action Hero* is so impressive because, while it has no more idea of the Real than any other Hollywood film, it nonetheless uses the unreal as a measure to plumb the questions of what reality might be, and how movies might deal with it. There's immediately a sense that we might want to reconsider our notion of what is tolerable when *Jack Slater*'s impeccably cruel British villain (Charles Dance) steps out of the screen and into Times Square; as he looks round at the everyday horror, you can see a faint thrill of revulsion as this cartoon Mephistopheles realises that his evil is not quite on a par with what our world has in store.

The film's choicest paradox is to bring the fictional Arnie face to face with the real Arnie – or, at least, the most convincing simulacrum of a real Arnie that it can muster. As Jack Slater – now exiled in the real world – arrives at the New York premiere of *Jack Slater IV*, he meets 'Arnold Schwarzenegger' himself, but as *Spy* magazine might parody him – a two-dimensional lunk with nothing on his mind but fatuous remarks about halving his films' body count, and desperate for a chance to plug his restaurant. When Slater appears, Arnie nonchalantly greets him with a deliciously obtuse flourish of megastar vanity, congratulating him on being his convincing double. But who's the double of whom? And which one are we rooting for?

You can see why the film has struck a dead note in the States – for one thing, because its indefatigable excess of *Looney Tunes* invention strains the bounds of a manageable narrative in just the same way that its star's a-charismatic oddness and unwieldy bulk strain the dimensions of the realist screen. And it's true that much of the satire is on a one-note level: all the in-joke jibing at genre conventions will quickly make the film seem as date-tied as, say, an 1830s skit on Romantic versification.

What *Last Action Hero* most successfully does is to dismantle the star persona as a product that is only marginally related to a real person with a real body and a real life, but intimately tied to a set of rules that govern how it is to be presented and consumed. A Schwarzenegger film is only possible if you find a framework strong enough to contain its star; the *Jack Slater* writers seem just about to have managed this. But once Danny has worked through the rules of how a Schwarzenegger film works – that is, how to watch one – there's no further need for Schwarzenegger. In the end, the image of Arnie that we retain from the film – the one that seems most real – is not the Jack Slater persona, nor the strutting Austrian at the movie premiere, but the Arnie that stands outside the premiere – the eighty-foot inflatable Jack Slater effigy. It was this effigy, bobbing placidly out at sea, that at Cannes this year caused considerably more of a stir than either the 'real' Arnie or the preview of *Last Action Hero*. And this season, Arnie as a giant-sized logo of himself is the only star likely to give the dinosaurs a run for their money.

30 July 1993

```
┌─────────────────────────────────────────────┐
│                                               │
│   S l i v e r  ·  B e n n y ´ s               │
│                                               │
│   V i d e o                                   │
│                                               │
└─────────────────────────────────────────────┘
```

Sliver is among the most accurately titled films ever – it's that slender, unlike Joe Eszterhas's payment as screenwriter, which is more like *Chunk*. In conventional terms, it has little to recommend it, unless you count its two most heavily marketed selling points – a song by UB40 at their whiniest, and the antiseptic spectacle of Sharon Stone enjoying a solitary writhe in the bath (surprisingly, Badedas have missed the obvious product placement opportunity).

What *Sliver* does have going for it, albeit fleetingly, is an interesting take on the modish theme of the moment – video surveillance. Since there's precious little suspense at work in the film's flabby mystery premise, it won't hurt to reveal (besides, you'll have guessed as much from the promo video for UB40's record) that *Sliver* features a character who surveys the tenants in an apartment block by means of a massive bank of surveillance monitors. This gives us the chance to watch a wide range of unsuspecting subjects at work, rest and play, usually in front of the bathroom mirror that conceals the camera. People yawn, screw, fight and generally drop all social formalities – there's even a generously unflattering glimpse of director Phillip Noyce mugging blearily through his morning toilette.

The video premise provides more interesting dividends than we're initially led to expect. At first, we're offered a rather hackneyed tease in the film's self-conscious appeal to the supposedly perverse drives that link cinema and voyeurism. As one character says, and the film's poster reiterates, 'You like to watch, don't you?' But there's nothing particularly pleasurable, nor convincingly perverse, in the watching we get to do – the fetishistically quick-spliced, decomposed electronic images in the bath-time scene, and later some (implausibly giggly) Manhattan sophisticates peering through a telescope at a couple making love in the apartment opposite.

The first – inadvertent – revelation that *Sliver* offers is that the simple act of watching is no big deal after all. Over the last decade, voyeurism has been built so solidly into the margins of mainstream cinema – from *Blue Velvet* to *sex, lies and videotape* – that the notion alone no longer packs any *frisson*. In this sense, *Sliver* is as inept at getting a charge out of its supposedly fail-safe risquéness as was the dreary Madonna vehicle *Body of Evidence*. But what *Sliver* does have to offer, in a remarkably powerful sequence, is an *excess* of vision. As Stone first walks in to find fifty screens simultaneously pumping out the realest form of 'reality programming' imaginable, the camera, as if drunk on the revelation, wildly scans the screens, on all of which *something is happening* – some event, some minor horror or spectacle or inconsequential anecdotal moment charged with absolute significance for the split second that you notice it. As the throb of the soundtrack music joins in, the effect is an overwhelming appeal to cerebral overload, a high-power narcotic.

That moment is over all too briefly, but it's followed by a sobering one. The drunkenness that Stone's character Carly derives from the simultaneous availability of so much apparently raw, unmediated knowledge palls when she realises that knowledge also carries a moral imperative. A man in one apartment has been sexually abusing his daughter, and there's a chilling exchange of glances when Stone gets in the lift with them and suddenly has a new vision of the social façade – the father's shield of normality suddenly becomes charged with evasive intent, while the child's paradigmatically 'innocent' look becomes a direct appeal to Carly as knowing subject.

There's no real debate on 'improper' knowledge – the issue is brushed aside, and the film effectively stops here. But for a moment, *Sliver* has transcended its transcription of glossy surfaces and taken stock of its implications as a vehicle for the image. The fact that nothing too sophisticated is going on is partly why it's interesting; you're reminded how very problematic things get when film tries to engage with video. These days, film increasingly measures itself against video as an instrument for capturing and/ or manipulating the real, and it's hard always to know what's at stake – whether it's a case of film being threatened by video's immediate access to the real, or envying its ability to reshape it. This is no longer a specialist subject restricted to the phenomen-ological wranglings of Wim Wenders or the moral debate of *Henry: Portrait of a Serial Killer*. Mainstream fiction now routinely has recourse to camcorder imagery – everything from Walter Hill's *Trespass*, which used it for enhanced grittiness, to *Falling Down*, which brilliantly captured the way that people use video as an unreliable lifeline to images of stability.

The most illuminating glimpses of cinema's uneasy relation to video are often the least fully articulated, rather than the more elaborated analyses offered by a film like Michael Haneke's *Benny's Video*. This Austrian production is a European art film of the most austere tradition, a blankly recounted parable about video's noxious effects. An emotionally blinkered adolescent, who lives only for his electronic images, kills a girl, incidentally capturing her death on his camcorder, and then transfers his guilt to his morally vacant middle-class parents. It's a stern jeremiad about moral and cultural devaluation, about the sins of the parents manifesting themselves in the children, and about a blinkered moral anaesthesia prevalent in the new Europe.

But the film is finally without real impact. That's partly because it occupies such familiar territory – in terms of its more obvious shock content, it's been pre-empted by *Henry* and the Belgian *Man Bites Dog*, both wittier and more perversely charming in their absolute blackness. But it also disappoints because there's no ambivalence at stake, no sense that the film, despite its loathing of video, might nevertheless allow itself to be susceptible to some of the form's seductions. That might not have made it more human, exactly, but it would have been more honest; instead, *Benny's Video* delivers its moralistic view strictly from the high ground – not least of all aesthetically, in its long takes from a static camera and absolute refusal of spectacle or stylistic rhetoric.

Benny's Video is part of a trilogy that Haneke describes as a 'polemical statement about the American sensational cinema and its power to rob viewers of their ability to form their own opinions' and 'an appeal for cinema of insistent questions in place of facile, erroneous answers'. *Sliver* is exactly the sort of film that Haneke rails against, and yet, in its brief flashes of interest, it is infinitely more suggestive of possible questions about video's attendant values than Haneke's film, which answers its own questions with frustrating decisiveness.

In all its idiot glossiness, *Sliver* provides much more of a sense of why video exerts its seduction. Haneke's young antihero repeatedly watches footage of a pig being slaughtered, but the image loses its horror the first time it's repeated; indeed, the film is about video as automatism, as reality drained of its emotive force. It demystifies a highly charged image from the outset. The monitor scene in *Sliver*, with its masses of casual domestic images, offers the appeal of a kind of random, on-tap reality, a reality not filmed with intent to interrogate the real, but supposedly caught *on the hop*, plucked out of the real and charged with status. In the last year, we have come to believe more and more in video's capacity to 'pluck' random moments out of the daily real, and extract from them *the truth* – to identify, for example, the blurry figures seen by British surveillance cameras accompanying murder victims Jamie Bulger and Emmanuel Spiteri. Rather than making definitive statements about the danger of relying on the video image, as *Benny's Video* does, there seems more scope in the occasional naive reminder that our appetite for the video-real is motivated as much by a taste for the glamour of 'reality programming' as by a desire for 'truth'.

20 August 1993

Blue

Throughout the entire duration of Derek Jarman's *Blue*, there's nothing to look at – nothing but a single shade of blue. Deep and rhythmic, it's the same blue – or as close as light through celluloid can get to it – as the colour patented by the French artist Yves Klein (IKB, International Klein Blue). Watch this single shade for the film's seventy-six minutes, and a strange optical effect takes hold, as the screen pulses, shimmies, reveals elusive shapes and dimensions. Theorists insist that in any film you see what you want to see, that the only real projections on the screen are those of the viewer's desire. For once, it's true. In this film, it's all in the eye of the beholder.

Blue is not some sort of conceptualist prank, to be read separately from the canon of Jarman's 'real' films. He hasn't chosen to show it as a gallery installation; instead, it's screening at the MGM Panton Street, and will be shown on Channel 4 with a simultaneous broadcast of the soundtrack on Radio 3. It is certainly a work that demands to be seen, in every sense; it needs the viewer to complete its fabrication.

See it in the cinema if you can – partly because otherwise you'll miss the full intensity of the colour, partly because the film so directly addresses the primal cave-dweller in every cinema-goer. Here the feeling of sitting in the dark bombarded with blue radiation on a big screen is as close as cinema gets to sensory deprivation, but the effect, paradoxically, is more like the opposite, sensory overstimulation.

Blue is simultaneously easy and nigh-impossible to describe. It's a blue screen, but what do you see?[1] What's happening? The question to ask is one that's usually elided in discussing cinema: what's it like to watch this film? Certainly, 'watching' becomes a rather different experience here, at once active and passive. You work to make sense of the film, and you have to concentrate – to assimilate this rather demanding experience and perhaps even to stay awake. But you also accept that your attention will fade in and out, as your own associations take you elsewhere. That drifting vision is an inescapable part of watching *Blue*.

Even if you're not a Jarman acolyte, able to make connections with his past work, the film is readable, for all its abstraction. It is unified by Jarman's own presence as speaking voice, as writing self, as autobiographical subject. The voices that speak and sing in *Blue* – in a complex sound patchwork designed by Marvin Black – are not always Jarman's own (the other speakers are John Quentin, Tilda Swinton and Nigel Terry), but they always seem to be delegates of the Jarman 'I'. This dislocated 'I', the postmodern self *in extremis*, comes to us in a series of verbal and musical fragments taking in impressionistic musings on the colour blue, mythical and pastoral evocations of a hero named Blue – a lost love? an idealised blue-eyed blue-jean boy? – and anecdotes and observations that could be fresh from the film-maker's diary.

The anecdotes mainly concern Jarman's treatment for symptoms related to HIV. Just as one single colour fills the screen and creates a multiplicity of colour metaphors in the text, HIV becomes the repeated subject that preoccupies Jarman here, a

[1] In cinema's use of 'blue screen' technology, the colour blue is normally what disappears; Jarman here is very literally showing us what is normally invisible.

single stable theme round which a multiple self revolves and dissolves.

The idea of imminent death haunts the work in a very concrete, painful way – in a long, discomforting litany of physical reactions to the drug DHPG, in a sardonic musing on the futility of buying new shoes. Blue itself becomes the colour of death, the 'blue-bearded reaper', and of the electric physical charge that attaches to the death-haunted body in a 'blue funk'. Above all, it is the colour of a change in vision: the flash on the film-maker's eyes as doctors carry out tests on his failing retinas.

The film is an attempt to communicate what, for a film-maker, could be considered as serious as death itself: the crisis of vision. 'If I lose half my sight,' Jarman asks, 'will my vision be halved?' The film is a wager on the possibility that a wilfully assumed constraint of the palette might make paradoxically for an amplified vision. 'If the doors of Perception were cleansed,' the film says, 'then everything would be seen as it is.' There's an element of mysticism in this utopian notion, which draws on one of the recurrent paradoxes of modern art – what is said when there's nothing on the canvas? Blank, or near-blank paintings have frequently risked banality to get at the transcendental (Klein in his blue paintings, but also especially Barnett Newman, a painter obsessed with the idea of the Sublime).

In *Blue*, Jarman is after nothing quite so abstract. The film attempts to evoke a particularly lucid, uncluttered view of things as they are. It conveys a near-physical sense of a subjectivity at once in retreat from the contingent world and shackled within the too-solid prison of a body. In a shocking passage, the narrator meets young Bosnian refugees, then remarks, 'What need of so much news from abroad while all that concerns either life or death is all transacting and at work within me.' It's hard to know how to take this: an admission of despaired fatigue, withdrawal from the world? A solipsistic self-aggrandisement, identifying his body as the locus of all earthly suffering? A feeling of impotence, of the impossibility of being at once in the world and in one's self? It's a feeling that we come to share while watching *Blue* – a sense that we too have retreated into our own confines and that the world ceases to exist, simply because it can no longer be referred to in the way that cinema usually refers to the world.

This hardly makes *Blue* a non-political film; and why assume that films informed by AIDS must be 'political' in a narrow sense? The political voice is one of the voices that run through the film, but it's not the palatable voice of reassurance. Jarman remarks on the slogan, 'Living With AIDS': 'The virus was appropriated by the well – so we have to live with AIDS while they spread the quilt for the moths of Ithaca across the wine-dark sea.' Together with this awkward verbal excess comes a more straightforward refusal of stiff-upper-lip 'courage', from a man who has had that publicly required of him more than is humanly reasonable. Some of the film's voices defy easy approval; that is part of the film's refusal to pin itself down. One song cuts rudely through the generally sweet ambience of the music soundtrack – a braying chant in which a football chorus roars its own evasion of definable identity: 'I am a cock-sucking/ Straight-acting lesbian man/ With . . . Spunky sexist desires/ Of incestuous inversion and incorrect terminology.'

Blue may be a boldly literal contemplation of the void, but it's also about a film-maker staking everything on one bottom-line attempt to see what film can deliver when all its contingent pigments are washed away. It gauges the possibility of retaining faith in the image even when the image has been reduced to its most intangible. We shouldn't be tempted, as we often are when faced with radically different films, to say that after this films will 'never be the same again'. Because of its radicalism, *Blue* can only be a marginal attempt to rethink cinema. But radical it certainly is, an attempt at a *tabula rasa* and a call to re-vision the world, to reinvent images that are genuinely personal and stripped of extraneous visual 'noise'. Here's where the political and the mystical meet, in Jarman's injunction: 'Thou Shalt Not Create Unto Thyself Any Graven Image, although you know the task is to fill the empty page.'

10 September 1993

The Tale of the Fox (Le Roman de Renard) · The Secret Adventures of Tom Thumb

It's the great linguistic quirk of art history that the French term for still life suggests its exact opposite – *nature morte*. The film term 'animation' is charged with the same paradox. The animator's art is less about revivifying dead matter, rousing still things to motion, than about the very deadness and artificiality that underlie the supposedly natural 'live' motion of cinema. We may believe that things on the screen are moving of their own accord, but really there's nothing happening – just still picture following still picture, enough of them per second to deceive us.

But animation, by its very contrivance, invariably lets its founding inertness show through. And the most philosophical animation does more than that – it actively displays itself falling apart at the seams, crumbling into its constituent still parts. That may be why animation, throughout its history, is so obsessed with representing death – from the singing skeletons that stalk through early Disney and Max Fleischer cartoons, to the million ritual deaths inflicted on that great metaphysical hero Wile E. Coyote, to the morbid decomposition of polymorphous clay heads in the work of Czech animator Jan Svankmajer. Where the 'Golem principle' of animation is about bringing dead clay to miraculous life, Svankmajer specialises in turning everything back into clay.

It's easy to forget all this now that drawn animation has become so adept at disguising its roots with high-tech trickery. Disney's *Aladdin* flows so liquidly, it's like pure organic electricity – you'd think the light had just generated itself. Two other current animation releases offer an antidote to this intoxicating slickness, but I'm not being Luddite or anti-Hollywood in saying that – just materialist. It's always welcome when film shows the stuff it's made of – literally – and a few creaks and groans can be stimulating indeed.

The Tale of the Fox is an extraordinary thing, as finely tuned, yet as endearingly rickety, as a Fabergé wind-up egg. It was made in France in 1930 by the great Polish animator Wladyslaw Starewicz. Starewicz is best known for his extraordinary insect stop-motion films, which took anthropomorphism to a bizarre extreme by casting bugs in louche melodramas. *The Cameraman's Revenge* (1911) is a tale of sibling rivalry, infidelity and voyeurism, in which two beetles clash over an inheritance of warm beer.

The mediaeval fantasy *The Tale of the Fox* is much closer to the funny-animal anthropomorphism of the Disney school – its characterisation is pretty much a precursor of *The Jungle Book* – but its obsessive meticulousness makes it quite extraordinary. Frogs, bugs and small birds still get a look in, but this time Starewicz is dealing with flesh and fur, with a taxidermist's fine eye. He really gets under the skin, moving his creatures not just on the outside but internally too, as if by hidden sinews. Fur bristles, nostrils twitch, a lion queen's bosom swells with passion as an amorous cat pays court (unsettlingly, they're Margaret Dumont and Groucho Marx to a whisker).

The very literary French text and bombastic diction, added in the early 1940s, detract slightly from the pleasure of the visuals, but they can't dilute the extraordinary mediaeval design and the sheer flexibility of Starewicz's universe. Everything is mutable here. At one moment, the animals seem enormous, grimacing and pulsating in close-up; the next, they're minute, isolated in stylised winter landscapes or crowding together in vast battle scenes. The textures keep shifting, too, between some sort of 'reality' and a dream world, like the animal heaven in which sausages and winged rabbit-heads float above the clouds.

There's also an extraordinary cynicism about it. It's pure folk tale, with the Fox as the traditional Trickster figure beloved of Propp and other analysts of narrative. That means we're asked to side with a hero who consistently outwits the other animals by snitching on them to humans, who are only too happy to bring out the cudgels and broomsticks (when the Fox's hapless victims get battered, rather dainty snowflake figures blossom above their heads). In the final showdown, in which the Fox wheels out an array of Heath Robinson war engines, he's as venomously sneaky as Macaulay Culkin beating the crooks in *Home Alone*. This is the limit-point of anthropomorphism – the Fox defeats the other beasts because he's more cunning, which is to say, more human. There's the same sort of Darwinism at work here as in Disney – the semi-human Mickey Mouse ranks somewhere in the evolutionary scale above Donald, who's way above Pluto, who's plain old dog and stuck that way.

Nothing so unfashionably anthropocentric in *The Secret Adventures of Tom Thumb*, in which animated matter takes its revenge on humanity in a big way. This hour-long piece by Bristol-based animator Dave Borthwick, from production company the bolexbrothers (*sic*) is creepy, dystopian stuff – what you'd get if Mother Goose swallowed *The Fly*. A mistake in a fertility lab leads to a woman giving birth to a Bendy Toy homunculus; the creature is shunted off to a research centre where it encounters a hellish cast of hybrid monsters – disembodied mouths and eyes, a gryphon made of batwings, wires and crocodile clips. The creations are grisly enough, but the real horror is in what's done with the live actors, who are animated in exactly the same way as the models. They're pixillated: that is, shot frame by frame and moved imperceptibly each time. Hence a jerky, dehumanising effect – the already grotesque characters lumber robotically around, fixed expressions contorting their faces, while the surface of their skin flickers and shimmies in small seismic ripples. Models and humans both move this way, and at the same time, so that you always get different types of motion going on in the same shot, to paradoxical effect. While inanimate matter – rolling newspapers, circling flies – surges with an uncontainable energy of its own, human flesh turns back to modelling clay, golemised.

This process is echoed self-consciously in the theme of the film, which concerns the artificial creation of life. The story itself is none too original, nor is the world it's set in – the now-familiar post-apocalyptic urban limbo inhabited by lurching Gumbies in singlets and Oxfam overcoats. The film's appeal, instead, is quite literally in the style – the *way* it's done, which creates its own language and determines the way we read it. But there are incidental touches that set the gorge rising pleasurably – the sight of fish (and worse) writhing on a plate, and the rather distressing figure of Tom himself, a cooing, piteous, earless blob. It's manipulative, of course, but if you wonder what David Cronenberg might have made of *The Clangers* it's certainly for you.

Starewicz's films are about pullulating life – they celebrate the uncontainable expansiveness of things. The bolexbrothers come right at the end of the line – theirs is a hymn to decay and deadness that reduces the human figure to silly putty. But arguably that's where live cinema's headed anyway – what are the muscle boys of the current action genre, after all, but overblown wind-up toys running on autopilot? As humans in Hollywood continue to do the work of automata, it's salutary to be reminded how much more lifelike real automata can be. It may be that humans in film were a complete distraction all along, and that Starewicz and his bugs figured it out back in the 1910s – stop motion is where the real 'live' action is.

3 December 1993

Heaven & Earth

Heaven & Earth is the proverbial 'tale told by an idiot, full of sound and fury, signifying nothing'. The idiot is not, I should say, the film's narrator and subject Le Ly Hayslip, on whose two autobiographical books the film is based, but Oliver Stone, who can always be relied on to go into hyperdrive. It's a safe bet that early on in his career Stone was taken by the phrase 'visual pyrotechnics' in a film review, and ever since has barely been able to shoot a scene without a couple of dozen Roman candles to hand. *Heaven & Earth* is pure Independence Day razzmatazz, rockets'-red-glare from start to finish. The irony is that, this time, he thinks he's not telling an American story at all.

Heaven & Earth is billed as the third chapter of a Vietnam trilogy, following on from *Platoon* and the overblown but compelling *Born on the Fourth of July* – American tales to the hilt. I was never much impressed with *Platoon*, which consolidated the stereotype of self-regarding sixties 'lost generation' angst: to think those fine boys could have been doctors, lawyers, rock musicians . . . But *Born on the Fourth of July*, a pure comic-strip version of liberal US history, was extraordinary, precisely because its earnestness knew no censorship and its symbolism no subtlety. There was something spellbinding in its frenetic inability to deal with any symbols other than the American flag – at every conceivable turn, Stone would wave a Stars and Stripes or stage a ticker-tape parade, just to hammer home the point that Old Glory was ragged and in need of a patching. Inarticulate neurosis writ large, the film was as American and as subtle as a fridge overstocked with chilli dogs and cantaloupes. In fact, *Heaven & Earth* itself features both a US flag, worn practically transparent and wafting in front of a melancholy sunset, and just such a fridge. And this is supposed to be a film about the experience of the Vietnamese.

Le Ly Hayslip, *née* Phung Thi Le Ly, is a woman who, as she puts it, has had more than her share of 'bad karma'. (I can imagine a studio conference in which the execs think, 'Who's man enough to take on this much bad karma? Ollie Stone, that's who.') Born in Central Vietnam in the early 1950s, the young Le Ly (Hiep Thi Le) enjoys an idyllic life in her secluded farming village, until the tanks start to roll. She joins up with the Viet Cong, but is captured by the South Vietnamese and tortured, in a remarkably unpleasant scene, with ants and snakes. She returns to her village only to be treated just as harshly by the VC, and raped by the side of what she's told is her own grave. Either it's grotesque pathetic fallacy, or it really happened in pouring rain – but this is a dreadful scene, not so much harrowing as embarrassing, as if the camera can't quite believe what it's seeing. It's the 'can-such-things-be?' element that makes it so awful.

Working as a bar girl in Saigon, Le Ly meets Steve Butler, a lonesome lunk of a GI, who will understand her pain and whisk her off to a new life. Of course, the minute you see Tommy Lee Jones in the part, you just know that a reel later he'll be having cold sweats and crashing into the furniture and those dried-raisin eyes will be popping out of his head, while Stone flashes up black-and-white flashbacks from Butler's own personal hell ('Psy-ops, baby!').

Heaven & Earth invites a cynical response because you can see so clearly what the film wants to do, and what it ends up doing. The truism about Stone's films is that he's the lyric poet of the US foreign policy guilt trip. This film does nothing to give that truism any extra depth; it's so manifestly his penance, both for the war and for making two films about the war centred entirely on the wounds of American youth. *Heaven & Earth* attempts to redress the balance, not only by representing the Vietnamese experience but also by being twice as bombastic as *Platoon* and *Born on the Fourth of July* put together.

From the start, the film is shackled to the stylistic weight of its precursors – *Platoon*, with its balletic firestorm extravagance, and, of course, the inescapable dazzle of what remains the most monolithic, and most problematic Vietnam movie, *Apocalypse Now*. Whatever problems you have with Coppola's film, you can't deny that its stylistic excess is solidly grounded in the proposition that war is showbiz – an idea that, whether taken as serious political insight or as a mere movie-brat conceit, at least dictates a certain visual logic. Stone is more high-minded than Coppola, but is equally besotted with spectacle. And he knows no other way to convey the irreducibly foreign experience that is Le Ly's story than by filtering it through American film lore.

Hence an opening sequence that spells out the 'paradise lost' image with staggering preciousness. We see gorgeous sunsets and flat picture-postcard shots of the rice fields; as a million strings swoon away (scored by Kitaro, a Japanese specialist in New Age wallpaper), the young Le Ly asks, 'Where did I come from?', her mother replies, 'From my belly,' and the two exchange winsome giggles. It's like a glutinous parody of *The Good Earth*.

Mainly, however, Stone is stuck in a rut decanting his own familiar tropes. From *Platoon*, we get the swoops of crossfire, the fiery arcs shooting across the screen. From *JFK*, we get the different visual textures, but the flashes of monochrome footage stitched into that film to create a sense of an elusive, many-textured reality here serve only to make everything faster and louder. Then there's a scene where the Viet Cong visit the village, trying to mobilise it; there's a hoedown, and Le Ly's dancing with two flowers in the fiery night; suddenly the camera cants, and we're right in the middle of a Venice Beach freak-out from *The Doors*.

When Le Ly goes with Steve to the States, Stone unleashes his wildest effects to show us just how, you know, *unreal* that country is. Steve's mother is Debbie Reynolds, perfectly pink and egg-like, attended by a flock of gremlin-like dogs. Everything is round, cornucopian – those melons in fish-eye shot cascading into your face, the drive-in fridge stuffed with the fat of the land . . . No wonder thin, angular Le Ly, from the land of airy, wafting rice fields, is out of place. Her drift from her own identity begins when she acquires a very un-Vietnamese bouffant hairstyle. When she returns home years later, it's that formidable Dolly Parton confection that marks her out as irreducibly different from her ravaged mother.

Stone is remarkable for his ability to make political movies that are only political in so far as they aren't political at all. That is, he can take a subject like Vietnam and strip it of all the specifics, turn it into a lament for lost boys, or make of the Kennedy assassination a drunken disquisition on the paranoid nature of film-making. But because they can't tackle their ostensible themes in any other way, they suddenly become immensely powerful unwitting statements about the American zeitgeist – films in which attempts to view the harsh realities of modern history can only take place through a confused, solipsistic optic. Addressing war, Stone can only function through the – ostensibly disturbing, ultimately reassuring – observation expounded by Michael Herr, Coppola and others, that Vietnam was a 'rock 'n' roll war'. With that in mind, Stone's Vietnam films are about bringing it all back home. Here too, there's a palpable swell of relief when Le Ly hits Saigon, and we get bursts of 'Mellow Yellow' and 'Judy in Disguise'. Phew, home at last!

Stone isn't able to say much about Vietnam except that it's not America, while America is too much America. His refusal to refer to cinematic codes other than Hollywood's is classic cultural imperialism, and his application of excessive, flattening energy to a very complex experience is emotional imperialism. In an interview in *Premiere* magazine, Stone has mused about Le Ly Hayslip, 'She's my counterpart. She's a mirror image, all the things that could have happened to me if my soul had been a woman's.' In the end, it seems as if Stone is looking to Hayslip for relief, to assuage all his own bad karma as well as his nation's. But Le Ly herself, despite Hiep Thi Le's tenacious performance, is swamped. It's too much, as if an overeager Stone had pledged to his subject to use all the resources at his disposal to tell her story. The result is a huge incoherent trailer, neither heaven nor earth but big, dumb purgatory.

21 January 1994

The Age of Innocence

The parlour game of the year has been trying to explain the incongruity of Martin Scorsese adapting Edith Wharton's *The Age of Innocence*. Of course Scorsese was attracted to a novel of tender passions in 1870s New York, one theory goes: it's a story of male desire tightly corseted by a façade that can barely contain it, and the hero Newland Archer is at heart a soul brother to *Raging Bull*'s boxer Jake La Motta. He simply wears fancier gloves.

Or, another version has it, the delicate construction of social hierarchy in Wharton's world runs parallel to the rigorously stratified underworld of *GoodFellas* and *Mean Streets*: the Mingotts and van der Luydens don't offer their victims cement overcoats, but they can inflict a social exclusion that sinks them no less definitively. Personally, I'm inclined to think that this project, with its spectacular opportunities for window dressing (the hats, the flowers, the precise alignment of the fish knives) is as close as Scorsese, cinema's most famous ex-altar boy, has yet come to indulging his nostalgia for liturgical impedimenta on screen.

But there's one moment in which we're granted a sudden, startling insight into what he is really doing. It comes when we suddenly see a house isolated against the New York skyline, and, miracle of miracles, there *is* no New York – just a gaping desolation of earthworks, the foundations of what will be Central Park. And we realise exactly what *The Age of Innocence* is: Scorsese's first science-fiction movie.

In this extraordinary matte shot, the whole film crystallises, and we realise why we've felt so ill at ease in it up till now. It is because Scorsese's film observes the laws of sci-fi, in which, however much we think we are in a known world, we always find ourselves adrift. This New York is effectively another planet, and its inhabitants aliens, however human they look. Like the famous revelation of the Statue of Liberty at the end of *Planet of the Apes*, this uncanny image brings the point home.

The sci-fi perspective also makes sense of the film's voice-over, a transcription of Wharton's narrative voice. It is read in august tones by Joanne Woodward, who plays up the text's coolly ironic hauteur so that you can practically hear the arching of her eyebrow. But it has the made-to-be-skipped quality of the 'Now read on . . .' introduction to *Star Wars*; it's a mere genre formality. It doesn't guide us in our relation to the visuals; rather it seems like a piece of music added to complement them, to accentuate the strangeness rather than domesticate it. The voice purportedly offers an entrée into Wharton's salon world and the relations between its habitués, but really it tells us nothing because the richness of the visuals effectively deafens us to it.

We don't want to hear, we want to see, and Scorsese's film is entirely about seeing. The film is predicated on a fundamental misunderstanding of the book, or, to give it its due, a wilful misreading – the assumption that Wharton's world is exotic. It isn't. Wharton casts a critical eye on a world of opulence, true, but of *regimented* opulence in which everything must justify its existence by signifying, in a strictly codified way: 'a kind of hieroglyphic world, where the real thing was never said or done or even thought, but only represented by a set of arbitrary signs'.[1]

[1] Edith Wharton, *The Age of Innocence*, Chapter 6.

It is *not* a world of wonders, but that is how Scorsese treats it. Towards the beginning, as Newland Archer (Daniel Day-Lewis) walks up a staircase leading to a ballroom, the camera seems alternately to give us his viewpoint and then to sweep aside so that we can pause and look in amazement at the paintings we pass. Are we looking, or is Archer? This dapper habitué of the scene probably wouldn't pause to look – and, if he did, would do so with a more coolly appraising eye than this energetic quasi-subjective shot tends to suggest. There's a thrill in the verve of the camerawork that suggests the viewer's presence as Newland's shadow – or, rather, as agitated cousin from the sticks, agape at this feast.

The same applies to the opening scene. We've already become conditioned to the fact that this will be a singularly florid film, by the luscious opening titles in which Elaine and Saul Bass create a rhapsody in explosive rosebuds. Now we're transported to the opera and, as one character scans the hall through opera glasses, we are shown what he sees in a sort of optical skid – a slurred vision, created by a mixture of stop-motion and printing. It charges the visuals with a libidinal energy that belongs less to the character than to the film itself. We're given similar effects throughout – a blush of red over the whole screen, or the superimposition of a finely calligraphed manuscript on the image itself.

Only the fact that Scorsese is so respectful of the text inclines me to read the film's tone against Wharton's. The problem is that he loses out on the spareness and the banality of Wharton's universe, because he is too in love with its glamour, and so he misses its fine distinctions, its irony. Where the novel is rigorously no-nonsense about this small world and its stilted mores, the film swoons over its props: the frocks, the fabrics, the paintings, the gentlemen's gloves neatly arranged in rows. Scorsese shows everything that the novel merely mentions: things become lovingly deployed fetish objects rather than the functional signs they are in the book.

But Scorsese is less interested in irony than in the 'real thing' that Wharton's characters can't mention: emotional discharge.

Everything in the film becomes eroticised, the emotions repressed in the drama displaced into the seeing itself – hence that plethora of swoons internalised in the very fabric of the visuals. Rarely did a supposedly naturalistic film have so much *body*, and be so erotically charged.

It's as if the film itself were perfumed. From the flowers onwards, the film is as much about scent as anything else, about catching a whiff of something – a historical period, an atmosphere redolent of certain costume films dear to Scorsese (*The Magnificent Ambersons*, *The Heiress*), or a womanly perfume more rarefied than any that his own films have yet contained. The scent subliminally evoked throughout is one of those fetish elements that attach to the story's women: the erotic charge of Michelle Pfeiffer's Countess Olenska is infused into the flowers that surround her and into the stronger, more exotic smoke that curls from her rakishly tilted cigarette.

The perfume is just one of the ways the film objectifies women. Its visible counterpart is their transformation into paintings, immobile objects of Newland's 'connoisseur' gaze. Two images stand out: the porcelain pink-and-white of Newland's fiancée May (Winona Ryder), less a woman than a conglomeration of rosebuds à la Tissot; and a fancifully exotic matte shot of Countess Olenska by a quayside, blazing in Turner gold. Both are remarkable shots, as artificial as each other, neither presenting, by any stretch of the imagination, a real woman. Both are exercises in displaying desire yet at the same time containing it in manageable, ceremonial form. They are academic paintings, and at heart – for all its fragrance – the film is an academic exercise, with all the uneasy repression that suggests.

28 January 1994

The Conformist
(Il Conformista)

It's not uncommon to come across films that completely bypass understanding. What *is* rare is a film that eludes it – a more troubling, devious matter altogether. Bernardo Bertolucci's re-released *The Conformist* is such a film. It tells a story (albeit one that we have to reconstruct from a complex structure of flashbacks), and it has a point to make about psychology and politics. Yet, much as it might make perfect sense on one level, on another – on the level of what it's actually like to watch – it doesn't quite make the sense we want it to. It's remarkably obscure – not surprising for a film with a central metaphor of blindness and darkness, but a little more surprising when you realise that the dominant visual tone of the film is a saturated, unbroken whiteness.

For whatever reason, this 1970 film has been somewhat forgotten – partly because of the vagaries of distribution, partly because its popularity was eclipsed by the *succès de scandale* of its follow-up, *Last Tango in Paris*, and partly because its predecessor, *The Spider's Stratagem*, seems in many ways much more complete and satisfying. Because we're somewhat estranged from it, *The Conformist* comes to us now with the force of a genuinely alien discourse.

It looks and feels like a film from another planet. It is from a time when films this complex and uncompromising seemed almost routine – when there was an audience for, and a way of talking about, the experiments of Resnais, Godard and Antonioni. Viewed from a world in which David Lynch is as far out as most of us are prepared to get, *The Conformist* looks as foreign and archaic and sophisticated as cave paintings.

Bertolucci's film cultivates its own unreadability, baffles us even while it plays a game of making perfect sense. For all its narrative dislocations, it tells a story, and has a simple point to make: the confluence of sexual repression and fascism. Based on a novel by Alberto Moravia, it is set in 1930s Italy, and tells the story of Marcello (Jean-Louis Trintignant), a young man who lives in the shade of a childhood trauma – he is convinced he killed a homo-sexual chauffeur (Pierre Clémenti) who tried to seduce him as a child. Horrified, he takes recourse in normality, or what he thinks of as normality – conformism stretched to its extremes. He marries Giulia (Stefania Sandrelli), whom he effectively despises, because he sees her as the very model of bourgeois empty-headedness. He signs up as a fascist agent, and undertakes to spend his honey-moon tracking down, and killing, his old professor.

Taken simply as a pathological explanation of fascism, the film would be banal. But it short-circuits its own obvious meaning at every step. Where Moravia's novel is linear, Bertolucci shuffles the events, so that, rather than just looking at Marcello, we are at once caught up with him on his literal and figurative journey, and far outside him, desperately trying to get a purchase on the big picture. The film is structured as a nest of flashbacks within the frame of Marcello's drive in pursuit of Quadri, the man he is to murder. Marcello also hopes to save Quadri's wife Anna (Dominique Sanda), whom he has apparently fallen in love with, and who has attempted to seduce Giulia. There follows a series of sequences that 'explain' how Marcello got where he is; they apparently take place in his memory, which casts a dubious light on their reliability. Marcello talks to his blind mentor in fascism, Italo; explores a strange, marble mausoleum of a fascist HQ; visits his drug-addicted mother in her crumbling mansion, and his demented father in his asylum; calls on Giulia in her apartment, a cluttered domain of stripes and window-blinds; and, in a sequence that Bertolucci originally cut from the film and is now restored, attends a pre-nuptial party at which all the guests are blind.

Added together, these scenes tell a clear story of who Marcello is, of his psychological make-up, of what he does and why. But the way it is constructed means that scenes undermine each other's claim to be reliable. There is also an overload of style that makes the film unreadable even when the letter of its meaning appears transparent. In practically every scene, the visual stylisation hints at some hidden rhetoric at work that we can't quite pin down. Marcello's visit to his mother, for example, takes in a dramatically canted camera angle; a sweeping, obtrusive tracking shot upward at an unexpected moment; an extremely artificial ground-level shot of a sudden dramatic surge of leaves in the wind. What we see is simple enough – but *why* it's done in this way is not immediately apparent.

There is the lighting, too. White dominates – the marble expanses of the fascist palace, the bleached, inhospitable vista of the asylum, the snow through which the car rushes, and in which the film's melodramatic climax takes place. And there is the bleached, flattening-out lighting of Sanda's broad Dietrich features – a blank space on which all things might be read, a page as inscrutable as Marcello himself.

The stylisation comes in the acting, too, undermining any consistent notion of character. At one extraordinary moment, Marcello, picking up his gun from a contact, suddenly breaks stride with the impassive, nervously scuttling figure we've seen up till now, and adopts a series of flamboyant gangster poses in a doorway. This is one of the film's many reminders that it is a film – as if Trintignant has suddenly taken time out from the narrative to oblige the stills photographer with some saleable shots.

You invariably end up picking out details like this, partly

because the film is so rich in them, but also because it is so wilfully diffuse. In this respect, it is completely unlike *The Spider's Stratagem*, which is equally dreamlike but more complete, more rounded off, with the claustrophobic, self-consuming quality of the Borges story that inspired it. *The Conformist* is much more a film about fragmentation, and is itself an act of fragmentation, shattering the novel it is derived from.

Cinematic allusion also gets in the way of concluding that *The Conformist* is 'about' anything other than film. A red light advertises Renoir's 1936 *La Vie est à nous* in the very first shot, a still of Laurel and Hardy is glimpsed in the window of a dance hall, and Marcello's felt hat, coat and icy demeanour in the first scenes relate him to the soulless, stateless loners of Jean-Pierre Melville's films. Bertolucci's desire to tell a story – and his willingness to work with Paramount, thereby shocking his contemporaries on the left – brings him into conflict with Godard's purist anti-narrative stance of the period; Bertolucci not only effectively snubs Godard by making the film's climax a homage to Truffaut (the snow scenes in *Tirez sur le pianiste*), but gives the marked man Godard's own address. And cinema is implicit in the film's central metaphor. Marcello and Quadri discuss Plato's image of the cave, in which shadows flicker before people's eyes, to be taken for reality. This is an evident image not only for cinema, but, as is made explicit, for fascist Italy and its illusions.

But if this is a political film, it is only in the most abstract sense. Its sexual politics are questionable, certainly, with Giulia and Anna presented as being at once Marcello's fantasy creations and absolutely tantalising objects he cannot control; they embody two extreme fantasies, a narcissistic one and a paranoid one. That paranoia extends to homophobia – the lesbian encounter between the two women, and the predatory, if not vampiric, role assigned to Clémenti's hermaphroditic chauffeur. It is hard to tell whether these fears are simply presented as part of Marcello's paranoid make-up or if we are invited to share them; they certainly make their presence felt by determining the film's sense of unease. They are also redolent of a style of 'decadence' that was a very modish factor in '60s and '70s fantasies of the '30s.

If the film is political, there is no sense of a real world in which politics exists. Fascist order is embodied in vacant architecture; Rome seems unpeopled (the reinstatement of the crowded party scene undercuts this impression) and only in Paris do we get the sense of a world with real people and landmarks in it. Fascism seems an abstract, imaginary power; it is only later, when Mussolini falls and crowds march in triumph through the Roman streets, that we are given any suggestion of a reality that is not entirely in Marcello's head.

The Conformist, then, is more about the politics of solipsism – its hero adopts a position because it suits his psychological make-up. That is what the title really means: it is not that Marcello wants to conform to society, but that he wants society to conform to him – hence the disruption that this apparently orderly man casts into the world. He wants to be the only observer of the world-movie that is running in the cave of his head.

Bertolucci remarked at the time of the film's release that, after May 1968, he had had a realisation: 'I wanted the revolution not to help the poor but for myself. I wanted the world to change for me.' This realisation leads logically to *The Conformist*'s de-mystification of right-wing idealism, and to the suggestion that, in a cinema of the left, you can't have Marx without having Freud. The banal Freudian 'explanation' is given cursory treatment here, but the sense of erotic stylistics, the fascination with surface, dominates the film. That stylistic lushness and complexity may defuse the film's ostensible lesson about sexual and political repression, but they defuse it to make the question more complex. And, in defying simple interpretation, *The Conformist* demonstrates a different kind of stance towards political narratives: that cinema is not to be a lesson, in which we are led by the hand towards a particular point, but a fascinated wandering through analytical wastelands. It's a wonderful reminder of the all-but-forgotten potential of borderline obscurity.

4 February 1994

Schindler's List

There is a lot that you have to get through before you can even begin to see *Schindler's List*. First there is the sheer disbelief at the thought that Steven Spielberg, of all directors, has taken on the Holocaust. Then comes the scepticism on reading the Oscar-fuelling adulatory reviews that greeted the film in the States. Once again, before even the first frame of a Spielberg film, you have to contend with its status as phenomenon – it's just that, this time, the stakes are immeasurably higher.

So let me just say that on many levels, *Schindler's List* gives ample cause to leave your scepticism at the door: it is a very fine film, a manifestly serious one, a film that may not entirely do justice to its subject (as if such an aspiration were possible), but one that certainly honours it. I also found it exceptionally moving, and not just because its subject matter automatically hit the distress button. I came out of the film feeling silenced, as if hushed reverence were the only possible response. But that feeling – like any intense feeling you have on leaving a cinema – subsides on reflection. I realised that the way *Schindler's List* moved me was akin to the way a funeral ceremony moves you: it demands that you suspend your thoughts for a kind of abstracted, almost *performed* emotional response. Indeed, this may be the only film ever designed specifically to elicit mourning as a single response.

That purpose becomes clear at the very end of the film, after the story has concluded. The war ends, and we see the last of Oskar Schindler (Liam Neeson), the German businessman who saved over a thousand Jews from the gas chambers by buying them as workers in his factory. Then the film shifts to the present day, out of fictionalised black-and-white history and into the real and colour. We see Schindler's grave being tenderly decked with commemorative rocks by the very people he saved, now frail and aged but very visibly alive, accompanied by the actors who play their younger selves. It's a brazen *coup de théâtre*, this sudden all-out appeal to the real, but it's quite irresistible – a moment of release that allows you to unblock the emotions that the film's monochrome sobriety has until now held back.

It's one of many moments at which the film goes full out to impress us with the seriousness and restraint of its intentions, to dispel the slightest suspicion of vulgarity, of Hollywood excess. God knows there's enough to live down – from the infotainment schmaltz of the *Holocaust* TV mini-series to the pernicious sentiment of Alan J. Pakula's William Styron adaptation *Sophie's Choice*, which managed to suggest that the Holocaust took place purely so that some nonentity American kid could become a great writer.

Spielberg rigorously expunges any sense of Hollywood and its conventions. But where the film nevertheless tends to sanitise is in its regard for beauty (which it seems to see as the 'truth'), incarnated in Janusz Kaminski's fine-grained black-and-white photography. In one early scene, the sunlight shines in through an office window in a perfect shaft, *just so*, and you realise then that the film will be fatally caught between its aspiration to the real and its love of elegance.

That contradiction comes out most strongly when Spielberg sets out to arrest us with moments of what you could call 'true horror'. He'll suddenly stop the quasi-documentary flow of images, often captured with dynamic immediacy in restless rolling shots, and make us look straight at a perfectly composed picture of awfulness. In one sequence, a boy takes refuge in a cesspool, only to find other children hiding inside; they tell him to go away, it's *their* place. It's an unthinkable, obscene image, yet so arrested is Spielberg by the horror that, even while heightening it, he has to make it aesthetic – that is, anaesthetic. The surface of the mire is deadly still, the inside of the box enlarged by cavernous chiaroscuro, the boy isolated by a shaft of light from above. It's horror, but it's poetry also – and we can only feel discomfort at having both.

The same goes for an image that has already become famous. Schindler, mounted on horseback on a hill, looks down on the routs of the Cracow ghetto. It's a horrific scene of turmoil, as the camera scans every way, lost like Schindler's gaze, and ours, in the abject chaos. Suddenly one figure is picked out – a little girl in red, her coat the only patch of colour in sight. Already we are blinded by the stridency of the symbolism – the little girl is life, about to be snuffed out in this monochrome world, by analogy with the only other colour we have seen, the Sabbath candle at the film's start. She will occur again – first, as she hides under a bed, with an earnest look of faith in her survival; later, with black inevitability, as a body carried off on a stretcher, in front of a mountain of charred corpses.

Why is this image so powerful, and why has it become the film's icon, even alluded to discreetly on the poster? Because it makes an immediate, irreducible point – red is the colour of life, but also of death; this innocent of innocents is both Little Red Riding Hood and the sacrificial lamb.

But it's so powerful also, I think, because of what it allows us not to see. We're allowed to attach all our feelings to this one image, which hides the mountain of nameless, faceless, dehumanised corpses. We are invited to cry for a dead child, and that allows us to elide the unmanageable enormity of death that is there in plain sight behind her. Somehow, that seems part and parcel of the film's project. It is after all a film about survival, about deliverance from evil; we accompany those who were spared, rather than those who were not. There is a limit to how far Spielberg can allow himself to go; hence his decision to take on Thomas Keneally's book with its essentially redemptive thrust, rather than any more despairing vision.

Bearing in mind that this is the film's project, *Schindler's List* is remarkably dense and suggestive, even when Spielberg's innate tendency to underline points gets the better of him. He can't quite handle the parallel between Schindler and the SS commandant Amon Goeth, even resorting to matched shots of them in shaving mirrors; it is down to the exceptionally subtle performances of Liam Neeson and Ralph Fiennes, playing a mutually seductive tennis game with each others' mannerisms, to make it work.

What to make, though, of a film in which the Jews play second fiddle to the sexy man of action who saves them? The film seems to be in love less with Schindler's humanity than with his 'super-humanity' – his vast energy as an entrepreneur, a deal-doer on a cosmic scale, a very Spielberg of caritas. It is no accident that the film is dedicated at the end to Steven Ross, the late president of Time Warner, nor that Spielberg once ludicrously claimed that if Schindler were alive today he'd be agency head Mike Ovitz. This Schindler, who does lunches for lives, is the last tycoon, and the film is inevitably flawed by this sneaking sense of Hollywood values where Hollywood should not be.

The fact remains that, whatever its subject matter, *Schindler's List* is a big-budget spectacle. Whatever the subtler ramifications of the debate on visual versus verbal recounting of the Holocaust (the film will inevitably be measured against *Shoah*, Claude Lanzmann's definitive collection of to-camera testimonies), I found myself worried on quite a pragmatic score. I've read the location reports, I've read how many extras were used, and when I saw the Jews herded into cattle trucks, I couldn't help seeing the extras regimented and coaxed by hosts of production runners armed with walkie-talkies. No matter how well they were paid and how lavish the catering laid on for them, I felt worried by the sense that somehow, however distantly, the same gestures were being repeated. I feel uncomfortable with this reaction, which is all the stronger for not being entirely rational. Would I have been as worried if I had been watching not a Hollywood film but a comparably ambitious theatrical reconstruction staged by some highly austere European director – a Tadeusz Kantor, say? I'm not sure.

It's true, there is nothing conventionally Hollywoodian about *Schindler's List*, much less Spielbergian. But its very seriousness, its monumentality, seems to have been achieved at a certain cost – not of repeating Nazism's actions, that would be a frivolous accusation, but in some way of reproducing its production values. This eloquent and absolutely honourable film is trying to live down its filmic nature and let us know that the Holocaust was not a movie. But I think it succeeds at most in telling us that it was simply a movie of a special kind.

18 February 1994

Short Cuts

The idea of making a ten-strand portmanteau movie of stories, starring a host of American cinema's great and good and called *Short Cuts*, might have seemed a dainty, manageable *Masterpiece Theatre* sort of idea to some directors. But not to Robert Altman. For a start, the title is a misnomer. The film may comprise a number of Raymond Carver short stories and variations thereon, but there are no short cuts here; the overall map is massive and labyrinthine, and you can only get from A to B by way of C, D and E. This is a film in which you have to take the scenic route – and with Altman's predilection for the scuzzy, the seedy and the downbeat, it isn't always that scenic.

The great thing about *Short Cuts* is that it's so low-key – it all looks as if it just happened, but the contrivance is enormous. You can imagine Altman and co-writer Frank Barhydt poring like military strategists over timetables and maps of Los Angeles, with coloured pins for the different characters.

What's extraordinary is that anyone should think of linking up Raymond Carver's stories at all. All his narratives take place in the same universe, a kind of dead zone, a middle-American junkyard in which dreams come home to die, or at least flop out on the sofa. But all his losers and dreamers are lost in their own world, and his famously minimal style creates a sense of airless downtime, in which explosive small events simply leave a slough of contemplative silence behind them (which is partly, I should add, why I find them practically unreadable, their evocation of inertia too uniformly stylised).

You can see why some Carver purists have railed at *Short Cuts*. The tone is completely different – not just in the way it favours the farcical, unruly comedy of embarrassment, but in the way it refuses to let its characters sit still, as Carver's can't help doing. Even the most inert figures, like Tom Waits's boozy chauffeur, can't stop twitching, doing little routines to scam the world into thinking they're still fully functional. This is not really an adaptation of Carver; Altman simply borrows the stories' cast and situations for his own use. It's rather like characters in a Pinter play being co-opted into *Waiting for Godot* and finding they have to do something as undignified as juggle with hats.

Oddly enough, the one story not taken from Carver, about a jazz-singing mother (Annie Ross) and her cellist daughter (Lori Singer), most directly evokes his themes of chances lost and communications not made, and it's the film's least interesting strand. It over-stresses the point to make Ross's nightclub act serve as chorus, with songs like 'Punishing Kiss' and 'Prisoner of Love' (among the composers: Elvis Costello, U2 and Dr John), but Ross's cynical, regretful bark is sparingly used and sets the tone.

So Ross and Singer have this pool, which is being serviced by Chris Penn, whose wife Jennifer Jason Leigh has a phone sex job, and his best buddy, Robert Downey Jr, is married to Lili Taylor, whose mom, diner waitress Lily Tomlin, has just knocked over the son of Andie MacDowell, who has just ordered a birthday cake from baker Lyle Lovett . . . What a strange, small world it is.

But it's not quite the same small world that Altman explored in *Nashville*, where all the characters seemed to exemplify an aspect of the legendary song city, and most of them aspired to be legendary themselves in its measure. *Short Cuts* isn't a portrait of LA in the same way, but draws on LA's very anonymity, the sense of its being not so much a city as a sprawling circuit board in which you can shuttle from place to place but never reach the heart of it.

These characters have homes to go to but 'no direction home' (to quote another songwriter who might profitably have been asked to contribute a number). They're always flying off somewhere else – blustering traffic cop Tim Robbins to visit his wayward mistress Frances McDormand, Fred Ward and his chums on a ghastly fishing trip – or turning up out of the blue, like McDormand's gleefully destructive husband Peter Gallagher, or Jack Lemmon arriving at the hospital where his grandson is critically ill. Lemmon's character walks into this painful crisis with his own entirely irrelevant agenda, as if someone had just flipped two pages in the script. It's an act of stunning incongruity, and the moment when the film's switches seem least contrived. Here's where it makes its point most bluntly and poignantly – that no life goes on in isolation, that crises happen alongside each other all the time, jockeying for pole position. These stories are like stations on a radio dial, all broadcasting at once, sometimes muscling in indecorously on each other's waveband.

This is why it makes sense for Altman to employ a moderately starry cast rather than unknowns. Because you recognise some rather than others, because some act in familiar fashion while others work flagrantly against type, he can invoke an image of society as non-stop performance with everyone reading from different scripts. As a variation on the old life-as-movie metaphor, it's infinitely more interesting than his much more overt *The Player*. Here, Altman doesn't have to wheel on Julia Roberts as Julia Roberts to make the point. Because you're star-spotting (as a couple of the characters themselves do, early on), you're not quite sure whether you're supposed to be seeing Lily Tomlin as Doreen Piggot working in a diner, or just Lily Tomlin working in an Altman film as a diner waitress.

Altman is simply highlighting a dilemma we always face (and

usually conveniently forget) when we see stars on screen, but uses it to make us aware that *everyone* is acting, more or less. These people dress the part, to work as newscasters, clowns, cops, bakers; but they also act the part of father or mother, pose for paintings in the image of themselves, change roles when they move into someone else's story. Yet they can't always tell the difference between life and pretence. We see what appears to be a horribly violent moment between Downey and Taylor, but the joke's on us – we've been had by a sick gag about American cinema's current appetite for pulp violence (Downey is just practising his skills as a special effects make-up artist). Then, just as we're prepared to imagine that it's all harmless make-believe, the theme returns in darker colours in an extraordinary, flagrantly contrived ending in which all the sexual tensions that have been building up erupt in one horribly cathartic gesture.

The theme also gets a lighter but equally nasty twist when Lili Taylor and Buck Henry, complete strangers, accidentally swap photos, and get a sudden, baffling glimpse into each other's imaginations. At moments like this, the film, for all its flip misanthropy, reminds us of its moral dimension. *Short Cuts* is largely about people casually fucking each other up in a lazy everyday way. You know at the end that life will go on the next day, and these people will still be at each other's throats. But, in its most farcical moments, it impresses on you that life is horrible enough without people aimlessly messing around with the genuinely unspeakable horrors. It's one long, beautifully cynical joke, and one that I'd take over Carver's punctilious solemnities any day.

11 March 1994

The Scent of Green Papaya (L'Odeur de la papaye verte)

Given that *The Scent of Green Papaya* can't actually give you what its title announces, it still comes remarkably close. It's a sensuous, evocative film on every level, plying you subtly with sounds, sights and textures, and the overall effect is something akin to an olfactory sense of place and things. It's every bit as fragrant as *The Age of Innocence*, in which Martin Scorsese conjectured a sort of *fin-de-siècle* Smell-O-Vision. But where that film got to the mind's nostril by bombarding you with the sight of fine lace and roses, Tran Anh Hung's film, it's truer to say, *suffuses* its impressions.

The debut feature by this remarkable Vietnamese director appears to be simplicity itself, but in a very complex, artificial way. Told in a skeletal narrative, it is the story of a ten-year-old country girl, Mùi, who comes to a quiet district of Saigon in the 1950s, to live as a servant in a family house. She gets to know the family, the courtyard and its cooking rituals; she develops a wonder-struck, almost microscopic view of its objects, flora and fauna – crickets, lizards, frogs, the papayas she skins and chops. And, except for the father's decamping and the family's descent into hard times, it seems a remarkably easy flow of time. Events occur but somehow their impact is never as cataclysmic as the hermetically sealed environment would lead you to expect. Time passes, and in a startling dissolve we jump ten years into Mùi's adulthood and her transfer to the house of a young musician – an effortless, absolutely satisfying change of key.

A conventional response to films that deal with sensuous minutiae is to assume that they are simple and leave it at that, all the more so when dealing with Third World cinema. But the simplicity of Tran's film is the result of elaborate artifice. It was filmed not in Vietnam but on a French sound stage. All bar one of its amateur cast were recruited in France, which meant that even gestures had to be learned – the younger cast members had never known the traditional posture of crouching on their heels.

This sense of unfamiliarity gives the film its peculiar alertness. Like Mùi, we have to be induced step by step into this world. The process begins with a long tracking shot that brings us and her down a street and into the courtyard where she will spend the next ten years. We never leave this sense of enclosure, and never see a sky. Effectively, the whole film dwells behind the fence, and the world is excluded, present only in the sounds it constantly transmits.

Set-bound films often have a mood of claustration about them, but that mood is rarely used so artfully. The sets themselves, as cluttered and segmented with frames, foliage, gauzes and screens as in a Sternberg film, hem in our senses even further, leading us into a small world that is at once an airy oasis and a complex, involuted labyrinth. The labyrinthine feel comes to the fore in the film's second half, when Mùi plays a tentative sexual game of tag around the house with her musician master, the camera weaving sinuously in between the walls.

Rather than inducing claustrophobia, the set-bound direction guides us in, allows the inner world to open up and reveal small, isolated marvels. Our gaze and Mùi's become one: seeing the small, white bead-like seeds of a papaya for the first time, or the glistening skin of a frog up close, we feel we are being shown something genuinely new and miraculous. The sense of revelation extends even to what might otherwise be clichés of sensuality: Mùi's delight in pouring water over herself might be a familiar picture if not for the way that Tran jump-cuts, creating a completely novel, energised image.

Like Victor Erice's *The Quince Tree Sun*, Tran's film is a rare example of the cinematic still life – a rebuttal of the assumption that cinema has to be about motion, when in fact it can be purely about time and its malleability. Allowing a space for stillness, these films restore cinema's contemplative possibilities, give it something of the empty time we experience in life, and encourage us not to escape from the immediate confines of our senses but to burrow further into them.

But it would be wrong to give the impression that the film is some wispy gossamer thing, a fragile vase (one of its few incidents, pointedly, involves a vase being smashed). It is also about shocks, small horrors, that nonetheless become strangely pleasurable marvels in Mùi's eyes. The younger of the house's two brothers wages war on her, farting defiantly, dangling a dead lizard in her face. But things we might conventionally expect to be horrific in this kind of domestic drama are transmuted into little comic pleasures. In this sense, her viewpoint doesn't seem at all passive, but a wry mechanism for making the world more than bearable.

What is perplexing, though, is the film's apparent elegy to the virtues of female servitude. Mùi's life may appear infinitely rich to us, but that is much to do with the way the film builds a mystique of everyday objects. We see the glistening papaya seeds only two or three times; Mùi sees them every day. Tran impresses on us the ritualistic nature of her life, and the repetition of objects in the film creates a sense at once of their unfamiliarity (to us) and familiarity (to her).

But is Mùi's apparent passivity, as a receiver of impressions, presented as a privileged way of seeing the world, or simply as a survival tactic? Mùi, by force of circumstance, rejects the external world, which after all seems to bring the family only grief. Or could we read the film as a sort of psychopathological case study, along the lines of *The Remains of the Day*? In James Ivory's film, the servant's self-denial was seen as an unequivocal ill, and the film's major flaw was the insistence with which it made its point. But Tran allows us no easy purchase on Mùi, who – as played first by Lu Man San, then by Tran Nu Yên-Khê – seems reduced to a sensuous recording skin of pure consciousness.

Mùi seems to be a consciousness entirely adequate to the world she inhabits, and she achieves a final, joyous apotheosis under the eye of a benevolently looming Buddha. Tran provides the most traditional of happy endings for a female servant's story, so much so that it fairly defeats interpretation. Are we to read this beatific soul as a distilled ideal of female consciousness, attaining Nirvana through her finely tuned senses, through immersing herself in seeing, serving and being invisible, getting her reward in the end?

Possibly, but, then again, Mùi's final golden moment arrives just as her world is passing, the old Vietnam's disappearance heralded by bursts of jets on the soundtrack and the increasing presence of Western culture – Khuyen, the adored musician Mùi goes to work for, and who finally marries her and makes her pregnant, is a Francophile and lover of Debussy and Chopin. Her story ends just as she breaks her silence, and when she first puts on lipstick, in emulation of Khuyen's skittish Westernised fiancée.

This myth of grace in servitude is so hard to accept as such that the film finally seems to be deploying an irony so oblique as to be barely readable. Tran allows these meanings to float only partly perceived, suspended in a liquid of pure impression. The film ends with what might be an ironic touch of self-reference, with one of the passages of Mùi's reading practice: 'If there's a verb meaning "to move harmoniously", it must be used here.' The face of the smiling Buddha that follows it might be assent or irony or gnomic blankness. How we are to read this harmony, it doesn't let on.

25 March 1994

Germinal

Emile Zola's *Germinal* is one of the few great novels to be remembered not for its opening sentences but for its ending. As its hero Etienne Lantier trudges away from the defeated mining community of Montsou, he hears the sounds of the miners hammering away beneath the countryside. The very earth is thick with the sound, literally pregnant with it ('*grosse*'), and Lantier is aware of 'a black avenging host . . . slowly germinating in the furrows, thrusting upwards for the harvests of future ages. And very soon their germination would crack the earth asunder.'[1]

It's a marvellous, millenarian vision, a last-minute flourish of apocalyptic triumphalism to redeem the day after a seemingly unmitigated defeat. The excessive imagery makes perfect sense in what is only nominally a naturalist novel, partly because of the chthonic theme that suffuses the book, which belongs to Zola's discourse of cyclical renewal – a discourse as much cosmological as political. But it makes sense in historical terms too. The rising

[1] Emile Zola, *Germinal*, trans. L.W. Tancock (Penguin, Harmondsworth, 1954), p. 499.

socialism that motors *Germinal*'s conflicts may meet a temporary defeat in the narrative, but was bound to make a spectacular comeback, if not in Zola's century then certainly in the next.

The ending, of course, makes *Germinal* perfect material for cinema, a form we tend to see in terms of endings rather than beginnings (we don't think of cowboys riding out of the sunset; no film was ever recut because its opening was downbeat). Zola's last line alone makes the book a movie: it's up there with 'Forget it, Jake, it's Chinatown', and 'Nobody's perfect.' Director-producer Claude Berri surely thought this, and respectful as his film is towards the book, its subtext is that we are watching *Germinal* as it was always meant to be: if Zola were alive today, he wouldn't be writing, but mounting 160-million-franc epics.

Zola's ending, which is Berri's too, ought to have acquired a powerful ironic thrust, given the benefit of 110 years' hindsight. With the notion of popular revolt soured on a global scale, and with a massive miners' defeat still echoing just across the Channel, Berri's film ought to carry a resonance of the embittered optimism that Zola's ending now suggests. But we're not in 1994 with this film; it wants us to imagine that we're still in 1885, when the novel was published. Historical distance lends it at best a *frisson* of nostalgist poignancy – the nostalgia being for a particular myth of French community that owes as much to Jean Renoir and Marcel Carné's crowds as it does to 1968, the Popular Front or the Commune. But this nostalgia itself enforces the illusion that we're getting the original novel unmediated; the historical distance is meant to remain invisible.

I should say I enjoyed *Germinal* thoroughly, but that's not the point; I was supposed to. It's the cinematic equivalent of a good read, and mercifully free of the softness you associate with Berri. He has come to represent in French cinema as much of a knee-jerk bogeyman as Merchant and Ivory do in Britain, for the marshmallow ruralism of his *Jean de Florette* diptych and for his production of Jean-Jacques Annaud's cretinous adaptation of Marguerite Duras's *The Lover*. The late, great French critic Serge Daney would periodically greet a film as the harbinger of the death of cinema; more than once, it was one of Berri's.

Germinal's spectacle is far from the glutinous prettification of the aforementioned – in look it's closer to his turgidly gritty *Uranus* – but it's certainly a prime example of imagination-deadening literalist cinema. It's what Daney, by analogy with 'filmed theatre', used to call 'filmed cinema' – effectively, the cinema is on tap before the cameras even roll, and the celluloid simply captures what's imagined to be 'there' in the text and the *mise en scène*. Here, once the mine and the village have been recreated as fully formed 'worlds' of their own, the work's half done. It's a cinema of transparency that takes the materials provided – text, sets, actors – as a template for what we see, as if the minds of film-makers and viewers alike were exempt from doing any work. Hence, *Germinal* is exactly as you picture a film of the novel to be – as you watch it, you can easily imagine it as a summa of the archival documentation, architectural plans and reports on miners' lung diseases that Zola studied, and Berri's team presumably did too. What we admire is the thoroughness of the research, the smoothness with which it has all seemingly been decanted straight into the frame.

Among the actors, too, Berri resorts to what they call *valeurs sûres* – fail-safe institutions who bring their own connotations to the parts they play. As the mining couple Maheu and Maheude, we have Gérard Depardieu and Miou-Miou, he a national economic resource and a cultural landmark as unshakeable as the Eiffel Tower, she a long-standing icon of intransigent feminist toughness. As Lantier, the observing catalyst of the drama, there's singer Renaud, a much-loved post-1968 nonconformist and social irritant. The gargantuan *bon viveur* Depardieu doesn't convince for a moment as an impoverished miner, but they all emote their butts off. Miou-Miou especially is hypercharged, convincingly extending her range into matriarchal fury.

Because the film hits us first with this familiarity, it's a lesser-known name who finally dominates – Jean-Roger Milo, as the treacherous slob Chaval, is the only figure who quite catches the volatility of Zola's melodrama. Gargling, twitching and rolling his eyes like a crazed Pulchinello, he has a touch of that great slippery Renoir villain, Jules Berry. Of course, the performance goes wildly against the grain of the film – that's why *Germinal* needs it so much.

Otherwise, everything is too easy. *Germinal* guides us around its horrors without making us experience any discomfort. When it takes us down the mine, plummeting an unimaginable depth, we feel the rush we might on a virtual reality theme ride – but we don't land anywhere really grim. The tunnels are filled not with tangible darkness but with a sort of impoverished daylight. Berri makes it easy for us to see what's going on. We're never left without a guide.

Zola is similarly scrupulous about guiding us in the right direction, but you'd think Berri might be interested in giving us a late twentieth-century perspective on nineteenth-century narrative rhetoric. As the weary mine owner, faced with a strike, learns he's been cuckolded, he sighs and mutters aloud, 'You think bread is enough?' Berri sees this as poignancy pure and simple; he seems unable to read it as melodrama and take that as his starting point. He wants us to experience such moments as if Zola had never written them first.

This one-dimensionality makes *Germinal* a formidable national monument, but not much cop as a film. João Botelho's modern-day Portuguese *Hard Times* (1988) showed how wonderfully displacement and anachronism could amplify a classic text. Even Christine Edzard's conservative two-part *Little Dorrit* played off knowingly against the familiar tradition of tea-time TV Dickens. *Germinal* simply invokes a great literary and cinematic academy and bids us nod respectfully. The leading French producer Daniel Toscan du Plantier spoke of it approvingly in *Le Figaro* as representing 'a great popular and artistic cinema, born out of a national cultural stock, conveying universal civilised emotions'. *Valeurs sûres*, for sure: back-to-basics cinema *par excellence*.

A key piece in the recent General Agreement on Tariffs and Services (GATS) debate about the future of European cinema, *Germinal* was seen as a national leviathan sent to do box-office and ideological battle with *Jurassic Park*. It too aspires to revive dinosaurs – the French cinema industry, and the mining industry too, or at least a memory of it. But it's far more of a lumbering monster than Spielberg's sleek DNA beast. The future of a national cinema isn't to be found in invoking the 'universal' or the 'civilised', nor in re-imagining cinema as if it were something that merely superseded literature. *Germinal* may not be the end of cinema, as Serge Daney might have seen it, but it's certainly a dead end.

6 May 1994

Priit Pärn:
Selected Films

Animation film lurks on the dark side more often than we realise, but we prefer to think of it making gentle dalliance with jolly bears and kittens in the nursery. British animation certainly has its share of venturers into the underworld – David Anderson, Joanna Woodward, the American expatriate Brothers Quay. But much as everyone applauds the massive overground success of Nick Park and the Aardman stable – after all, who can't find a place in their heart for a Plasticine penguin? – their prominence only makes it easier to forget that animation can explore the unwelcoming areas that live-action film can't always reach.

It would be naive to think that animation simply has no boundaries, that it can claim total artistic licence. As with live-action film, there are economic limits – whatever medium you work in, there will always be controlling interests waving warning fingers. But there aren't star egos to contend with, you can jettison the demands of narrative altogether, nothing ever needs to be justified by reference to the real world and, unless you're Disney, you're never going to please the good folks of Des Moines anyway, so why try? There's the added advantage that non-animators simply can't figure out what animators are up to – so they're treated with the mystified awe due to mediaeval alchemists. Despite the proportionally extravagant budgets it requires, animation is largely allowed to get on with its own odd concerns in its own odd corner. It's the last space left for the monomaniac auteur.

The work of Estonian animator Priit Pärn is a prime example of the sort of extremity that you don't find anywhere else. In live action, we think of Lynch or Greenaway or Tarantino as being extreme. No, *this* is extreme – but a different kind of extreme. It's the extremity you find in political cartooning at its most desperate (which is where Pärn started out) or in the more cut-throat surrealist humour (Pärn has more than a touch of the French illustrator Roland Topor). The three films collected on the *Selected Films* tape (Connoisseur Video) are dazzling work – rebarbative, nightmarish and violent, but also hard to pin down to any message, even when the theme ostensibly seems clear.

On the most obvious level, these works, dating from 1984 to 1991, are about the Soviet Union, its excesses and its downfall, and its relation to the West, *its* excesses and *its* downfall. But there's nothing schematic or reassuring about the way their messages come across. Pärn may use the language of political satire – but what do these films actually mean? Their structures are too complex, too much driven by the repetitions of nightmare to deliver comfortable parables.

Breakfast on the Grass (1987) is dedicated 'to artists who went as far as they were allowed', but the artist in the film is a scuttling, lascivious Picasso figure, who, while being dragged off by the secret police, is concerned only for his lost shoe. There's no idealisation of art: in the second of five sections, Georg, a grinning photocomposite medallion man, lives surrounded by lavishly framed old masters. His world is art history seen through Old Spice ads – at one wonderfully reductive moment, a female nude torso heaves mechanically into view over a generic sunset.

The four protagonists of *Breakfast on the Grass* eventually take their place in a reconstruction of Manet's painting, but only after various travails: Anna to brave blank, Smiley-faced crowds in her search for an apple, Berta to find her lost face, which is temporarily replaced by lipstick scrawl ... They find their moment of epiphany, but then it's the train home, and the film ends with the artist lying steamrolled into a blur of paint.

Breakfast easily accommodates the standard epithet 'Kafkaesque', with its depiction of a grey, joyless city, and its deflation of the high-art utopia as a dream of escape. In a wonderful sequence, Georg's pristine world, depicted in golden photoassemblage, suddenly melts into the scratchy grey murk of Pärn's cartoon universe. But the style is too excessive, too exuberantly scabrous to deliver a univocal message. There's more going on than meets the eye – which is the let-out we usually grasp at when we argue that a political work is not specific but 'universal', and thereby depoliticise it.

Pärn's work, though, can't be that easily depoliticised, because it is so much about the politics of animation – about the myths that different kinds of image, visual styles, even textures, can be made to represent. The extraordinary *Hotel E* (1991) could be read as an allegory of East and West or, as its title suggests, as a representation of Estonia, but neither interpretation quite exhausts its relentlessness. There are five or six radically different styles at work here; one of Pärn's arguments seems to be that animation has to resist the lure of the smoothly homogeneous.

Hotel E begins with two cryptic sequences depicting legends – one about a Stone Age outcast, the second a kitsch idyll in lurid oil paints, in which a bunch of smiling bliss-heads (trendy '70s Christians? ex-members of Steeleye Span?) exchange cups. Then comes the main section of the film, entitled 'The American Dream'.

In one of two rooms, a group of swanky exquisites loll around, play mini-golf, raise quizzically flirtatious eyebrows – all in cloying, supersaturated psychedelic pastels, all outlines and no shading. (It's reminiscent of a famous Situationist graphic, which

Pärn may or may not be alluding to, but the spirit of which he definitely shares.) Seductive as this world appears, the repetition of slow-motion gestures, the monotonously poised pastiche-Bach soundtrack (by Olav Ehala, whose antagonistic scores are a key part of these films), and, above all, the marshmallow colours, all add up to a vision that just stops short of being physically nauseous. (If you ever see *Hotel E* on a big screen, you'll realise I mean this quite literally.)

In the next room, hell is jumping. In a storm of scratchy grey, scratchy grey men raise their coffee cups frenetically while a swarm of hellish flies bombs round their heads (on close inspection, you realise they're iron filings – that's how tactile these films are). Life here takes place at buzz-saw speed, with desperate actions executed in a hail of black static. Both this frenzy and the adjacent languor are accentuated by the cutting between them; at last, their uneasy proximity gives way to the inevitable entropy. Pärn signs off with a reckless flourish of cute-animal cartoon pastiche, Bugs Bunny gone apocalyptic.

The great appeal of *Hotel E* is that it leaves you shaken and yet completely mystified. You start off twigging to the obvious point it seems to be making – that title 'The American Dream' is surely overstating things. But then you realise that the obviousness gets you nowhere, and by the end that dream seems less definable than you imagined it could possibly be. Fascinated, you wind the tape back and watch it again. This is how political cartoon transcends itself to become provocation.

Even when Pärn's work seems lightweight, as in the short *Time Out* (1984), there's something distressing going on. This is a breezy lark with free-flowing metamorphoses, playing wryly on nursery cartoon conventions, as a cat escapes its daily round of hell into a skittish *Yellow Submarine* world. But even here, life's a war of attrition (as it is in the best of 'Toons), and he's soon fated to return to his mechanical drudgery, a helpless tool of the animator's hand (which briefly appears, a baleful *deus ex machina*). *Time Out* is a wonderfully equivocal entertainment, which gives diversion with one hand and takes it away with the other. Animation can be intoxicating escapism, Pärn is willing to concede – but we'd better be prepared to sober up for the other, tougher things it can do.

10 June 1994

Kika

There's only one decent joke in John Waters's recently released *Serial Mom*: an *Oprah*-style TV show on 'Serial Hags: Women Who Love Men Who Mutilate'. It's funny because it encapsulates in a pithy headline the mix of tabloid sensationalism and day-to-day suburban mundanity that the rest of the film so laboriously strives to elaborate.

It also shows up the redundancy of Waters's brand of satiric outrage, which was so effective in his *Pink Flamingos* and *Female Trouble*. There's no longer anything strange about the idea that such a show might exist on American TV, or that the 'straight' media might resort to such flagrant camp-speak. What's 'weird' in *Serial Mom* is no longer the manifestly outrageous behaviour of Waters's former cast of antisocial freaks. Instead the freak is Mom herself, who is monstrous not because she murders, but because she's excessively, archaically normal.

The reason that Waters's barbs now seem so directionless is less that he has run out of ideas than that the very institution of camp has become redundant. Reading Susan Sontag's 1964 essay 'Notes on Camp' in the newly reissued *Against Interpretation*

(Vintage, London, 1994), you're struck by how many facets of what was once a marginal, rarely articulated aesthetic/ideological stance have become, thirty years later, deeply embedded in the mainstream imagination – part of what we would now call post-modern self-consciousness.

The intervening developments of gay politics and theory make it hard now to celebrate camp as purely a 'dandyish' stance that, as Sontag puts it, 'incarnates a victory of "style" over "content", "aesthetics" over "morality", or "irony" over "tragedy"'. The political needs of gay communities, together with the mainstream recuperation of camp, have changed camp's value. If it can still have a value, it is most likely to be as a rhetorical weapon, no longer divorced from morality but intimately bound to the articulation of new moral discourses.

Camp, like any counter-culture language, tends to be not only assimilated but also institutionalised. Whatever is brought to light and celebrated, having begun in the margins, risks being canonised, and often actively pursues a parodic canonisation in order to pre-empt such a fate. Hence, on the one hand, the cults surrounding John Waters or *The Rocky Horror Show*; on the other, the path from Warhol's Factory to the Warhol Museum. The latest example of this tendency is the Madrid company El Deseo S.A. (Desire Ltd), which presents itself as an industry selling a specific generic product – the 'Almodóvar Film'.

The 'Serial Hag' joke has an exact counterpart in Almodóvar's *Kika*. Andrea Caracortada (Scarface), played by Victoria Abril, is the presenter of TV 'reality show' *The Worst of the Day*, which features real-life atrocities that she films with a camera mounted in her rubber carapace. Andrea is public voyeurism incarnate – Shaw Taylor in bondage drag, peddling a familiar brand of titillating moralism. Before tickling her viewers with the latest hot-off-the-street sleaze, she warns, 'It'll shock your sensibilities – if you still have any.'

On one level, Almodóvar is straightforwardly critiquing the excesses of tabloid TV, in a form that's not so far from the real thing. But, at the same time, Andrea's taunt is an anxious wink to

Kika's audience: Almodóvar is asking us whether *our* sensibilities are dulled yet – whether we can still be galvanised by his films, or whether their power has long since worn off.

Alas, it has. Taken in isolation, *Kika*, on paper at least, appears rich in perverse conceits; as Almodóvar's tenth feature, it is a weary retread of tropes that were already threadbare two films back, in *Tie Me Up! Tie Me Down!*. Now the flouting of narrative coherence and the courting of shock value are so transparent that it looks as though El Deseo is running a sort of market survey, to see which tricks work and which don't.

Kika's remarkably cluttered plot concerns an irrepressibly jolly make-up artist (Veronica Forqué, whose toothy sexiness is pure Barbara Windsor); her cataleptic beau; his American stepfather writer (Peter Coyote); a brain-damaged porn stud; a lesbian maid (the ineffably beaky Rossy de Palma); and as many other incidental oddballs as Almodóvar can cram onto the latest of his stylishly garish posters. In fact, *Kika* seems to have been created not so much to exist as a film as to generate its own promotional baggage – poster, tantalisingly funky trailer, fashion-plate stills with Abril modelling Jean-Paul Gaultier's bespoke cyber-splatter collection.

Almodóvar has described the film as a 'jigsaw', and indeed the narrative appears almost random in its refusal of order. It starts off as a false whodunit, in which the original crime is either unstated or forgotten, and unimportant anyway because crimes, in this luridly grim world, are all around. A baroque construction of flashbacks and inserts, the plot seems capable of going any-where, and by all accounts nearly did – one abandoned story line involved Rossy De Palma in a wax museum, dressed up as Morticia Addams. The Oedipal detective story that starts the film gets lost in a forest of parallels and repetitions from which it never emerges.

Rather than the 'depth' provided by narrative motivation and character psychology, we get Almodóvar's customary super-ificality. Alfredo Mayo's photography and the designs of Javier Fernandez and Alain Bainée flatten everything out, repelling the eye. Expanses of blue and orange wall push us out of the picture; in one shot, characters are separated by flamboyantly obtrusive red and yellow orchids.

Not only the film's look is surface. Kika is a make-up artist, and her world is 'made up' in every sense. Andrea wears her scar, the badge of her badness, like a tattoo; the lesbian maid, when dragged up in glam gear, declares, 'I'm authentic!' But event, too, is superficial: no matter how momentous, what we get is cartoon event. The controversial scene in which Kika is raped by the escaped porn star is neither shocking nor funny; it's entirely without affect, a farcical gesture as empty of meaning as the film's incidental references to Sarajevo and Somalia. 'Real' experience transmutes into glib commentary on media gloss: Kika's ordeal happens simply so that she can protest about it being used to sell milk (Andrea's show is sponsored by a milk company). The film's most representative moment is its full-frontal shot of the glamorous transsexual Bibi Anderson. A 'scandalous' spectacle that isn't, it is a *reductio ad absurdum* of striptease, the film's avowal of its own castration. What is on display is the very fact that there is nothing to see.

Absence of meaning is always relative. In his book on Almodóvar, *Desire Unlimited* (Verso, London, 1994), Paul Julian Smith argues that these films cannot be divorced from their specific origins, that 'frivolity can be seen in a Spanish context as a political gesture'. It's true that aspects of *Kika* – the TV satire, notions of identity and 'authenticity' – gain in meaning if we apply them to a specific Spanish context rather than reading them as, in some vague way, universally applicable. (Outside Spain, of course, the 'Spanishness' of these films functions as a particular kind of exoticism – something of which Almodóvar is cannily aware in addressing his international market.)

But the apparent emptiness of *Kika* seems to be a function of the film's anxiety about its effectiveness as a political gesture. What is Andrea's show – omnivorous, perverse curiosity incarnate – if not a de-moralised representation of Almodóvar's own flashy scandal tactics? In that case, *Kika*'s own audience may prove as desensitised as hers. *Kika* finally offers its heroine's indefatigable optimism as an antidote to Andrea's rapacious cynicism. But it seems an empty gesture in the face of the film's underlying anxiety that Almodóvar might have ended up selling milk like the rest of them.

1 July 1994

Wolf

The trouble with reviewing a film called *Wolf* is that, even before you've seen it, you find yourself reaching for that mental file card marked 'Lycanthropy, Film images of' – and you're halfway to writing that think-piece that has already effectively been written into the film. Then you yearn for some lost Edenic age in which Hollywood's unconscious really was unconscious – a time when monster movies were just monster movies, and it was left to the critics to unpick the thorny undergrowth in which stirred the murky, unspeakable Repressed.

Now it's all done for you. There seems little mileage in explicating what films are 'really' about, because it's invariably written clear on the surface. Hollywood movies are made by people who've been through film school, boned up on their Bettelheim, and come to a subject fully armed with subtext. What was once cinema's unconscious has simply risen to the top, leaving little for critics to do but tick off the salient points. Francis Coppola's *Bram Stoker's Dracula*, for example, was such a knowing exercise in meta-Gothic – it was actually inspired by a scholarly annotated version of the novel – that you could just sit there ticking off the most up-to-date Repressed Top Ten: castration anxiety, yes; AIDS, OK; homophobia, present and correct . . .

So you pretty much know what you'll get with Mike Nichols's *Wolf*, and what will be done to give it that '90s twist. The werewolf myth is about letting the beast break through the veneer of civilisation: hairy chests, howling at the moon. *Ergo* we're talking about a project pitched at the people who put Robert Bly's *Iron John* at the top of the best-seller lists.

The one daring thing about *Wolf* is that it turns its back on the dominant target audience of teen-twenties multiplex-goers, and courts a generation that wants to be reassured that you can grow older and still feel tough, sexy, sophisticated – the older set of *Vanity Fair* readers, say. Its hero is Will Randall (Jack Nicholson), a weary, middle-aged book editor who gets bitten by a wolf, feels those old lycanthropic twinges, and then starts living a little. Rejuvenated overnight, he gets mad *and* gets even with his nasty new boss, his creepy work rival and his unfaithful wife, then makes out with Michelle Pfeiffer, the boss's daughter. He acquires vastly improved repartee and terrific business acumen, and gets to outleap and gore deer in the woods. It's not so much a wish-fulfilment fantasy as a Five-Point Self-Realisation Package. Feel that bite! Howl that howl! You know it feels good – you'll shed unsightly pounds too!

But there's no resonance in the myth once it's stripped of all the disturbing things that traditionally come in the package along with the fangs and side-whiskers: the self-fear, the sense of punishment, of possession as curse. An expert in matters lupine tells Will, 'The demon wolf is not evil,' and spins a lovely Bly line about 'power without guilt'. But what a weedy fantasy it is – how blandly therapeutic. It's so *efficient* – every wish realised, every score settled and the slate left perfectly clean. Indeed, Will even gets to clean up the city: in one scene that gives away the film's true allegiances, he metes out fang-and-claw justice to a gang of black muggers in Central Park. Here are the forces of darkness in service to white middle-class paranoia – the children of the night signed up as good citizens with Neighborhood Watch.

Initially, though, *Wolf* promises something quite engaging. Apart from the considerable pleasure of seeing Jack Nicholson exude unusually warm gravitas in an elder statesman role (his most subdued and human performance since *The King of Marvin Gardens* in 1972), there's considerable relief when what looks set to be a boogly-eyed horror film takes a rather elegant detour into the real. We find ourselves immersed in the tawdry daily politics of the publishing company where Randall is the last old-school Man of Taste (he told Judith Krantz that no semi-literate fourteen-year-old would read her books). For a while it looks as though an injection of moon madness into this urbane milieu will have a nice satirical pay-off. At the party held by the new boss (Christopher Plummer), things get interesting: it's just when Will has lost his job that he finds the horses shying away from him, as if he'd become *persona non grata* even in the stables. Later, fully wolfed up, he vengefully pisses on his rival James Spader's shoes and sweetly announces, 'Just marking my territory.'

The film is best at moments like this, where the hoary apparatus of genre horror becomes a vehicle for a novel take on the professional jungle. Then the banal old fantasies come to the fore as Will starts sprouting John McCririck whiskers and makes for the woods. But the forces that emerge in him aren't that interesting. Will simply does what every middle-aged guy caught in the rat race dreams of doing. It's hardly the rampaging Id set free; more like desire whitewashed as some sort of manageable will-to-fun. We find the same thing in the current release *The Mask*: its hero turns into a cartoon monster when he dons an ancient mask, which, as a psychiatrist tells him, has the power to unleash repressed desires. But where the original Dark Horse comic let rip the nihilistic spirit of massacre, the film version of *The Mask* turns its psychotic ghoul into a Bugs Bunny fit for family viewing.

The same for *Wolf*. Nothing Will does horrifies us; we only want to root for this regular guy coming into his own. The only twist is that he isn't turning into a wolf at all – he's actually turning into Jack Nicholson. We're treated to the strange, frustrating sight of an actor playing interestingly against type, then becoming predictably like himself. This self-referential appeal to star persona is the film's only interesting twist on the theme: where most Wolf Men and Hydes have started out recognisable and then morphed away from the norm, the character of Will is simply a delaying tactic before good old Jack, bristling and sniggering, jumps out of the mild-man skin. How much more interesting it would have been to see him in *Curse of the Mummy*, as a rampant extrovert who gets unnaturally wrapped up in himself.

What's happened to the Repressed in all this? It's not that Hollywood no longer has an unconscious. It's simply that it prefers to give vent to an old unconscious that's long been worked over and classified (the unconscious of the traditional horror film), in order to repress the current anxieties that it can't quite deal with. *Wolf* is the conservative man's riposte to the uncontainable antisocial drives of modern American culture – the drives that emerge in Quentin Tarantino's films, or in gangsta-rap records (the sort those Central Park muggers probably listen to). *Wolf* attempts to tame the wild imagination by bringing it onto the surface, domesticating it as healthy therapy – legalising it, in other words.

But what shows through in such emollient fantasy is a new Repressed. There is one thing that *Wolf* can't handle – something that, having initially addressed, it has to brush under the carpet of mere spook-fiction. It's that complex negotiation of language and mood and style and the everyday, which emerges here in the first half hour, in some of the barbed amorous dialogue between Nicholson and Pfeiffer, and in those scenes where the film actually bothers with language. *Wolf* only breathes when it's a comedy of manners that works around the werewolf theme instead of gasping under its dead weight. Take away the banal high-concept pitch that is the film's main selling point, and you get that risky excess that only one in a hundred Hollywood films even attempts to deal with (Peter Weir's recent underrated *Fearless* was one). I hesitate to give it a name, but at a pinch you could call it the real.

19 August 1994

The Lion King

Once the world was young and things were simple, and there were just two points of view about Walt Disney cartoons. Either they were as natural and indispensable a part of childhood as gripe water or Marmite soldiers, or they were the Great Satan. If you didn't take it as read that Bambi and Snow White belonged on the nursery wallpaper, then you saw them as emissaries of a sinister conspiracy, importing poisoned ideology into young minds under cover of button noses and goo-goo eyes. Bambi was a propagandist for the nuclear family; Dumbo an apologist for the imperatives of conformity; and Snow White taught little girls that, while waiting for their prince to come, they could do worse than tend to the everyday needs of any seven pint-size patriarchs they happened to encounter.

Yet sooner or later, even the most devout Disneyphobe would break down and admit that, as a child, they'd shed an elephant tear or two for Dumbo's mummy; or felt their nose growing Pinocchio-style every time they fibbed about the dog eating their homework; or simply swooned at some gooey gouached sunset.

There's no use fighting it. Since the day we were born, we've all ingested Disney along with a lifetime's E-additives and carbon monoxide. Besides, these days, we're too sophisticated to be paranoid about Hollywood brainwashing. We're so adept at the art of reading films against the grain that we can make even Charles Bronson and Leni Riefenstahl into funky, subversive, queer icons if we damn well please. And as long as we don't actually part with good money going to EuroDisney, then our ideological purity can rest unimpaired.

With *The Lion King*, though, things get a little complicated, and it's probably safe – or, at least, salutary – to start worrying about Disney again. I couldn't get too hot under the collar about *Aladdin's* supposed racism, partly because its more hackneyed Arab stereotypes were crammed apologetically into the first five minutes, then shunted aside so that Robin Williams could do his shtick unimpeded. And you had to applaud *Beauty and the Beast*, tepid as it was, because Beauty's feisty, literary, protofeminist stance looked like a fairly sincere attempt to compensate, in one vigorous song routine, for all of Snow White's sins of simpering.

But *The Lion King*, Disney's biggest hit in ages, is just weird, and not a little dishonest (not to mention stomach-turningly kitsch). It's best to forget the press-kit rhetoric about its 'powerful, allegorical story', and all you've heard about its timeless echoes of *Hamlet* – it's best summed up as described early on in its inception: '*Bambi* in Africa'.

Here's the tale: Simba, a little boy lion cub, is born and his father Mufasa, King of the Beasts, waves a paw at the veldt and tells him, one day, son, all this will be yours. But evil Scar, Simba's uncle, has his eye on the throne, and lures Mufasa into a computer-generated wildebeest stampede, killing the king and traumatising his rightful heir, who dashes off into the jungle. There, with shades of Prince Hal, he lives a leisurely, bug-eating life in the company of an insouciant meerkat and a flatulent warthog, while Scar and his coterie of hyenas rule it over the now-crestfallen noble cats. Soon, of course, Simba must return to save the day, so that a new king will reign, a new cute boy cub will be born, and the glorious hymnal chorale of Elton John and Tim

Rice's 'Circle of Life' will ring out, filling the air with the chime of a thousand candyfloss machines.

In a curious volte-face from the last three films – *Beauty*, *Aladdin* and *The Little Mermaid* – all the things we expected to find in classic Disney are back in force: anthropomorphism, sexism, the advocacy of the divine right of kings. Homophobia, too: wicked Scar is not only a European nasty, voiced by a magisterially sneery Jeremy Irons, but also camp to the hilt and the only lion who doesn't mate, who therefore impedes the Circle of Life ('You're so weird,' marvels the cub; 'You have *no idea*,' smirks Uncle). The racism is pretty blatant, too: of Scar's trio of mad, bad hyenas, one is characterised as black (voiced by Whoopi Goldberg), one as Hispanic (Cheech Marin), the third as a dribbling, gibbering crackhead. When Simba gets lost in the elephants' graveyard where they hang out, he's a little white kid who's wandered into the bad, black part of town – like Sherman McCoy in *The Bonfire of the Vanities* taking the wrong turn and finding himself in the Bronx.

The film seems to outwit itself, though, when it has Scar's ranked hyenas doing an unmistakable goose-step. Is Disney trying to alert us to a black gay Nazi conspiracy? This hardly makes perfect sense, and it's not supposed to. The only rule of the exercise is to use whatever image will be most powerful, and if that results in something less than coherence, that doesn't matter. *The Lion King* uses whatever meanings it needs to, for quite unashamedly commercial purpose. It appeals to *everyone*'s favourite myths, *everyone*'s pet paranoias; it wants to make a buck out of *everyone*, and seems to have succeeded. The Disney studio, in its attempt to milk the widest possible demographic, here thinks nothing of placing all its old reactionary commonplaces alongside its overtures to a black audience; for this is, in effect, Disney's first black film.

Hence the discrepancy of the film's appeal on the one hand to an exotic Euro-American image of Africa as lush Safariland, and on the other to post-*Roots* Africanism (the soundtrack features vocal arrangements by South African musician Mbongeni Ngema, of the anti-apartheid musical *Sarafina!*). Throughout, Disney gives us jarring messages. Simba's dad is voiced by that icon of black gravitas James Earl Jones. The young Simba's voice (Matthew Broderick) is pure baby WASP, but when he sings it's with the hiccuping lilt of a Michael Jackson.

What's more, *The Lion King* takes its moral rhetoric straight from the codes of the new black US cinema, with its recurrent themes of the absent father and the need for young men to wise up, get serious, Be King. Like the cocky homeboys in *Juice*, Simba wants to cruise through life fuelled on testosterone ('I Just Can't Wait to be King'); but his dad explains that with power comes responsibility, just as super-patriarch Furious Styles does in *Boyz N The Hood*. Later, when it's time for Simba to leave his funky hedonistic friends – bug-eaters and therefore not his people – it's his girlfriend who reads him the riot act, just as in *Straight Out of Brooklyn* and *Menace II Society*.

The reactionary clichés may be more transparent, because more familiar, but it's these borrowed black codes that dominate the film and make it readable in a way that's more current – and, to a young African-American audience, far more 'archetypal' – than *Hamlet* or *Ulysses* or whatever grandiose precedents the Disney script analysts may claim for it. There's no conspiracy to it. This really is *Bambi* in Africa – the same old Disney story, but aimed at a wider audience than ever. In Disneyland, no-one gets left out; *everyone* has to buy a ticket sooner or later. Maybe we do have cause to get paranoid again.

7 October 1994

Three Colours: Red (Trois Couleurs: Rouge)

There's a trick sometimes used in recording studios to determine how sturdy a pop song and its production really are. Instead of trusting to the profligate luxury of a thirty-two-track mix blasted through state-of-the-art speakers, the engineer will play the work in progress through a cheap mono transistor radio. If it still sounds like Phil Spector on a good day, then you possibly have a hit on your hands.

It's widely thought that the same principle applies with film. It's all very well, the theory goes, to sit cradled in the dark with several hundred other people engrossed in the quasi-religious glory of Panavision and Dolby stereo. But to be a real film, it's got to hold up on the small screen at home.

This method quite often works, but sometimes it can reveal the absurdity of even thinking that film and video make in any way for related experiences. I've now seen Krzysztof Kieślowski's *Three Colours: Red* twice, once on screen, then on video. The first time I was quite awe-struck; I felt not only that I'd witnessed something genuinely magical but also that all my misgivings about *Blue* and *White*, the preceding parts of Kieślowski's multinational trilogy, were misplaced. On the second viewing, however, I began to wonder whether I'd simply let myself be conned by the film's considerable art, and whether all its apparent depth was purely illusionist's sham.

I'm still not entirely sure whether *Red* is a profound achievement or a dour, tendentious piece of stuffed-shirt metaphysics. At a pinch, I might still tend to the first opinion, if only because these days the very fact of making a genuinely ambivalent film, one that isn't cut-and-dried, has to stand as some sort of profundity. *Red* is by far the warmest and the most satisfying of the trilogy, pointing in the direction of integration and reconciliation after the chilliness of *Blue* (which was about a woman cutting herself off from society) and the lugubrious cynicism of *White* (in which a hapless innocent learned to play society at all its own meanest tricks).

Set in Geneva, *Red* is about chance and control: Valentine (Irène Jacob), a young model, by chance runs over a dog, which leads her to an encounter with its owner, embittered retired judge Kern (Jean-Louis Trintignant); he plays a godlike role, eavesdropping by radio on people's telephone conversations and drawing a mental map of their lives and those lives' contingent causes. The story is rife with evident contrivance, as befits its ambivalent weighing-up of randomness and design – for example, it's implied (only a second viewing makes this apparent) that Kern's radio-hamming is itself the indirect cause of Valentine's running into the dog. The story is rife with the echoes and mirrors that underwrote Kieślowski's *The Double Life of Véronique*.

There may be a simple explanation of why I liked *Red* less the second time: it may be that, once you've pieced together its jigsaw narrative, there's simply no picture left. It's almost a disappointment to find things falling into place. But part of the film's story is about the gradual discovery that finally there *is* no real story – not much happens on screen, the main events serving to bring people together so that they can tell each other about past events or make prognoses for the future. But my main reason for liking *Red* less (and I can test this theory out if I ever see it a third time, on screen) is that on video there really are dimensions lacking that narrative alone can't account for. For a start, Kieślowski's films depend, more than most others, on the communal experience of being in a cinema, sitting silently for ninety-six minutes, prepared to take things seriously. (It's precisely Kieślowski's contract with the audience, this promise of serious content in exchange for serious attention, that lays him open to attacks as a retrograde high-art obscurantist.) In films that largely concern society and individuals' ability or failure to interconnect, there's a very poignant sense that cinema is one of the few things that can, if only for an hour and a half at a time, mould us into micro-communities, congregations.

In addition, if there is a sense that there's less to Kieślowski's films than meets the eye – and what meets the eye is precisely the immediate impression that there's *more* than meets the eye – it's because Kieślowski is entirely speaking the language of cinema. His films contain arguments that solicit our intellectual responses, and *Red* at times expresses them more bluntly, if not crassly, than usual. The issue of the judge as disabused god carries dispiriting echoes of Camus's *La Chute*, and the arguments about the ethics of surveillance look simplistic beside the average police procedural thriller. But what gives his films their genuine intellectual content is that they bypass the verbal and go for the emotive, the tactile, the visual – they present *plastic* arguments.

Mystificatory though this may appear, it amounts only to this – Kieślowski might not be a great thinker, but when he is great it's because he's thinking in cinema. The moments in his films that strike chords are the moments that are most purely tactile, that can't easily be spelled out. *Dekalog*, his massively lauded but almost entirely unwatchable series based on the Ten Commandments, was dense with banal allegorical moments – my favourite being a wasp slowly struggling out of a glass, at the bedside of a recovering invalid. But when Kieślowski gives us moments *as* moments and no more, then his films occasionally achieve the transcendent quality his adepts claim for them: these are the moments when he captures a certain hazy reflection in an amber paperweight or catches Irène Jacob's face in the rain (both in *The Double Life of Véronique*), or when he lets Zbigniew Preisner's music swell up in particularly rapturous fashion. All he's doing is giving us cinema to the hilt – and just as *Jurassic Park*'s dinosaurs don't carry their full weight when shrunk into twelve inches square, so you need the full cinema screen to properly catch the generosity and fine definitions of Kieślowski's films. They are music that you can't listen to on a car radio, and I use the analogy advisedly; the fact that Kieślowski aims for music's abstraction is signalled by the way that the recurring artist figures in his films are musicians – notably, the apocryphal Dutch composer Van Den Budenmayer, who figures once again in *Red*. (A tentative theory about the trilogy: it's structured around the sensations – *Blue*: sight; *White*: touch, i.e. ownership; *Red*: hearing.)

Kieślowski clearly is one of the few directors around who *scores* his films on every level. Piotr Sobocinski, his cinematographer on *Red*, has attested to the unusual closeness of his collaboration with Kieślowski, not just in the film's lighting but in its whole conception; and it's clear from every shot just how much the look of the film is thought right through it. It's fair to say that the colour red, with its various registers, is the film's true setting, rather than the city of Geneva.

Blue was spoilt for me, though, by a certain over-reliance on rhapsodic visual language, and here again I find it hard to trust entirely. Kieślowski's poetry of the luminous may be more thoroughly integrated into the shape of his films than the superficial neon-ism of a Besson or a Beineix, but it may ultimately be of the same nature. Kieślowski relies massively on a certain glamour, most obviously in his use of the iconic beauty of Juliette Binoche in *Blue* and Irène Jacob here and in *Véronique*; there is something calculating in the presentation of the numerous small ecstasies that Jacob seems infinitely susceptible to.

Watching her swoon in the rain in *Véronique*, or gulp joyously at a glass of water in *Red*, there's an uncomfortable sense that we're being coerced into falling in love with her, in classic Hollywood fashion. *Red* ends with Jacob's face on a massive hoarding, an advert for chewing gum; this could be the most sophisticated film ever to use what are effectively the seductions of advertising. Then again, Kieślowski – who has announced *Red* as his farewell to cinema – could be one jump ahead of us: the brand of the gum is 'Hollywood'.

11 November 1994

Dear Diary
(Caro Diario)

How to sum up the uniquely skewed sensibility of Italian director-star Nanni Moretti? Actress Jennifer Beals tries to get it right when she and her husband encounter an excitable Moretti in the street (Moretti's life, he claims, was changed by seeing her dancing in *Flashdance*): 'Off – crazy but not quite . . . Whimsical – almost dumb.' *Off* is about right for the director whose film *Palombella Rossa* contemplated the fate of the Italian Communist Party in the form of a game of water polo. And *Dear Diary*, in which the above scene appears, is the most uniquely *off* film I've seen for some time. 'Off' is what Moretti's humour and persona are – not eye-rolling manic like his fellow Italian director-comics Roberto Benigni and Maurizio Nichetti, but oblique, pensive, and not a little discomforting.

Moretti has a lot in common with Woody Allen – both derive much of their humour from a sense that clowning is perhaps not the most dignified thing for an intellectual to be doing. But where Allen's wit has always been about aspiring to be seen as an intellectual, Moretti comes across as the real thing: partly because his career has evolved out of an approach to independent film-making as a political voice (he recently contributed to a collective film-polemic against Silvio Berlusconi), partly because he's so evidently committed to cinema as a medium of thought – not just argumentation but reverie as well. Like Woody Allen, Moretti has a concern for his own mortality that borders on the narcissistic (but how narcissistic can a man be who mainly shows you his back for the first third of a film?). In *Hannah and her Sisters*, Allen played a man as hypochondriacal as Allen is famously known to be. Moretti goes one better – he actually films his own chemotherapy treatment.

Dear Diary presents itself as three slices of the life of 'Nanni Moretti'. That is, the man in the film is and isn't Moretti – he undergoes the same medical treatment as Moretti did a couple of years ago, and Moretti produces documentary evidence in the form of his chemotherapy footage and reams of prescriptions made out in his name. But Moretti has stretched the self-portrait somewhat; he's sworn in interviews that he never really wanted to dance like Jennifer Beals.

Dear Diary may present some thorny problems for analysts of autobiographical cinema, but we are never less than convinced that this is a genuine *mise en scène* of Moretti's inner life. The minute we see him write the rather childlike words 'Dear diary', we accept that the film is going to be a sort of magic slate on which Moretti sketches a version of his life and thoughts. Not the definitive self-portrait, though, but a provisional sketch in three loose and vaguely related fly-sheets.

From the first shot of Moretti on his Vespa swaying through the streets of Rome to a song by Angélique Kidjo, *Dear Diary* comes across as a beautifully casual film. It's a *flâneur*'s movie, restless, distracted, but apt at moments to let its mind go perfectly blank. In Part One, Moretti rides around the deserted summer streets of Rome, visits the duller parts of town, wonders why there's nothing on in the cinema except bad Italian films and *Henry: Portrait of a Serial Killer* (which he hates). He goes on to berate the critic who recommended *Henry*, dances a bit of salsa, and finally, in a sequence of elegiac beauty, rides out to see the spot where Pasolini died.

In Part Two, he and an island-dwelling Joyce scholar head out across the sea in search of a quiet place to work, only to encounter manic social organisers, anguished mayors, one-child families and anchorites. They finally give up the quest, because Moretti's friend contracts an addiction to American soap operas. And in Part Three, Moretti soberly recounts his long illness, which led him through an endless series of doctors and ointments; after being operated on for a lymphoma, he finally declares his faith in a glass of water taken every day with breakfast. That's the last shot of the film, and it's astounding that anything so simple (and apparently bathetic) can have such joyous resonance.

That's what makes *Dear Diary* so surprising – the way that simple things gain the most extraordinary power because Moretti persuades us that his entire being is invested in them. *Dear Diary* is all those things traditionally associated with the canon of 'great films': serious-minded, philosophical, humanist, rooted in a particular place and a particular sensibility; but at the same time, it often seems irredeemably trivial, self-regarding, whimsical. I'd say this makes it an utterly radical film: it's a film about nothing except its own thought processes and rhythms.

The first segment is the most extraordinary in its distraction. Where *8½* was about a man trying to make a film, Moretti starts off by daydreaming about the films he might make, loses interest, then moves on to the films he's glad he didn't make. The scene where he reduces a critic to tears by reading him the critic's own excruciating eulogies of David Cronenberg is the film's least funny moment because it's so overstated, but you accept it because you feel that this complaint came into Moretti's head on the spur of the moment and therefore has its legitimate place in the film.

Certain other things jar: in Part Two, for example, the laborious gags about TV soaps and only children. But there are moments that offset them because Moretti evidently isn't working too hard; he's just letting his mind sway the way his bike does in the long Steadicam shots of Part One. On one island, he starts bobbing absent-mindedly to the rhythms of a Silvana Mangano film on TV, then muses about what a strange film it was. Later, in a beautiful *trompe-l'œil* shot, an ocean liner drifts languidly across a football field, and we just watch, letting our minds go as appreciatively blank as Moretti's, who's observing it.

No single section would mean quite the same if not for the other two, and it's the no-nonsense lucidity of the third section, 'Doctors', that gives the film a completely different impetus. The film ends on a note that could seem utterly glib – the realisation that doctors know how to talk but not to listen, and a glass of water is good for you – but doesn't, because it's utterly touching that Moretti has taken the trouble to document the pettifogging quotidian hell of prescription forms, and has the heart to shrug it off in a moment's closing gesture. *Dear Diary* casually pulls off, in the spirit of whimsy, what was once the grand project of cinema's avant-garde – to make films that were portraits of the thought process. *Dear Diary*, with all its narcissism, its flippancy, its off-ness, is just this. We may be tempted to think, so what, it's just cinema; Moretti makes us think it's also just life.

25 November 1994

Junior is the very definition of a high-concept movie: it has one measly idea and milks it for all it's worth. It's a comedy about a man getting pregnant – surely a droll enough conceit to keep us amused for ninety minutes or so. Make that man Arnold Schwarzenegger, however, and you're upping the ante somewhat: not only do you provide the punters with a visual paradox to make the head spin – those biceps, that jaw, that belly! – but you instantly send critics everywhere scurrying off to bash out think pieces about the Crisis of Masculinity. Everybody's happy . . . or would be if *Junior* weren't such a dreary piece of work – shoddy, smug and a little late in the day. Late because *True Lies* has already proved that there was no fun to be had out of Arnie as a big soft family man; and because *Mrs Doubtfire* said all there was to say about boys being girls with the aid of funny rubber attachments.

The trouble with high-concept movies is that they invariably boil down to a single sentence – 'What if . . . ?' – and so you invariably end up with a single-sentence answer. What if a man got pregnant? Why, then he'd start eating pickles, wearing pastel colours and getting all soppy. You'll believe that Arnie can be a big girl's blouse!

Junior reunites Schwarzenegger with Danny DeVito, his partner in *Twins*, as Hesse and Arbogast, a pair of scientists working on a pregnancy wonder drug, Expectane. When their grant is cut off, and a rival project, headed by Emma Thompson, hustled into their lab, they decide to carry on research anyway. Schwarzenegger is injected in the gut with a cocktail of Expectane and eggs from an unknown donor (a scene weirdly reminiscent of Uma Thurman's nasty syringe moment in *Pulp Fiction*).

The payoff is a long time coming, but it comes with heavy inevitability. Arnie is pregnant, and grows a huge prosthetic belly. He also starts complaining of sore nipples and a bad back, develops an odd waddling gait, and starts getting testy when DeVito is late home from work. What starts off in effect as a drag act finally becomes one literally, when Arnie has to don a floral smock and a wig and pass himself off as a former East German athlete zapped up on hormones.

It's easy to say why the film falls flat – because the jokes are obvious, lamely executed and telegraphed miles ahead; because Schwarzenegger now takes himself so seriously as a comic turn instead of the rumbling cyborg he should ever have remained; and because director Ivan Reitman has taken too much inspiration from the baby theme, cloaking the whole film in clinical nursery pastels that lull the eye into a queasy languor. But why the central joke itself fails is more of a problem. What seems like a sure-fire gag, a hilarious 'man-bites-dog' set-up, backfires and leaves us feeling curiously uneasy, as if we're being asked to laugh at something we'd really rather not be seeing.

What makes *Mrs Doubtfire* an entertaining charade is that it announces itself from the start as a charade, a film about a jolly play-actor – it's simply a variant on the pantomime dame tradition, with a thoughtful spin given in the direction of the decline of the nuclear family. *Junior* has no such spin. It has no questions to ask about the structure of the family, about what makes men men and women women or vice versa. Its premise stands or falls entirely on the question that haunts all Schwarzenegger films, whether he's a cyborg or a Cimmerian or a civil servant – the question of his *impossible body*. The idea of his being transformed by prosthetics is from the very start a redundant one, because that excessive frame is already prosthetic. Arnie with a little extra, male or female, isn't remarkable; Arnie with a little less *would* be, and the day he gets to play a hunger striker, we should all sit up and take notice.

Junior is different from *Mrs Doubtfire* in other ways. In that film, the Robin Williams character proves himself in some ways to be a 'better' woman – more maternal, whatever that means, than his own ex-wife. But the film wasn't so much about testing modern ideas of womanhood; rather, in a roundabout, very 1990s-Hollywood gooey liberal way, it was about a guy learning new ways to be a guy. You want to be a real man? Go and be your granny for a week.

Junior appears to be about this too, but only up to a point. On the surface, it's about dry, academic Dr Hesse becoming a complete person, getting in touch with his body and his emotions, learning to lighten up and love life (the many awe-struck glimpses of foetuses on scanners make this a pro-life film in more senses than one). But at the same time, he's actually made incomplete – he starts acting irrationally, feeling all manner of physical discomforts, losing his sense of himself as a man. As he says to DeVito, 'I feel so humiliated, I feel I've lost control over my body.' *Junior* is effectively a horror story, a male nightmare about how being a woman means being debilitated in some way. (See Arnie's look of coy bemusement on the poster – what is it but sheer terror?)

The film's two principle female characters are represented as being out of control in different ways. Thompson's Dr Reddin – a surprisingly gamy turn in her brisk Joyce Grenfell mould – is a scatty boffin-buffoon, who invariably has cheese smeared over her face and toilet roll hanging off her shoe; while Arbogast's ex-wife Angela (Pamela Reed) is herself pregnant but, in what appears to be the ultimate lapse of control (or at least taste), it's by a member of Aerosmith's entourage. They're both oddly defeminised – Angela because she's played by Reed, who brings to the film a trace of the asexual-buddy tough-cookie role she played opposite Schwarzenegger in *Kindergarten Cop*; and Reddin by virtue of being so common-sense and English public school, with her stout-chap jumper and slacks (also, of course, an allusion to Katharine Hepburn's typical garb in her screwball comedies). Effectively, Arnie is the *only* woman in the movie – the crowds of fluttery moms-to-be wafting around in neat frocks are simply there as so much flowered wallpaper.

When Dr Reddin learns what's been going on, she angrily complains, 'You think men don't hold enough cards? You're trying to take this away from us?' The line falls flat, because it's so obviously tossed in as a well-meaning bit of tokenism, the implications of which the film has no intention of following up. In one sense, Arnie does have all the cards – he's so much more than a man that he can also be that much more of a woman. The film can operate on its light, engaging level precisely because we see Schwarzenegger as a superbody and not as a person at all. If the film had starred any actor who appeared vaguely human, that actor's body *would* be at issue. By the flip wheeze of featuring Schwarzenegger, the film refuses to acknowledge that there are questions to be asked about how men's and women's identities are defined by their bodies. But it's actually that refusal that makes *Junior* rather uncomfortable to watch, as if it were repressing something it didn't want to think about. That something is the fact that, if not for Arnie, it would have to take itself a little more seriously. It would have to be a David Cronenberg film, with gags.

9 December 1994

Wes Craven's New Nightmare

No-one likes it when a genre gets too self-conscious, and partly for good reason – a genre that can't play itself straight knows it's on the verge of collapse. Look at the frosty reception that greeted the Arnold Schwarzenegger meta-vehicle *Last Action Hero*, which was almost universally felt to have overstepped the bounds of clever-dick self-referentiality. That film may have been rejected out of hand by critics and punters alike, but you couldn't deny its corrosive power: after it, Schwarzenegger's subsequent film, *True Lies*, which did at least half take itself seriously, looked all the more transparent and witless.

There are certain bounds within which such mirror games are held to be acceptable. Self-reflexivity in fiction is permissible in the realms of high art, where it's always been OK to get ontological about things (Woody Allen when he's serious, Godard, Fellini) or in comedy (Woody Allen when he's not so serious, Mel Brooks, or the priceless 1953 Chuck Jones cartoon *Duck Amuck*, in which Daffy Duck falls off the frame and gets erased by the animator's hand). The greatest meta-fictional burlesque of all, beating *8½* hands down, is the

1941 Olsen and Johnson vehicle *Hellzapoppin'*, a kamikaze assault on showbiz-movie conventions, and a veritable encyclopaedia of film-within-a-film tropes – the *Tristram Shandy* of backstage musicals.

The one field where you might expect such trickery not to work is in horror. To be effective, you would imagine, horror has to be taken on some level as being 'for real'. But horror buffs – especially the academics among them – will tell you that to be a true fan is to acquire a specialised competence in the genre's history and conventions. That's why most of us regard horrorphiles as irredeemable nerds – not because they actually believe in the oogie-boogie stuff, but because, while we hide behind our sofas in terror, they sit there reeling off the complete CV of special effects artists like Screaming Mad George, or telling you how many different titles some Dario Argento film has been released under.

But here's a film that works brilliantly as a horror film – it's not that scary, perhaps, but it is ingenious and startling, it works as a meditation on genre conventions, and it asks what motivates both the fans and the makers of horror films. *Wes Craven's New Nightmare* is not, strictly speaking, another sequel in the *Nightmare on Elm Street* series, but a commentary, from outside the canon, on Craven's original *Nightmare* and its five vastly inferior sequels. In fact, this is probably the first film that explicitly examines the Sequel as a genre in itself.

Craven's original *A Nightmare on Elm Street* (1984) was based on a premise that from the start implied a commentary on fiction and its effects. Nocturnal ripper and revenant child-killer Freddy Krueger, he of the animatronic manicure, had the power to haunt people's dreams; only by staying awake could they elude his fatal fingertips. The trick of the film was to con us that we were in dreamland when we were in the waking world, and vice versa; the whole film was a cruel play on that weary fictional let-out, 'only a dream after all'. But from sequel to sequel, the *Nightmare*s, once out of Craven's own hands, became tamer and tamer, and Freddy increasingly became a comic-cuts bogeyman, a wise-cracking hobgoblin no more threatening than Count Duckula.[1]

Now back at the helm, Craven has recharged his ghoul's shock potential by distancing us even further from Freddy. Here he reveals Freddy from the start as a paper ghoul, and defies us to find him frightening – and, despite the odds, he is. This time the game of mirrors is dizzyingly convoluted, just short of arch. Ten years after the first *Nightmare*, the heroine of the new film is Heather Langenkamp – played by Heather Langenkamp, who played the teenage heroine of the first film. Now with a child of her own (Miko Hughes), Langenkamp is still haunted by Freddy – in her nightmares, on television (the original film seems to be showing every night, at all hours), and in real life. She can't get away from Freddy, even on a chat show where all the audience members are dressed as him and where she's joined by the actor who played him, Robert Englund – played by Robert Englund. It's a wonderfully telling scene: when Englund bursts onto the set to riotous applause, Langenkamp shoots him an equivocal look, not only because he is her nightmare incarnate, but also because he is getting more attention – the king of the night lording it over a minor daytime soap star.

Langenkamp is summoned to the (real-life) New Line Productions, where its (real-life) president Robert Shaye wants her to be reunited with Englund in 'the definitive *Nightmare*'. Wes Craven (Wes Craven) is working on a new script: its gist is that a timeless spirit of evil has been released by the termination of the *Nightmare* series – now the demon wants to play Freddy one more time. Fade to black, on a cut to Craven's word processor, on which we see the script of the film we are watching . . .

If you are a student of Gide, Robbe-Grillet, Borges and the

---

[1] The other *Nightmare* films were *A Nightmare on Elm Street 2: Freddy's Revenge* (Jack Sholder, 1985); *A Nightmare on Elm Street 3: Dream Warriors* (Chuck Russell, 1987); *A Nightmare on Elm Street 4: The Dream Master* (Renny Harlin, 1988); *A Nightmare on Elm Street 5: The Dream Child* (Stephen Hopkins, 1989); and – at last breaking the title pattern – *Freddy's Dead: The Final Nightmare* (Rachel Talalay, 1991).

like, all of this is fairly routine stuff – you just don't expect to find it in a horror film. This is not just formal play, however; Craven uses it to make a serious point about the repetitive, addictive nature of the horror genre. Horror, we tend to assume, is about the unexpected, but Craven shows how much it can be about the *expected*, by overtly repeating shocks from the earlier films, giving us Freddy's greatest hits one more time – the tongue in the telephone, the dragging-the-victim-up-the-wall trick. They're the same but, because of this singularly odd context, crucially different.

On an explicit level, the aim is indeed to give the punters more of the same – but Craven is also asking, *why* always the same? The film is about its own necessary bad faith – about the repetitive obsession that motivates not only Freddy's fans but also his creators (at least the fans can't be accused of being in it for the money). Ten years on, A *Nightmare on Elm Street* is still Langenkamp's biggest success; Englund, who graciously plays himself as a ham buffoon going through the motions, can't get himself taken seriously in any other role, trapped by his own steel claws just as Leonard Nimoy was by his ears; and Craven hasn't come up with anything as good since. If Craven must give in to market forces and the death of inspiration, then he intends to take everyone with him, not least of all New Line, who roundly get the blame for the bowdlerisation of Craven's initially potent concept. A story dies, explains Craven, when 'someone waters it down to make it an easy sell'. There's certainly something strange about a hideously scarred child-killer becoming a kiddies' favourite – 'like Santa Claus or King Kong', as Langenkamp puts it.

Craven does indeed ask some timely questions about children and horror – timely in view of the panic that surrounded the video *Child's Play 3*, cited as a *possible* bad influence on the child killers of Jamie Bulger. Are horror videos bad for children? Perhaps, and in this case perhaps literally so – Freddy seems to be getting at Langenkamp's son Dylan through *Nightmare* revivals on TV. Or is it more a case of adults projecting their own fears onto children? Langenkamp is concerned that her role in the series may indirectly be a cause of Dylan's trauma, but she's no less apprehensive about reading him 'Hansel and Gretel'. Yet it is through repeated readings of that supremely horrific yarn that Dylan is able to acquire a necessary understanding of evil (Freddy's defeat, in a stunningly baroque finale, brilliantly merges that fairy-tale with the first *Nightmare*'s own myth of Freddy's origin).

In a brilliant twist on the first film, Langenkamp is accused of traumatising Dylan through her attempts to guard him from an imaginary demon, by depriving him of sleep – a neat reversal of the series's golden rule that, in order to survive, you had to stay awake. While Langenkamp is made out to be a neurotic, her judgement addled by her role in a foolish film, her child becomes the hero. The child's ambivalent role in horror fiction – as prey, hero or monster, the focus of all family terrors, preying on adults' own infantile imagination – is brought to the fore in a series of allusions to *Poltergeist*, *The Exorcist* and other canonic demon-child tales. And the fact that, conversely, any nightmare can have its cosy, reassuring side is brought to light by the fact that Dylan's personal guardian, who drives Freddy away, is a stuffed dinosaur called Rex – so much for *Jurassic Park* traumatising kids.

6 January 1995

Natural Born Killers · Bandit Queen

A director working on a screenplay for a love story recently told me how much he wished he could break the rules of the genre. If only he could bring a gun into it somewhere, then he could get finished so much faster. Produce a gun at any point in a plot, he said, and things simply happen. You might add: produce a gun and people immediately know where they are.

Violence, in real life and in the cinema, is unequivocal. It sorts you out, stops you in your tracks; you know what it means. That, at least, is what Oliver Stone is counting on when he uses violence – both its power to repel and its box-office allure – as the basis for his satirical argument in *Natural Born Killers*. Despite the high ketchup factor, *NBK* is far more violent formally than it is in what it shows. It's a hyperspeed-edited flash-fry of lurid imagery, much of it sampled from TV and film.

Stone's argument is that we no longer know any moral absolutes because the onslaught of media imagery has left our judgements scrambled from a cacophony of interfering signals. His antihero lovebirds, young psychotic killers Mickey and Mallory (Woody Harrelson and Juliette Lewis) are innocents simply looking for spiritual stillness among the radio noise. They are 'lost in a world of ghosts', says the film's one moral centre, a wise old Native American (Russell Means) who can read the words 'Too much TV' projected on their chests.

In Britain, *Natural Born Killers* has become headline news for contingent reasons – its certification was delayed after media speculation that murders in France may have been directly triggered by the film. But films, all the evidence suggests, don't trigger violence; what they do trigger, and on the slightest provocation, is media generalisations about violence. It is enough to know that *NBK* is about two young homicides who become pop heroes, and that its leads play up the amoral thrill-kill sexiness to the hilt – and, whether or not anyone has seen the film, it's deemed unarguably Bad For You.

NBK probably is bad for you, but only insofar as it's bad for film. It certainly represents some kind of breakthrough in terms of the speed and intensity with which it marshals its images, but it does so without any sense of rhetorical complexity. By throwing enough extreme images at you, it aims to prove we live in an extreme world. You shall know the truly evil because they're ugly and bloated and sweaty, or wear hideous houndstooth suits and demonic little moustaches. *NBK* is a clumsy, stupid, extremely tiring film that leaves you numbed and disinclined to form any complex judgements.

NBK's breakneck dementia is a form of violence in itself – the violence of bad rhetoric. But it is also a technological refinement of a basic violence that has always been fundamental to cinema. The very act of editing images together, forcing them into incongruous promiscuity, is based on a very material violation – the severing of continuity, the cutting of the strip of celluloid that records real acts, so that it can be recut into a reality that never existed. The act of editing film forcibly directs our sensibility, constantly prevents us from following the vagaries of our own attention, goading us with the cut away from one image to another.

It is perhaps because of this symbolic mutilation that cinema has so readily embraced violence as a subject matter; but it has also always been regarded as an act to be approached with caution. The best respected action directors are the ones who cut fast and clean. And the mistrust with which some theorists have traditionally regarded montage, as opposed to the extended shot, may go hand in hand with an awareness of film's expense – there is both a formal and a financial puritanism at stake.

What makes *NBK* a case of genuinely gratuitous violence is the editing itself – Stone's use of the Lightworks system, a computer-based method that makes it possible to cut short and fast without laborious concrete cutting-and-pasting. All cuts are therefore provisional and immaterial (perhaps in more senses than one). Editing becomes something like automatic writing, or, rather, like zapping between channels – a sense that Stone explicitly gives it in his constant recourse to the imagery of US television (adverts, sitcoms). But the violence his editing inflicts on the viewer is also inflicted on the image itself; each image is promptly bled dry of its significance, which is invariably primary and immediate, then tossed aside.

It is easy to make the leap from distaste for this kind of MTV rhetoric to a paranoia about film's infectious power. There is a powerful fear of being affected subliminally – perhaps literally so, by the much-demonised and probably apocryphal subliminals, flash messages that only the unconscious reads. But Stone's use of comic-strip shorthand actually defuses the power of violence altogether.

There are some great films that set out to brutalise the viewer – notably Shinya Tsukamoto's two *Tetsuo* films, which make you feel as if you've been set upon with a sledgehammer for ninety minutes apiece. But the really artful exercise of screen violence tends to deflect the blow away from the viewer, to produce a more devastating effect than mere revulsion can produce. In the ear-cutting sequence of *Reservoir Dogs*, we never actually see the cut, because the camera veers away; we all but think we do. In the Belgian black comedy *Man Bites Dog*, a far blacker exposé of media complicity than *NBK*, the camera crew accompanying a personable killer wake up the morning after a night of slaughter to realise they themselves have taken part. The fact that we have missed the action only makes us feel more involved in their horrific lapse of consciousness. In being out of it, we become part of it.

But sometimes too we just have to be there. The current release *Bandit Queen*, by Indian director Shekar Kapur, features violence that is painfully hard to watch – not just the rape and beating of the heroine, but the moral opprobrium and caste discrimination that go hand in hand with it. Her ordeal explains her fate – how in real life Phoolan Devi became a feared bandit and folk heroine. Kapur's film may have the stylised feel of a spaghetti western. Yet what shakes you is that the violence doesn't end in a burst of ketchup and a quip, but in suffering, shock and lasting moral damage. After several months on a diet of cartoon bloodbath films like *Killing Zoe* (by Tarantino associate Roger Avary) and the lamebrain subtleties of *Pulp Fiction*, *Bandit Queen* feels like a slap in the face from the real world.

24 February 1995

The Silences of the Palace (Les Silences du palais)

Curiously, the two recent films that immediately come to mind watching *The Silences of the Palace*, by Tunisian director Moufida Tlatli, are Chinese and Vietnamese – Zhang Yimou's *Raise the Red Lantern* and Tran Anh Hung's *The Scent of Green Papaya*. All three are about women in servitude in enclosed, cellular societies on the brink of destruction – the Tunisia of the Beys, feudal 1920s China, pre-war Vietnam – and all three are austere and measured in a way that is generally alien to Western cinema. There is the temptation to make the leap here into some spurious generalisation about Third World cinemas and images of repression, and yet these films do share important structures that shape their portrayal of the world. All are set in *huis clos* households, they all involve a literal Inside and Outside, and a literal or figurative Upstairs and Downstairs – oppositions that their respective heroines (Tunisian servant's daughter, Chinese bride, Vietnamese maid) have to resolve for themselves and within themselves.

Of the three films, Tlatli's addresses these questions most severely. Where Zhang creates a lush, heightened image of a dreamlike past, and Tran applies Proustian exactitude to his heroine's sensuous perceptions, *The Silences of the Palace* is the most abstracted film in terms of its structures, and the most sparing in its narrative, although its story is conventionally melodramatic. It is both *Bildungsroman* and detective story: the heroine returns to the palace she grew up in and reviews her adolescence. She wants to solve the mystery of herself, but she is also looking for clues about the nature of Tunisia. It must be said that the film is weakest when it makes those connections obvious. 'You're like the country itself,' the young heroine's suitor tells her, 'indecisive.'

The story begins in the 1960s, as singer Alia (Ghalia Lacroix) performs at a banquet. She goes home with her lover Lotfi, by whom she is pregnant. 'Every eye accuses me as if they could read my face,' she complains – and in fact the film has begun with a close-up of her, daring us to read these beautiful, exquisitely made-up features that we don't yet know. The film is about reading the surfaces of things – of rich decor, of social convention, of women's faces with and without make-up. Like the younger Alia, who spends all her time looking, we are encouraged to see behind these things, and behind silences, to learn what they conceal.

Alia returns to the palace she left ten years earlier, where her mother Khedija (Ahmel Hedhili) was one of the servant women in a household of Beys (princes). Alia's name has not been mentioned there for ten years; she is herself the first silence we learn about. The film flashes back to her childhood, and the silence is briefly broken by her scream at birth, but it still surrounds the identity of her father. As Alia grows up, her life is marked by a desire to escape, to break the house silences, which the precise soundtrack, isolating dialogue in a sea of muteness, makes powerfully literal.

The possibility of breaking silence in a way that is specifically female – although fraught with danger – is represented by music. Young Alia (Hend Sabri) dreams of being a singer and playing the lute. When her mother presents her with a lute of her own, she carries it rounded body out, like a pregnant belly; the image intersects with the film's recurrent theme of childbirth, achieved or aborted. Upstairs, where the princes live, is the realm of silence; downstairs, the servant women sing, drum and squabble. But for Alia, finding a musical voice will be perilous – it will make her an object of predatory lusts and her mother's jealousy, and will also lead to the scandal that causes her name to be silenced.

The lute is a representative image for the film: its rounded soundbox suggests the way themes resonate with each other inside the closed world of the drama. The overwhelming sense of enclosure makes these themes considerably less schematic than they might appear. Music is not only a gift but also a curse. The women are trapped in their roles, but far from being passive, they are engaged in fierce unspoken struggles – jealousies between generations, between the princes' favourites, between the mistresses and the wives. The princes may be jailers, but they are also prisoners, an effete dynasty protected by thin walls from the world outside, in which French rule is about to crumble before the nationalist uprising.

As in *The Scent of Green Papaya*, where change is announced only by the distant sound of a fighter plane, so here the fall of the Beys' world is announced only by alarms from outside – radio news of strikes, the harbouring of a young militant. Another too-explicit moment makes plain the community's incarceration: as curfew is announced, one woman complains that their life is already a curfew. But Tlatli all along shows us that in her long, measured takes; in the way interiors are framed like stage sets, evoking the claustrophobia of a Chekhov play; and in the way even exteriors in the palace gardens and courtyards seem enclosed, too oppressively laden with light – they are sun traps.

The Silences of the Palace uses the familiar strategy of weighing an adolescent's perceptions against the portrait of a society ripe to be demystified. The film is most directly powerful, but again most conventional, when young Alia watches her world's secrets from behind curtains. But Tlatli shows a fine, troubling judgement in the maturing of young Hend Sabri from a diffident, volatile little girl into the confident, mighty-voiced beauty that the Beys begin to desire. The film's time scheme is based on the creeping awareness that, at some point, Alia must intersect with her older self, and that the hatching out into her butterfly self won't necessarily entail freedom. The film opts for a traditional melo-drama conclusion, as Alia finds some kind of answer for herself. But what resonates when the film is over is precisely that lingering silence that Tlatli meticulously and suggestively constructs, and the closing freeze-frame implies that everything still remains to be asked – which for that rarest of schools, women's cinema in the Maghreb, it of course does.

10 March 1995

Eyes Without a Face (Les Yeux sans visage)

Commenting on Henri-Georges Clouzot's Hitchcockian shocker *Les Diaboliques*, Georges Franju, that other French master of the ghastly *frisson*, commented, 'The trouble with Clouzot is that he tries to knock the audience's head off. That's wrong; you should twist it off.' Seeing Franju's 1959 *Eyes Without a Face (Les Yeux sans visage)*, you wonder what he was thinking; if this is an exercise in persuasive subtlety, my name's Sam Peckinpah. In fact, for all its brutality, Franju's film does something remarkably subtle: rather than twist your head, it attempts to slice off your face.

This is a film that can still make you squirm – still an 18 certificate, thirty-seven years after it induced a fainting epidemic at the Edinburgh Film Festival. In fact, except for one notorious scene, Franju's film is as discreet in its nerve-twisting as the legendary Hollywood horrors produced in the 1940s by Val Lewton (*Cat People*, *I Walked With a Zombie*), which showed nothing but always suggested the worst. Franju's tactic is different: he shows plenty, but leaves it to you to decide what it's really about.

Eyes Without a Face is a variation on the Beauty and the Beast myth: brilliant plastic surgeon Dr Génessier (Pierre Brasseur) has caused the hideous scarring of his daughter Christiane (Edith Scob) in a car accident. Determined to reconstruct her face, he sends his assistant Louise (Alida Valli) on missions to pick up likely face donors, unwitting girls who all happen to have Christiane's blue eyes. On first viewing, the film may seem superficial, more fairy-tale than horror, or stiff and fusty, a museum piece. In fact, its rather solemn deliberation adds to the clinical ghastliness; it's matched by the self-satisfied dignity of Brasseur's walk, which reminds us that the prince of surgery is also the provincial quality butcher.

The film's sense of dread comes in the way it slowly reveals what its horror is about, as if lifting a mask. The opening sequence is brilliantly deceptive. Accompanied by Maurice Jarre's eerie calliope music, Valli drives down a country road at night. The conventions of horror tell us that she is the one facing a menace; and when we see a mysterious figure in a coat and hat slouched in the back seat, we assume it is an interloper. But it turns out to be the disguised body of the girl Valli is disposing of. From the start, our certainties are disturbed, and such reversals and ambiguities run through the film. With Génessier and Louise playing both her protective parents and her tyrannical jailers, Christiane is at once a fairy-tale princess and a monster. She is the lovely minotaur in Génessier's labyrinthine house, wafting around in a white alabaster mask that inscrutably replaces and mocks her lost beauty, and a robe that is half surgical gown, half wedding train (her own engagement to a young doctor has been interrupted by her 'death').

Meanwhile, the innocents whom Louise 'auditions' in a series of conceivably Sapphic encounters become the faceless stand-ins to Christiane, this transcendent screen star, a star who is herself the screen; their own features are peeled off like so many flimsy disposables. In the film's most distressing sequence – still horrifying despite blood oozing in monochrome, rather than spurting scarlet – Génessier and Louise perform a typical operation, briefly becoming faceless themselves, as their eyes peer out from behind surgical masks. It's a painfully protracted scene, performed with clinical application, and the film dares us to stare intently at what we can't really bear to witness.

Franju does show us everything here, and mercifully, as the scene reaches its apogee of horror, the screen blurs over and the image fades. But it's already too late, as it clearly was for that Edinburgh audience. Compare the rather more discreet use of the unwatchable in a scene that's become just as famous – the ear-slicing in *Reservoir Dogs*. Tarantino builds up his scene in such a way that we think he can't possibly back down from the horror; then, just as we think we're going to see the terrible deed, the camera jerks away. Franju, however, goes one step further – he takes us beyond what is tolerable, then fades out in a way that mimics our fainting in horror at having seen too much. (I'd be interested to know how much this scene influenced the French performance artist Orlan, who has spent much of the last decade publicly being sliced up in the name of her inquiry into the body cosmetic.)

Too much is indeed what the film is about. Génessier – cast in the mould of the classic Promethean ghoul – does too much and it destroys him. Similarly, we see too much for our own good, and it compromises us. The mask of delicacy we wear as cinema-goers is peeled off by our willingness to sit unblinking (if we can) through a spectacle that taste and compassion demand we shut our eyes to – the skinning of an innocent. We're asked to make a conscious decision about what we look at, and, once we decide to go with Génessier, we've signed up on the side of the ghouls.

This trick has been used bluntly in countless horror films since, but most slasher movies simply address the brutish adolescent in us, our desire to prove we're game enough not to duck behind the sofa. Franju was not one of the first to do it; there was, of course, the eyeball-slashing in *Un Chien andalou*, although that was so abrupt that it gave the audience no choice in the matter. But he does it in the framework of a complex play with the theme of looking, of masks and eyes.

What, after all, does the film's title mean? It implies the lack of a face, but in fact there are too many faces in this film: faces scarred, removed, replaced with masks; faces that themselves become masks, like Génessier's impassive scowl, or beatific Louise, whose face is literally a mask, the result of Génessier's last experiment. Christiane's gentle, hieratic white features are more fully a face than any other in the film: they represent an abstracted ideal of beauty which Edith Scob's real features, seen elsewhere, seem hopelessly to aspire to, just as Pygmalion's live creation can never live up to the statue.

The importance of the eyes is suggested by a bizarre loose thread – the victims are chosen to replace Christiane's face because, like her, they all have blue eyes. But why should that matter? After all, the eyes are the only part of the face that they won't be donating. But eyes are traditionally the manifestation of the soul, and if they are absent then the soul is traditionally considered not to be visible in the body. So the victims can give Christiane back her face, but never her soul. In the remarkable final shot of her as the madwoman loosed from her attic, it is as if she has finally given up her soul, or become a lost soul herself, free-floating without anchor. Throughout, the film conveys a sense that being and appearing – having a soul and seeming to have one – are two entirely separate things, and that the self and its manifestation are never to be found in the same place. (We only ever see Christiane's original face in a briefly glimpsed photo on her fiancé's table, a reproduction of a self that appears nowhere else.)

The surgery and Christiane's final apotheosis with doves fluttering around her are the images that have become legendary in this film, but there is another that really sticks in your mind, and crystallises the title's meaning. It is a close-up of one of the victims, who has leapt to her death; all we see is her bandaged face, eyes wide open, gazing in impassive grace or horror. No face, just looking, which is all we are left with as viewers. Looking into the abyss, Franju seems to tell us, leaves us abysses ourselves, disfigured, de-faced, staring.

21 April 1995

Outbreak

The biggest scare a film ever gave me came directly after Philip Kaufman's 1978 remake of *Invasion of the Body Snatchers*. It wasn't so much the film itself that got to me, with its story of parasitic alien spores reducing earth's population to hordes of shuffling, blank-eyed zombies. Rather, it was emerging from the auditorium a little shaken, and looking around the foyer to realise that I was among hordes of shuffling, blank-eyed zombies.

It has often been said that video culture is destroying what is most specific about cinema-going: the congregational nature of the experience. When we think of ourselves as parts of an awestruck multitude gazing at the wonders of the movie palace, what we usually have in mind is some sort of sacramental experience, as if the cinema had to be either a glorified funhouse or a church.

That may be fine for *Singin' in the Rain* or Tarkovsky. But a more alarming aspect of film-going, which from the start has contributed to cinema's social disrepute, is the idea of the mob – a mass squeezed promiscuously and, potentially at least, uncontrollably into a small space. It's a notion that makes for both excitement (who doesn't dream of some impossible, truly orgiastic form of cinema?) and terror. Hence the regimental nature of multiplex architecture – keep them ranked and filed at all costs.

One extension of this is the idea of cinema as plague ward, the place of epidemic and its containment. Kaufman's *Invasion*, and Don Siegel's 1956 original, play brilliantly on the menace of the crowd as a constituent part of movie-going. It is generally taken as gospel that cinema is best enjoyed *en masse*, with reactions spreading from one part of the auditorium to another. But going to the cinema is in this sense a perilous undertaking – you have to be prepared to open yourself up to contact with other people's emotions. (This is an experience that critics, who attend quiet, well-behaved press shows, habitually miss – which may be why so many repressed, defensive types become film critics.)

Antonin Artaud made a similar observation about theatre, in 'Theatre and the Plague', a wonderful essay in which he describes the body bubonic as surging and pulsating with black, noxious fluids, then tells us that theatre has much the same effect on an audience. Artaud didn't really extend the argument to cinema – although he did write a delirious encomium to the Marx Brothers – but cinema is the epidemic form *par excellence*. On stage, actors attempt to communicate their passion directly to us, but the surpassing wonder of the cinema epidemic is that it comes to us out of nowhere, out of light, thin air. What are the dust motes suspended in the projector beam but Siegel's alien spores, noxious microbes?

It's hardly surprising, then, that cinema has taken the theme of contagion very much to heart, and there is a rich vein of plague paranoia movies – from Elia Kazan's *Panic in the Streets*, to David Cronenberg's cycle of sex-parasite chillers, to Todd Haynes's *Poison*, in which a body-mutating virus becomes the vehicle for a complex argument about otherness, queerness and AIDS. By the time of *Poison*'s release in 1991, it had become a critical commonplace to assume that all contagion movies could be made to yield an AIDS-specific reading. (The same goes, with dreary reductiveness, for vampire films: see Coppola's tiresomely literal *Bram Stoker's Dracula*.)

Clearly, cinema's affinity with contagion makes it the perfect vehicle for AIDS debates and metaphors. But to rely too much on the AIDS reading is to limit the resonance of this particular quality of cinema. Plague cinema's particular strength – and one that clearly lends itself to articulating the social ramifications of AIDS – is its ability to make us aware (almost physically, as horror and suspense films can) of the connection between physical proximity and mental contagion. It can trace the subliminal motions of mass hysteria. Plague films always produce some sort of diagnosis of the social body, even if it's only through what they avoid saying.

One such case of avoidance is Wolfgang Petersen's new epidemic thriller *Outbreak*, in which the US Army moves in on a small town infected by a deadly virus. The scenario seems to owe a lot to George Romero's *The Crazies*, in which martial law is similarly imposed on a town where its poisoned inhabitants are taking leave of their senses. *The Crazies* begins with a tender scene in which a husband and wife prepare to face the night's ordeal, good people who are clearly fated to save the world. But they don't; they tear each other apart. There's something infinitely more cathartic to Romero's absolute, circular nihilism – another town, another apocalypse – than there is to Petersen's blockbuster. For a start, we can be sure of *Outbreak*'s ending – you don't pay millions for Dustin Hoffman and then deny him the chance to be humanity's saviour.

Outbreak is the plague movie in its extreme degeneracy – stripped of any real paranoia, reduced to the anaemic shades of the straight-up action movie. As such it gives good value, but only in the way that action movies always do: it knows how to handle pathos, humour and helicopters. But as a film about what it purports to be about, it's a void: *Outbreak* is about the epidemic as much as *Disclosure* is about sexual politics. It's an example of genuinely parasitic cinema, with the plague genre acting as living host to the mortifying blockbuster bug. It comes with a clipboard-full of genre commonplaces, each neatly slotted into place. The plague comes from elsewhere – from Africa, which chimes with a popular tradition of AIDS paranoia – but its spread is occasioned by US military skulduggery, and, apart from one transmitting kiss, it is entirely stripped of any sexual overtones. From AIDS culture, the film simply draws the fear of epidemic; it painstakingly avoids making any comment on it. As in *The Crazies*, the military presence that aims to save the world has first to destroy the town ('Be compassionate . . . but be compassionate globally,' as Donald Sutherland's general ominously commands).

But where Romero forced us to be paranoid all round, making us at once identify with the townspeople and fear them, the innocents here – the great American public – are simply faceless pawns who supply a chance for plucky scientist Hoffman to redeem himself, win back his estranged wife (Rene Russo) and do a lot of fee-enhancing copter-jumping. *Outbreak* is a strange thing – a body-horror movie without horror, a feel-good movie about feeling bad, Apocalypse Lite. It does get one thing right, though. The plague first breaks out in a cinema.

28 April 1995

Clerks

According to a recent article in *Variety*, there's a simple explanation for the return of dialogue in American cinema. The new generation of directors is not emerging from the film schools, as Scorsese and his movie-brat contemporaries did; instead, they learned everything they know about cinema from working in video stores. The trouble with being a video clerk, however, is that you don't get to stand and watch movies all day; you have to turn your attention away from the screen every now and then and serve the occasional customer. But with a trained ear you can still catch all the dialogue while you're looking elsewhere. Hence a generation of young cineastes who haven't entirely evolved a visual aesthetic all their own, but boy can they remember the best lines from their favourite movies.

As loopily reductive theories of film-making go, this is inspired, but not entirely convincing. One of the article's subjects, Quentin Tarantino, can hardly have been a model assistant, because he somehow seems to have absorbed plenty about both dialogue *and* visuals (mind you, he probably knew every tape's serial number by heart, too), while his colleague Roger Avary, judging from his film *Killing Zoe*, must have been too busy with customers altogether, except when the shoot-outs came on. Kevin Smith's *Clerks* does seem to bear out the theory pretty well, with highly wrought dialogue and a devout visual minimalism. And yet the character in the film who actually is a video-store assistant doesn't seem inclined to pay attention either to customers or to tapes, and prefers to spend his time hanging out in the drugstore across the road. Make of that what you will.

Since the terms 'slacker' and 'Generation X' have come to denote a certain film genre – i.e. anything made since 1992 in which white kids wear their caps backwards – then, yes, *Clerks* is a slacker movie. It contains a lot of rancid thrash metal music, its characters sit around doing nothing but whingeing for much of the time, and its director and producer are likely to end up being, oh, at least as rich and famous as slacker-pic doyen Richard Linklater. Linklater is currently enjoying a more mainstream success with *Before Sunrise*, which sees him taking a rather suspect turn for the literary and Europhilic; he'll be ditching the Aerosmith T-shirt yet and making Jane Austen adaptations, just you wait.

I can't quite see Kevin Smith doing that, somehow, if only because none of Austen's novels provide opportunities for im-promptu hockey games or litanies of hard-porn video titles. But as far as the language goes, Smith's scriptwriting is already as poised and lapidary as Whit Stillman's, or Eric Rohmer's if he hung around the quieter parts of New Jersey. This rather belies the widely-touted impression that *Clerks* is a sort of live-action *Beavis and Butt-head*. It may be coarse and infantile, packed with jokes about beer and cigarettes and blow-jobs, and it may climax with the most unbelievably black sex-and-death joke ever told on film, but the comparison ends there.

In fact, the much-discussed New Dumbness in American cinema doesn't come into it. Smith's lead characters – hapless shop assistants holding their own against a hostile and cigarette-hungry world – may act dumb, but only because they're smart enough to know when to face the world with the blankness it deserves. When idiot customers are in the shop, pelting them with cigarettes, testing each egg for perfection, asking for ice in their coffee, they react with all the fatigued peevishness they can muster; as soon as they can get a quiet moment, they're plumbing the mysteries of love, death and the role of roofing contractors in *The Empire Strikes Back*, with exemplary rigour.

The leads – Brian O'Halloran as harassed Dante, Jeff Anderson as his joyously malevolent video-store buddy Randel – rise to the occasion, rattling off their shamelessly overwritten lines with glee and some apparent discomfort, at top speed, as if they knew it was the only chance they'd get. At the time, it probably was: *Clerks* was shot on a paltry $27,000 which Smith and producer Scott Mosier raised themselves, largely from credit cards and Smith's comics collection. They shot the film on overnight sessions in the New Jersey store where Smith was working at the time (hence Smith's own weary demeanour as a silent loiterer hanging around with Russian heavy-metal singers and other manic lowlifes). The film features the most succinct example ever of a low-budget film turning the strictures of its making to good advantage. Because of the night shoot, the store shutters needed to be permanently lowered, hence a running gag about how they have been jammed shut with chewing gum, the first of Dante's infernal ordeals of the day.

Structured as a series of madcap, excruciating vignettes, *Clerks* is like the best, densest sitcom you've ever seen, but without any of the sentimental pauses that US sitcoms routinely feature by way of lip service to 'real' life – this despite some tender but pithy play between Dante and his girlfriend Veronica (Marilyn Ghigliotti), who plies him with lasagne and sexual revelations. In fact, the comedy it most resembles is the surreal, claustrophobic British night-watchmen show *Nightingales*, but with a more naturalistic take. By the time the guys lock up for the night, leaving a trail of breakage, scandal and obscenity behind them, you feel you've been through the day's rigours with them; you're just aching to get away from the cigarette counter. In fact, Smith clearly felt the same, since he breaks the enclosure twice – with a rooftop hockey game and a disastrous rush to a funeral parlour. So it flouts the unities – what did you expect? Corneille?

5 May 1995

Jefferson in Paris · *Bad Boys*

The lunatic diversity you find in even a modest week's worth of cinema releases mocks the notion of any coherence in a film reviewer's job. Most literary critics wouldn't have to deal with a Mallarmé sonnet in the morning and a Barbara Taylor Bradford after lunch. But this week it struck me that I'd had two intensely unpleasurable experiences from two entirely different films. Both filled me with a sense of not just boredom but gaping emptiness; both epitomise my idea of cinema as hell; and it occurred to me that they were so far apart that somehow, according to the law of circularity, they had to be essentially of the same kind. You may feel that, under cover of seeking out hidden affinities between two unconnected films, I'm actually attempting a quite spurious rhetorical exercise. That may be, but for a critic boredom is the most grievous affront of all (after all, we're talking about two hours out of someone's life), and sometimes rhetoric is the only retaliation you have.

The films in question are *Jefferson in Paris* and *Bad Boys* – one a historical drama of the grand school, by the reputable firm of Merchant, Ivory and Jhabvala; the other a flying-glass action movie by the equally renowned team of Don Simpson and Jerry Bruckheimer, the producers of *Beverly Hills Cop* and *Top Gun*. I say *Bad Boys* is 'by' them, because their names are highlighted on the publicity material and in the film itself, at the expense of its efficient and hitherto unknown director Michael Bay – which gives a new twist to the idea of anonymous direction.

So, one lofty offering from the most eminent team of Sunday-supplement auteurs, and one chunk of fodder so transparently factory-farmed as to have no auteur at all. In fact, both are the product not of directors but of establishments: they carry not signatures but brand names. I'm inclined to think of 'Merchant-Ivory' and 'Bruckheimer-Simpson' as resembling not the old Hollywood studio insignias like Paramount or MGM, but culinary labels, so attuned is their work to easy recognition and digestion. It may be Fortnum and Mason in one case and Burger King in the other, but it's all fodder; it's hard to see either film as anything but the latest flavour in a successful line.

Both films are in instantly recognisable genres with all the accoutrements: fine brocades and fine acting in one; guns, girls and jovial effing-and-blinding in the other. In fact, the costume drama and the action movie are arguably the only stable genres that currently exist in mainstream cinema, the only ones impervious to the ebb and flow of reinvention and cross-fertilisation. Otherwise, 'pure' genre largely exists only in the straight-to-video market, where you find strains like the real-life problem movie (*Oprah* operas) or the curious mix of psychodrama and lingerie ad known as the erotic thriller.

Jefferson and *Bad Boys* are as purely generic as they come. *Bad Boys* simply ups the ante on *Beverly Hills Cop*: not one feisty, *witz*-spouting black cop, but two: a harassed suburban husband (stand-up comic Martin Lawrence) and a muscular super-Lothario (sometime 'Fresh Prince' rapper Will Smith) at comic loggerheads. They bust jaws, smash cars, question each other's dick size, and get next to a variety of faceless vamps – business as usual.

It may seem cynical to suggest that the painstakingly crafted

Jefferson in Paris is every bit as routine a product as *Bad Boys*, but I believe it is. Ismail Merchant and James Ivory simply offer a refinement of the familiar, a new bloom of gravitas they haven't handled before: the eighteenth century rather than the early twentieth, Paris rather than the Home Counties, fact (supposedly) rather than fiction, Nick Nolte rather than Anthony Hopkins. But we're still being sold the same values: diligently researched authenticity, sumptuous tableaux, the work of several 'distinguished' players – in short, the knowledge that we are in the hands of experts. Watching both films, we trust in the capabilities of technicians: in *Jefferson*, a reputed trio of what the blurbs usually call 'expert storytellers'; in *Bad Boys*, armies of specialists in ballistics, stunt driving and the deployment of blue neon lighting.

The trouble is, when you know you're in good hands, you tend to lean back and settle into the ride: fundamentally, these are both in-flight movies that lull you into a trance while you're in transit from start to finish. One may hypnotise you with exquisite landscapes after Boucher, the other with bangs and crashes and small-willy jokes; one may be overtly dumb, while the other proclaims itself as 'thought-provoking' (stimutainment?). But both encourage you to leave your critical faculties at the door.

In his book *Flickers*, Gilbert Adair says of the school of 'high culture' drama that Merchant and Ivory's films exemplify: 'It's a type of cinema which excludes us from what might be termed the materiality of film as effectively as a sweet-shop window excludes a craning child from the goodies within – our noses are flattened against the screen.'[1] You could extend that metaphor to the *Bad Boys* school, which excludes us by repeatedly making us start back from the window in alarm – by forever showering broken glass in our faces. Whether it remains augustly intact or splinters in shock after shock, in both cases it's ultimately the window itself that we're aware of; it's the window that displays the name of the firm

[1] *Flickers: An Illustrated Celebration of 100 Years of Cinema* (Faber, London, 1995), p. 29.

running the show. So it wouldn't be too much of a surprise if one day Bruckheimer-Simpson were to sink their millions into a historical epic, or Merchant-Ivory to make an action movie: the world's first flying-porcelain blockbuster.

16 June 1995

```
┌──────────────────────────────────────────┐
│                                            │
│   Batman Forever ·                         │
│                                            │
│   Casper                                   │
│                                            │
└──────────────────────────────────────────┘
```

Bad as it was, the live-action version of *The Flintstones* did have one saving grace – it wasn't afflicted by the psychologising New Age sensibility that's creeping into Hollywood these days. We'll never know how close we might have been to seeing Fred and Barney stalk off into the petrified forest with their drums and brontosaurus bones to contact the caveman within, *Stone John* style.

It's become increasingly common for the most mainstream films – particularly ones aimed at family audiences – to have a therapeutic factor built into the narrative. This can be as straight-forward as having a psychiatrist character explain those under-pinnings of the plot that we might have had more fun figuring out for ourselves, like the shrink in *The Mask* who lectures the shape-changing hero on masks as instruments of wish-fulfilment.

But it's more and more common for the dramatic structure of problem and cathartic resolution to be elaborated into extensive textbook exercises in family therapy. Family melodrama has always been an effective device for attracting parents to otherwise innocuous children's films; the narrative of estrangement and reconciliation provides a certain educational appeal, giving children a sneak preview of the burdens of adulthood. *Mary Poppins* is a prime example, in which both children and parents become more fulfilled Edwardians through Mary's lessons in self-expression through responsible play. The dogmas of '60s primary-school art teaching can probably be traced directly to the influence of Julie Andrews.

Melodrama has now been supplemented by a more programmatic catharsis, through the language of psychotherapy. I became aware of this new film rhetoric when reading one of those books that reveal the ten key points for writing screenplays-that-sell. One of its recommendations was to give a screenplay an 'embracing' ending – 'embracing' being synonymous for the new three Rs of the Hollywood screenplay: reconciliation, reunion and redemption.

The most successful therapy movie so far is *Mrs Doubtfire*. It may have been conceived as a rollicking excuse for pantomime-dame jollity, but, in the new Hollywood, laughs have to be dignified by a moral lesson and an emotional purging. By the end of the film, Robin Williams's arrested-adolescent daddy has made proper contact with his children, and learned to be both good father and good mother, by strapping on comic breasts. The fact that he isn't reunited with his wife is part of Hollywood's new therapeutic realism; the film offers its viewers reassuring help in reconciling themselves to the end of the nuclear family. It's not so much a movie as a communal counselling session.

Robin Williams is Hollywood's specialist at coming to terms with the Child Within – something even a therapist needs to do (see his glutinising of Oliver Sacks in *Awakenings*). He was the Child Within in Spielberg's *Hook*, in which he played Peter Pan, grown up and estranged from the memory of childhood. It was a disastrous film for several reasons: because of its hectoring insistence that we all throw away our cellphones and dream a little; because it took Williams's image as a comfort bunny to nauseating extremes; and above all because it was so explicit an expression of Steven Spielberg's much-publicised anxiety about growing up. [1]

Now therapy seems to get thrown in as a commonplace. In *Batman Forever*, Batman/Bruce Wayne falls for a psychiatrist who is fascinated by his duality; she has obviously done her homework and read all those 'Dark Side of the Superhero' articles inspired by the first Tim Burton *Batman* film. Here, Batman – a brooding prisoner of his adult repression – not only defeats the childlike villains, Id-ridden kids Two-Face and Riddler, but comes to terms with his primal trauma, the killing of his parents. Among origin myths in the comics pantheon, this moment has something like the status of Oedipus's roadside tussle with his dad. *Batman Forever* culminates in Bruce Wayne remembering the image he came to fixate on fetishistically – a bat looming up out of the dark. And *voilà*, the emotional block is lifted.

Batman's exorcism may be a little desultory; *Casper* goes the whole clinical hog. Not content to be just another flash SFX movie for kids, *Casper* has aspirations to heal. The pretext is the notion that ghosts are human spirits with unfinished business on earth – that is, that haven't completed their therapy before dying. Bill Pullman plays a ghost therapist, who doesn't exorcise phantoms so much as encourage them to exorcise their own phantoms. His daughter Kat (Christina Ricci) is in denial over her mother's death, and Casper himself – a blob of marshmallow ectoplasm so twee he makes E.T. look like the Alien – is suffering from prolonged babyhood, having died before reaching adolescence. By the end, everyone has benefited: Casper has learned to mourn his own family; Kat is ushered into adolescence by doing a slow dance with Casper's mortal incarnation; and Pullman has become a better father by completing his mourning for his wife, and conquering his overprotective anxiety about Kat's burgeoning sexuality.

[1] Williams also appears in *Jumanji* (Joe Johnston, 1995) as Peter Pan crossed with Ben Gunn – a little boy sucked into a board game who emerges later as an adult and must do symbolic battle with his father. In *Jack* (Francis Ford Coppola, 1996), he does his ultimate man-boy act, as a boy prematurely grown into the body of a man.

This could have been designed expressly as a kids' film for a new generation aware of all the hitherto-unpublicised new strains of family trauma that *Oprah* has revealed to us. It can't be long before sexually abusive parents become legitimate plot commonplaces in Hollywood children's films. *Casper* is a prime example of Hollywood's current predilection for films as all-in redemption packages, a ghastly refinement of its perennial fixation on the feel-good factor. Bill Forsyth's ill-fated *Being Human*, released straight to video in Britain, illustrates this. The last story in this portmanteau has Robin Williams again playing a father estranged from his children. He takes them to the beach to bond, and everything is angled towards catharsis with swelling strings. But Forsyth, committed to the downbeat, rebels against it; it's clear that, whatever bonding takes place, the father will go back to his isolated life. When Forsyth met the studio executives, they were outraged that a dad didn't immediately hug his kids; in order to get the film made, he wrote in a hug, as ambivalently sour as he could get away with. 'The $20 million dollar hug,' he's called it.[2] I'd say he got away lightly.

14 July 1995

[2] *Sight and Sound*, August 1994.

The Big Sleep

The big sleep, in Raymond Chandler's novel of that name, is death. But when Peter Bogdanovich asked director Howard Hawks what it meant, he replied, 'I don't know, probably death. It just sounds good.' In fact, in Hawks's 1946 film, the big sleep could well be just sleep. Watching it is like being in a hypnotic state, walking blearily through a labyrinth where no paths ever seem to connect; in which shady figures appear and disappear; in which no stories – and God knows there are plenty of them in this ramshackle funhouse of fiction – ever make sense.

Famously, Hawks and his writers – William Faulkner, Leigh Brackett and Jules Furthman – could quite never figure out the story; when Chandler was consulted, he couldn't explain it either. 'The scenario,' Hawks recalled, 'took eight days to write, and all we were hoping to do was make every scene entertain.'

The Big Sleep is about what you could call the ultimate form of entertainment, the Big E – dream. The plot doesn't make sense because the Production Code wouldn't allow it to. Chandler's novel could be explicit about sex and drugs; Hawks couldn't, and the Code office supplied him with an alternative ending which he liked so much that he used it. It's dreamlike because so much is suppressed – for example, the nature of 'the usual vices' that Philip Marlowe's client, General Sternwood, attributes to his daughters. Marlowe (Humphrey Bogart) finds the younger Sternwood girl, Carmen (Martha Vickers), adjusting her stockings in a trance with a corpse at her feet, observed by a bronze Indian head (it contains a spy camera). More than a 'compromising position', it's a dream image: uncanny, inexplicable, straight out of a Max Ernst collage, and it's that because the film can say no more.

The film's central image, briefly glimpsed, is the rush of the roulette wheel. Characters appear at lightning speed, only tenuously linked to the people around them, then vanish – like Elisha Cook Jr's small-time hood, who no sooner appears than he's been poisoned. Each new character seems to be the terminus of Marlowe's quest; each, in turn, proves to be just a signpost leading further down the road, telling him which fork to take.

In that respect, *The Big Sleep* is not unlike another great dream film, *The Wizard of Oz*. But whereas Dorothy ends up meeting the Great Oz, who is promptly unmasked, Marlowe *starts* from an interview with the big daddy, Sternwood – who, although he disappears from sight, proves to be the story's only reliable figure. Dorothy ends up in her back yard after Oz is demolished; Marlowe himself participates in the slow demolition of his own back yard – corrupt, nocturnal Los Angeles.

Plot connections form, than fall apart; Marlowe keeps throwing plausible stories, hypotheses, into the air, then discards them a second after. It's as if it were all play to him. At one point, he winds up in the classic predicament of the solo private eye – he's still working on the case, even though he's been dropped from it. When Sternwood's daughter Vivian (Lauren Bacall) asks him, 'Why did you go on?', he replies, 'Too many people told me to stop.' When a shamus talks like this, it's usually read as an existential profession of faith, or the statement of a Beckettian impasse ('I can't go on. I'll go on'). But really, it's because the case has become a source of heady pleasure, and he won't give up the drug simply because it's been prohibited.

For sure, Marlowe gets more fun out of the case than Sam Spade ever did out of his – *The Maltese Falcon*, with its ascetic interiors and endless verbal confrontations *à huis clos*, looks like Racinian tragedy compared with Marlowe's crazy-paving adventure. For one thing, Marlowe meets more women – the Sternwood daughters, assorted flirtatious taxi drivers, waitresses and hat-check girls, and a bookshop assistant (Dorothy Malone), with whom he has a chance encounter that turns into something more interesting, again protected by the Production Code. It's raining; he's got the whisky; she shuts up shop and takes off her glasses; 'Well, hello,' he says, before the fade. Marlowe's world is an ever-open sexual playground; he taught James Bond everything he knows.

In this world, the rules for survival, or redemption, are simple: you have to be quick-witted enough to enjoy yourself. Both sisters have 'the usual vices' but Vivian, unlike Carmen, is saved. Why? Because she's verbally and imaginatively creative. Carmen falls at the first fence; she's mystified when Marlowe playfully announces himself as Doghouse Riley, but Vivian's made of smarter stuff. She joins him in an Abbott and Costello routine on the phone to the police; she engages him in an extended bout of innuendo built around horse-racing (and added eight months after the rest had been shot) that is as close as 1940s Hollywood gets to the *Carry On* spirit. 'You got a touch of class,' Marlowe says, 'but I don't know how far you can go.' 'A lot depends on who's in the saddle,' she replies.

The losers are the ones not smart enough to join in the fun: Agnes, the bad, grouchy bookstore girl, as opposed to Malone's larky good one; a variety of poker-faced lunks. The winners are the good talkers, like Sternwood himself, a gamy old stick with a flair for strange metaphor: 'I seem to exist on heat,' he says, 'like a newborn spider.' *The Big Sleep* depicts an amoral world, all right – one in which people's redemption is measured by their acumen as scriptwriters, their ability to spin yarns, to spiel. Back to the roulette wheel – they're spielers, but they're also *Spielers*, in the sense of gamblers, staking everything on a good line. And what are good lines for in a film like this? Watch Bacall's strange slouched position in the seat of Marlowe's car, when Vivian tells him she loves him. They keep you awake through the dream; you come out the next morning, alive and still talking.

4 August 1995

Apollo 13

A few weeks ago, Channel 4 screened the infamous 'Roswell' footage – grainy black-and-white film that purported to show an autopsy performed on a genuine extraterrestrial. There was a time when the media would have been in a frenzy over even the possibility that there might be evidence of life elsewhere in the universe. These days, however, such cosmic imponderables seem like a quaint side platter of *National Enquirer* fodder; even if the High Plenipotentiary of Alpha Centauri had landed this week in Trafalgar Square with a full cadre of purple people-eaters, the event would have had less tabloid space than Prince Will's schooldays or the launch of the latest cable porn channel.

The success of Ron Howard's *Apollo 13* – it's so far taken $200 million world-wide – is less to do with our fascination with space than with a collective nostalgia for the days when space was still fascinating. We can most of us remember a time when the infinite *seemed* infinite – before Neil Armstrong had walked on the moon, before the famous photo of the glowing earth had become a money-spinner for Athena Posters. It was a time before *Close Encounters*, *E.T.* and *Star Wars* – and the political appropriation of that term – had domesticated the idea of space, brought the alien uncanny into the realm of suburban kitsch.

It's commonly accepted that space ceased to be transcendental the moment that Neil Armstrong took his one giant step for the recyclable sound bite. *Apollo 13*, with some degree of regret, shows space travel as being firmly on a human footing. Its nicest touch is that Armstrong and Buzz Aldrin appear in a very domestic light – they are brought in as jovial neighbours to distract Jim Lovell's old mom from the Apollo 13 crisis. It reminds you that, although they always seemed destined for demigod status, Armstrong and Aldrin, in the cosmic icon stakes, somehow ended up lagging somewhere behind Yuri Gagarin and Laika the dog.

Apollo 13 is an account of human bravery so everyday and pragmatic as to be altogether banal. It's a story of failure snatched from the jaws of defeat – a story in which nothing *really* happens. Jim Lovell, Fred Haise and Jack Swigert (Tom Hanks, Kevin Bacon, Bill Paxton) set out for the moon in 1970, ran into problems *en route*, and made a perilous return to earth, missing the moon entirely. It would be a wonderful basis for allegorical farce, and there is indeed a degree of bitter humour in Ron Howard's film, largely directed at the blasé media of the time, who refused to cover the mission until it became a life-and-death nail-biter.

But by and large the film is played absolutely straight, with one eye on the human factor – the brave boys and the hugely undercharacterised little ladies at home – and another on spectacle and authenticity. The film-makers had unprecedented access to NASA facilities and advice, in a deal that has handsomely paid back the budget-beleaguered space agency in good PR.

Curiously, gripping as it is, *Apollo 13* is a non-drama. It's a suspense story with an outcome we already know, so its appeal lies entirely in putting us through the events for ourselves. (In fact, John Sturges's *Marooned*, a fiction film that did have the benefit of unknown outcome, and which anticipated the Apollo incident, suffered from being released just as it was happening.) But precisely what appeals is the inexorability of it all – the sense that there can be only one outcome, and that it will be good. At one point in the rescue attempt, Mission Control boss Gene Kranz (Ed Harris) manfully declares, 'Failure is not an option.' One hell of a catch phrase, this was recently quoted with approval by Bill Clinton.

Rather vacant as drama, *Apollo 13* nevertheless functions quite adequately as a theme-park experience that lets you feel what it might like to be marooned in space with no certainty of returning. The idea of theme-park simulation has been desperately over-worked as a paradigm for the spectacle movie of the '90s, but it's peculiarly applicable here. The heroes are actually saved from death by a feat of imaginative projection on the part of their colleague Ken Mattingly (Gary Sinise), who spends his time locked in a flight simulator trying to figure out what he'd do in their position. Watching the film, it could be us in that simulator. When the astronauts are saved, there's no catharsis, surprise or moral payoff – simply the feeling we would have if we were stepping out of a fun capsule at Universal City. We heave a sigh of relief and head for the cold-drinks stand.

Since American politicians are always looking to appropriate pop-culture images to illustrate their own ideal of national spirit (cf. *Forrest Gump*, Bruce Springsteen's 'Born in the USA'), it's no surprise that *Apollo 13*'s can-do premise has been endorsed both by Clinton and Newt Gingrich. It speaks of America's current crisis of self-image that the tale that has stirred the nation is not triumphalist, as the Apollo 11 story might have been, but a real spit-and-polish piece of pragmatism muddling through in the face of confusion – reassurance for a nation with a sense of siege culture.

What is missing, curiously, is a sense of what the astronauts have left behind on earth, and what they hope to return to. The 1970 we see is never real, but as much a simulation as the journey itself. Howard gives us not a feeling of a real past, but period effect – history denoted by hideous wallpaper and bouffant hairdos, the sort of kitsch stylistic nudge Hollywood uses to represent what it thinks of as more innocent times. But the sense of what 1970 might have felt like to live in – other than a joke about the Beatles break-up – is largely absent. Space is something we can handle, but the past really is *terra incognita*.

22 September 1995

The Neon Bible

In the opening sequence of Terence Davies's *The Neon Bible*, the fifteen-year-old hero, on a train journey, reaches up and lays his fingers on the window, as if actually touching the vast white moon reflected in it. We immediately think of two things: first, that it is an extraordinary image, perhaps too obviously extraordinary; and second, that it is an image of cinema. This is partly because the window is shaped like a cinema screen, partly because cinema is by nature a lunar art: we fondly imagine that the screen radiates light whereas, like the moon, it simply reflects light from elsewhere.

But above all, this image is suggestive of the way that cinema allows us to touch in our imagination things that are unimaginably distant; we are able to precisely because the screen separates us from them, just as the window separates the boy from the moon. This is what it feels like to watch *The Neon Bible*. At first you feel the film gives you a more direct experience of its subject than it really does; then you realise that Davies's direction distances us from it as surely as that window. Even the aspects of the story that might lend themselves to sensationalism – a boy's

experience of death, violence and madness in the Deep South –
seem frozen in aspic. The first time I saw the film, this reserve
impressed me immensely; the second time, I realised that it allows
the film to give us too many unequivocal signals about how to
respond. Contrary to the belief that such distance frees the
viewer's imagination, *The Neon Bible* actually gives us too little
room to manoeuvre, enough only to witness and contemplate.

The Neon Bible is the story of a boy growing up isolated and
pained in the 1940s Bible Belt. It is based on a precociously lucid
novel written at the age of 16 by John Kennedy Toole, the New
Orleans writer who committed suicide in 1969, aged 31, and
achieved posthumous fame with his comic novel, *A Confederacy
of Dunces*. The Toole legend is part of a weight of mystique that
the film carries, which might from the start incline us too easily
to respectful awe. There is the mystique of Terence Davies himself,
of whom British critics are peculiarly protective; he has been
landed with an image as our cinema's noble poet, a sensitive man
who evokes a fraught inner life with Proustian precision and
delicacy plus a sense of Blitz-spirit good cheer. And the film's lead
is Gena Rowlands, whose work with the late John Cassavetes has
given her an unimpeachable status as an actress unusually in
command of images of pain and intensity. All this predisposes us
to feel that *The Neon Bible* is in some way going to be the real
thing, the unadulterated cinema of emotion.

But some of the film's least effective moments are those that
directly solicit our emotions. In a disastrous scene, not in the
book, young David's mother (Diana Scarwid) appears bedraggled,
singing a maudlin Irish lullaby; it jars not because, as some critics
have complained, Davies should have known that Steve Martin
sings the same song for laughs in *Housesitter* (I mean, if we're
going to niggle about movie-quiz trivia . . .) but because it looks
like the worst mad-Ophelia scene you can remember. (This
reference may be intentional: she does after all carry a bunch of
pine cones, standing in as rosemary for remembrance.)

What does make the film fascinating, however, as well as very
problematic, is its commitment to artifice; for a start, the way in

which Davies has decanted all his trade marks (the stillness, the evocation of spiritual endurance, the concentration on everyday objects invested with meaning) into a form that appears quite alien to him – in effect, an American costume drama. For *The Neon Bible* is a genre piece at heart, and so too is the novel, as opposed to the 'true story' of Toole's childhood: the blurb on my American paperback copy reads, 'If you liked *To Kill a Mockingbird*, you will love this.'

It is hard not to read the film through the window of genre reference. The visual allusions to Edward Hopper and the iconography of folk Americana reminds us how much the film is of a piece with other cinematic, artistic and literary imaginings of the Deep South. The central sequence about a travelling evangelist only reminds us how difficult it now is to detach the image of the Southern preacher from a range of cultural references: *Wise Blood*, *Elmer Gantry*, the excesses of US cable evangelism, Nick Cave lyrics, Steve Martin again in *Leap of Faith*. Davies's take is different for its restraint: his preacher is no ranter, but a portly huckster who mouths along complacently with the Tannoy as it announces him. The hypocrisy is made too explicit, but it is made explicit in stillness, which at least is something unfamiliar.

The problem, I think, with *The Neon Bible* is that Davies is supremely aware of cinema, but not of other films. He seems to react to commonplaces by distancing himself from them, with austere distaste – almost as you imagine David, the serious child, distancing himself from other rowdier kids.

Davies has an extraordinary skill for isolating objects and making them signify: the moon, the pines waving with theatrical stiffness outside a window, or, in a remarkable sequence of images built around the theme from *Gone With the Wind*, a single white sheet on a line, another numinous avatar of the cinema screen. But we're aware that these things are meant to signify, before they actually do; our awareness of their status as image somehow blocks our apprehension of them. This is one of the great problems of cinema, and a terribly subjective and erratic one. What makes an image work? Why do certain images signalled *as* images (in

Kieślowski films, for example) send shivers down our spine, while others raise the hackles?

What makes Davies's most powerful images so frustrating is perhaps their sense of a double-layered quality: they signal themselves as cinema, but at the same time suggest that, once we recognise them as cinema, then we can have access to the deeper truths they contain. I think we may be more won over by self-conscious cinema that carries itself as if cinema alone were the most important thing in the world, but here are touches of artifice that gesture at something loftier than mere celluloid, at the spiritual or the metaphysical. It is as if these images themselves, as cinema, were not quite enough. These are very vague musings, and I'm not quite sure where they leave us with *The Neon Bible*. It's a very fine film, there's no denying that, but it makes you review your misgivings about fine films and what they can do for us.

13 October 1995

Crimson Tide

To state the obvious first: *Crimson Tide* is a submarine movie, and therefore entirely about penises. The USS *Alabama* and its Russian counterpart surge through the depths in a way that can only be called priapic, discharging manfully streamlined torpedoes at each other. When the US craft strikes a leak, it doesn't so much sink as detumesce. Just to drive the point home, fearless captain Gene Hackman – never without a correspondingly thrusting cigar close at hand – retorts when he's told that the enemy craft is loading, 'You don't put on a condom unless you're gonna fuck.'

There was a time, decades ago, when it was possible to imagine that film-makers didn't know what they were really dealing with when they played with boats and planes, and that it was the job of the discreet Freudian to explain it all gently to them. These days, Hollywood scriptwriters probably attend weekend seminars on 'Penile Innuendo Within the Three-Act Structure'. Director Tony Scott certainly knows the score: he made *Top Gun*, which may have been the most explicitly phallic war movie ever made, until now. Last year, Quentin Tarantino had a cameo role in a comedy called *Sleep With Me*, in which he expounded feverishly on *Top Gun*'s homoerotic subtext. That must have appealed to Scott because, having already filmed Tarantino's *True Romance* script, he's now enlisted the wunderkind for an uncredited rewrite on *Crimson Tide*.

The screenplay is actually credited to Michael Schiffer, although Tarantino's work on it is supposedly more extensive than is apparent. What strike you, though, are the single lines that seem to reveal the Tarantino touch. Watching *Crimson Tide* in a cinema full of critics is an extraordinary experience – at certain points, you could feel a thunderous wave of nudging pass round the stalls. The lines jump out at you – a reference to *Star Trek* here, the Silver Surfer there, a busful of Navy men chatting about the films of Hardy Krüger. Who knows, maybe these bits are all Michael Schiffer originals, but the effect is the same you get from any Tarantino script. You wonder whether anything at all exists outside pop culture.

In *Crimson Tide* this is a pertinent question, because the central issue of the film is nothing less than the fate of the world. The plot is simple: a US sub goes to war against the enemy. Nuclear fire power is evenly matched: gung-ho Captain Ramsey (Gene Hackman) wants to blast the other side out of the water, knowing that the result will surely mean world destruction; his second-in-command Lieutenant Hunter (Denzel Washington) would rather be circumspect and await future instructions. It's not that complex a plot option: either the world will end or it won't. What's interesting is not the outcome but the amount of scowling and jaw-clenching our men will have to do to reach it.

What's also interesting is that *Crimson Tide* is an almost indecently eager welcome-home to the Cold War movie; the bad guys, for the first time in ages, turn out to be Russian. The end of the Soviet Union was an uncomfortable day for Hollywood, which was suddenly obliged to think up convincing new international villains. If it wasn't Alan Rickman in a vague German accent, the Arabs had to be the safest bet, calculated to set middle America hissing and flinging popcorn at the screen. However, that option seems to have been soured for the foreseeable future, first by the exceptional racism of the portrayal of Arabs in James Cameron's *True Lies*, and second by the embarrassing haste with which the US media jumped the gun in hypothesising Arab perpetrators in the Oklahoma bombing.

How reassuring it must be, then, to have once again for your villain a crazed Russian war-hawk. It's a bit of cobbled-together topicality calculated to offend no-one: knock up an extremist Vladimir Zhirinovsky figure, make him some sort of maverick off on his own track, replace the sinister Red Army with a sinister rebel faction of the Red Army, and it's business as usual. The film takes self-conscious pains early on to let us know that dusting down the Red Peril genre is absolutely its primary concern: 'I hope you enjoyed the peace,' Hackman tells his men, ''cause as of now we're back in business.' You can imagine producers Don Simpson and Jerry Bruckheimer summoning their staff and saying the very same thing.

Crimson Tide is a very effective nail-biter, and compellingly tackles the defining limitation of the submarine genre – the fact that sub films can't show us much more than a bunch of men cooped up in claustrophobic proximity, with the odd periscope popping down and cramped, visually austere sets rocking from time to time. You imagine that directors take on sub movies for the same reason that theatre people do Racine: for the challenge of the constraints. Scott gives us a few choice moments of under-water action, but not so much that it seems like copping out of the sub movie's more ascetic formal requirements. *Crimson Tide* is very much about talk, as befits an oedipal drama: the best clashes between Ramsey and Hunter take place at the dinner table, father and rebellious older son quietly but furiously squaring off in front of the younger brothers, the other officers.

What you remember of *Crimson Tide*, in fact, is not the action but the words – the one-off lines like Ramsey on cigars ('I don't trust air I can't see'), the left-field routines like the already-celebrated eleventh-hour exchange about Lippizaner horses, and the pop-culture riffs. In one way, *Crimson Tide* is an encouraging sign: it seems to signal the advent of the primarily verbal action movie, in which words speak louder than flying glass. But neither the words nor the action finally add up to that much; you come out of it feeling thrilled, only to realise that you've seen something a lot more staid than you thought: *Crimson Tide* is one step away from being the courtroom drama that it forms the back-story to. When they make that film, let's hope Quentin's around to give the judge some good innuendo about gavels.

3 November 1995

La Haine (Hate)

Salut les mecs – or should that be *yo homeboys?* The first shock in Mathieu Kassovitz's *La Haine* comes in the subtitles. 'Don't diss my sis, butthead'; 'Quit snoopin' round the hood.' Reading the words, we could be deep in Bed-Stuy or South Central. But this isn't an inner-city drama; it's outer city, the *banlieue*, the dreary housing estates of the Parisian suburbs, where immigrant communities, youth unrest and unemployment are shunted safely out of view in one of the most PR-oriented cities in the world. They are safely out of the way of most French cinema, too, which is why *La Haine* has come as a salutary blast, both to the international film circuit – a corrective to the delicate psychologism that is still France's main celluloid export – and to French society. Stylish and funny as well as simply incendiary, Kassovitz's film has been massively successful and controversial in France, where it has itself been accused of fuelling the kind of youth–police confrontations it anatomises.

La Haine is about three young men hanging out in the suburbs the day after a riot. One's African, one's Algerian, one's a Jewish skinhead; they're deeply pissed off and edgy, as they wait to hear news of a friend who is in hospital after a police beating. They play incredulously with a police gun one of them has found, eat merguez at a rooftop party, then head into Paris where they get stuck overnight. There's a run-in with a crazed coke-head acquaintance, a casual police beating for two of them, and finally a return home to the showdown the whole story has been working towards. The film starts with a story about a man falling from a rooftop, telling himself, 'So far, so good . . .', and running through it is the ticking of a clock, so we know when to expect the crash. When it comes, it's with a beautiful ironic gesture – it happens under a mural of Baudelaire, an emblem of social dissent, but also of an old French culture these kids are irrevocably excluded from.

La Haine is less about racism than about the possibility of coexistence. The police are the racists here, and they're hated in turn as if their job constituted them as a race apart. Kassovitz's argument is that the new France is, if not exactly a melting pot, with all the '60s utopianism that phrase implies, then certainly a place of multiple identity and exchange. This was also the theme of his first film, not released in Britain, *Métisse*, a tale of love rivalry between an African student and a black-identified Jewish kid (Kassovitz himself). In a neat barb, one character accused him, 'You think you're Spike Lee?'

Kassovitz doesn't think that, but he's certainly interested in what it might mean to work like Lee in France. *La Haine* has been described as a French *Do the Right Thing*, and it does operate in a similar mode of disaster held perilously in check. It also owes a lot, I suspect, to Joseph B. Vasquez's film *Hangin' With the Homeboys*, in which a similarly multiracial posse of guys wind up out of their depth in Manhattan overnight. Kassovitz's gang miss the last train from Gare du Nord, in what might be a wry homage to the plight of so many bridge-and-tunnel kids in New York movies.

Kassovitz may be drunk on Americanisms, but he doesn't want to be an American director. Rather, he's fascinated by the French fascination with America, and wants to know what's specifically

French about it. Vinz, the aggressive, addled skinhead (Vincent Cassel) has an amazing routine facing himself down in the bathroom mirror, playing at De Niro: '*C'est à moi que tu parles?*' And his African friend Hubert (Hubert Kounde), alone in his wrecked gym, boxes in slow-motion *Raging Bull* style.

So it's at once oddly appropriate and something of a disaster that the subtitles Americanise the dialogue so completely. If these characters spoke American, it would be homeboy-speak. But what's lost is the Frenchness and a lot of the meaning. Some of the translation produces a comic incongruity. 'Your sister sucks Donald Duck'; in the original, it's Smurfs. A cop says, 'You think you're in Disneyland'; the original has 'EuroDisney', which is a fine but telling distinction. There may be a veneer of glamour still to US Disneyland; but for the French, its Paris branch is the crassest of the crass, a grotesque alien encampment. More grievously, a pithy doggerel about '*le pénis de Le Pen*' gets lost altogether. It seems the subtitler just didn't have faith in the script. When the boys have made a boorish irruption at an art opening, attended largely by snooty types who might have stepped out of a film by Eric Rohmer or Claude Sautet, the host benignly shrugs; 'Troubled youth,' the subtitle reads. What he in fact says is '*malaise de banlieue*', which is no less condescending, but more acute and certainly more culturally specific.

What you lose in the dialogue, you gain in the visual energy. Shot in lucid black-and-white that really suggests the feel of a hangover after a hellish night, *La Haine* never lets up in its invention. Kassovitz deals in trickery for the sheer play of it, but his effects can be as subtle as they are often extreme. He uses everything from slow, dreamy tracking shots to violent jump cuts, no trick left unused in a kind of hormone-drunk approximation of the characters' own strung-out confusion. One minute, everything is happening at once: a cop crashes repeatedly, silently through plate glass, as Vinz imagines blowing him away with his fingers. The next, there's a brilliant evocation of dead time: the boys sit in front of a video wall in a deserted precinct, watching the bad news about their friend. Kassovitz cuts to that ticking clock and an intertitle telling us the time – then back to the boys. No time has passed, but it feels like an eternity.

La Haine is less ambivalent in its prognosis than Do the Right Thing – it's a populist film almost in the Renoir tradition, suggesting that the people could get it together if only the system would get out of their face. Lee's conclusion was that things had gone too far for such hopes. But there's no sloppy humanism here: Kassovitz confronts cultural tensions head on, knowing that without them there's no cinema. It's not a pleasant lesson, but it's a massive depth charge to the complacency of French cinema.

17 November 1995

The Museum at Night: The Brothers Quay

Last year, the reclusive animators the Brothers Quay made a rare venture into the outside world to shoot their first live-action feature *Institute Benjamenta, or This Dream People Call Human Life*. Except for the occasional commission in opera design, the Quays have rarely worked outside the confines of their studio, Atelier Koninck, a South London industrial unit that over the last few years they have turned into a cramped, labyrinthine antiquarians' den – a modestly sinister clutter of marionettes and mirrors, rickety cameras, discarded limbs and ligatures.

But the Quays managed to take their surrounding sense of enclosure with them. Over a summer, they transformed a gutted mansion near Hampton Court into a trick box of their own – a scaled-up version both of their Atelier and of the toy-sized theatre sets in which they stage their animations. Nondescript corridors were rigged by cinematographer Nic Knowland with eerie siren lights to suggest the passing of phantom trams in a *fin de siècle* Europe; an antechamber became a forest clearing, the walls painted with an anamorphic tableau of rutting deer, the floor scattered with pine cones. The inversion of space and size was completed by the transformation of a basement room into an attic with a false floor, its contracted dimensions centred around a cyclops-eye fish tank.

The Quays slept in the real attic for the six-week shoot, sealing the house's transformation into a prosthesis of their own domain. It's typical of the way they work: never bowing to the objective impression of how things are, but bending the shapes of things to the transforming laws of their universe. More than most film-makers, the Quays have a universe that is entirely their own, and in which they can genuinely determine everything – the shape and motion of things, even the path of the viewer's gaze. It is a peculiar privilege that animation has over other forms of film, and the Quays have seized it with obsessive eagerness. They were drawn to animation, they have said, precisely for the possibility of controlling everything 'literally object by object, limb by limb and frame by frame'.

Since their first 16mm experiments in the early 1970s, when they were students at the Royal College of Art, the Philadelphia-born twins have elaborated an exacting style of stop-motion animation that has sometimes been written off as fanciful surrealism or as an extended homage to the Czech animator Jan Svankmajer. The Brothers pay tribute to him in *The Cabinet of Jan Svankmajer* (1984), but in recent years have preferred to play down the comparison. Besides, Svankmajer is a card-carrying Surrealist – a member of the still extant Czech Surrealist group – while the Quays are weary of the label. 'Oh, for a bit of "neo-realism",' they say.

If there is a simple difference between their style and Svank-majer's, it is this: Svankmajer, with his clay heads and infinitely malleable objects, is fascinated by the elasticity of things, their hidden capacity for life; the Quays, preoccupied with the im-material properties of light and motion, are drawn to things in their deadness and fixity. They are fascinated with objects that can be transformed because they have exhausted their potential for life. Hence their use of eviscerated, tarnished toys, rust and dead metal, fragments of now-dead organic matter. They have most in common, perhaps, with the Russian animation pioneer

Wladislaw Starewicz, who in the 1910s staged grotesque anthropomorphic dramas using dead insects.

However, the Quays' militantly non-anthropomorphic work is not about bringing dead things to life, but about dramatising their deadness, their will to entropy. That will takes violent form in *Little Songs of the Chief Officer of Hunar Louse, or This Unnameable Little Broom* (1985), obscurely based on the *Epic of Gilgamesh*: in a box mysteriously suspended in space, a grinning clockwork clown torments and finally kills a beautiful androgynous creature, part bird, part moth. Their medium-length film *Street of Crocodiles* (1985), based on the stories of Polish writer Bruno Schulz, is set inside a mechanical peepshow, in which a harassed, cadaverous mannequin is pursued by a phalanx of blank-eyed china dolls. (The Jewish Schulz was shot dead by a Gestapo officer during the Second World War, and it's not hard to read Holocaust imagery into this film, or into the striped-fabric motif and skeletal figures of their 1988 film *Rehearsals for Extinct Anatomies*.)

To breathe life into their pocket golems, the Brothers work painstakingly through frame after frame of static postures, building them up into the semblance of motion. This paradoxical fabrication is the basis of all cinema, but live action tends to conceal that; the Quays never let us forget it. The critic Paul Hammond has called their technique 'nudged *nature morte*', and their work always reminds us of the troubling equivalence of the terms 'still life' and '*nature morte*' – as if the viewer were forever forced to decide whether the objects on display are to be seen as life briefly suspended or as death caught in a moment of objectification. The Quays' puppet figures – botched-up chimeras of clockwork and cloth, feather and fishbone, battered toys that have uncannily outlived their purpose as fetishes of affection – are things that have died and been recomposed, like miniature mummies. They are ghosts, living uncannily beyond their natural lives – true 'found objects' in the Surrealist sense, divorced from the original context of their use and from the desires and meanings originally invested in them. In their new ghostly lives, they inhabit the phantom landscapes – cities, theatres, forests – that the Quays construct in table-top boxes with complex *trompe-l'œil* perspectives (often suggestive of Joseph Cornell pieces taken to a baroque degree of elaboration).

Described in these terms, the Quays' work might seem to be simply a staging of fetishistic rituals. What gives these films their extraordinary power is the increasing importance accorded to the viewer's role. In the Brothers' films, the eye – or its surrogate, the camera – has increasingly become the central character. 'For us,' the Brothers have said – in a curious Freudian slip that appears to reveal how much they view themselves as players in their doll-dramas – 'the camera is the third puppet, in a sense, the motivator.' The Quays have been increasingly concerned with the play of the lens; they favour complex, staggered tracking shots and sudden shifts that always withdraw the objects they promise to reveal; they use lenses that minimise depth of field, causing objects to distort completely as the focus shifts. The eye's attempt to locate and identify objects, to make the world briefly stable, becomes a narrative theme in itself.

The Quays have sustained themselves by working in the contemporary world – commercials for Honeywell Computers and other companies, channel ident clips for BBC2, commissions for MTV and much pop-video work, including an uncharacteristic sequence for Peter Gabriel's 'Sledgehammer' promo (a homage to the baroque illusionist painter Arcimboldo). But their iconography really belongs to an imaginary past, the sort of phantom time Bruno Schulz writes about; 'the apocryphal thirteenth month, those tracks that lead off into time suspended, it's ideal for animation,' say the Brothers. They draw from German Expressionist cinema, from Romantic and Surrealist literature, from the traditions of a Europe that these American expatriates have largely invented for themselves. 'We think of ourselves as European by wish. We like going for long walks, metaphorically, in whatever country we go to.'

One key reference is the German Romantic writer E.T.A. Hoffmann, largely responsible for putting automata on our imaginative map, and whom the Quays have long planned to devote a project to. Another is the Swiss writer Robert Walser (1878–1956), a precursor of Kafka, whose short, melancholic novel *Jakob von Gunten* (1908)[1] forms the basis for *Institute Benjamenta*.

Entirely at odds with the literary-adaptation tradition that still dominates British cinema, *Institute Benjamenta* is less a 'version' of Walser than an evocation of his book's mood. The Quays and co-writer Alan Passes have taken Walser's novel as a skeleton, eliding it with some of the writer's shorter texts. They have also worked in concerns entirely their own, such as a running seam of deer iconography that turns the house into a fairy-tale forest.

The hero of the novel is the scion of a wealthy family, who, in his desire to abnegate all elements of his self, enlists at an institute that claims to train young men to be servants. There he learns to lose himself in a series of monotonous, pointless classroom exercises. Walser's text is deeply ambivalent, with its narrator who on the one hand celebrates the joys of life in naive, almost infantile fashion, and on the other embraces nullity and abjection with terrifying zeal.

The film's most radical departure from the book is its near-total erasure of signs of the outside world. The Institute becomes instead a decadent sealed sanctum governed by its own opaque rituals. The Quays saw the building itself as the film's main character; the other lead player is light, which has rarely been so mercurial on film. Throughout, light from outside is caught in the Institute's refracting trap and distended, distressed. Passing light from trams behaves like an ornate, mobile fan grazing the walls and floor before folding in on itself.

Combining live action and miniatures, *Institute Benjamenta* has allowed the Quays to take their illusionism into new areas. One scene shows a vast, ghostly gallery; it is a purely phantom composite, digitally mixing a real walkway with an image taken from an inverted picture of a Bavarian cathedral interior. The film's space, maze-like and infinitely extendable, might conventionally be labelled as Gothic, but the brothers insist,

[1] Published as *Institute Benjamenta*, trans. Christopher Middleton (Serpent's Tail, 1995).

'"Gothic" has the wrong connotations for us. "Baroque" is much more painterly and imaginative. The idea of baroque was to make the sheer materiality of concrete feel weightless.'

The appearance of humans in a Quays film comes as something of a surprise, although live performers have made fleeting appearances before. The Quays set out to use their cast not so much as actors but as dancers; people here behave almost like puppets, going through automatised motions in the ritual world of the Institute. It only works for some of the time, however – in the fussed, jerky choreography of the classroom, and in the striking presence of lead actor Mark Rylance, whose halting gestures and terrorised expression make him a reincarnation of the beleaguered mannequin hero of *Street of Crocodiles*. But, finally, the film is perhaps more expressive in human terms than it needed to be – it's haunted too much by the delicate literariness of Walser's language, and by the emotiveness that entails. *Institute Benjamenta* does, alas, rather play into the hands of those who have accused the Quays of preciousness.

The Quays are not planning to abandon animation altogether for live action. They have further to go in exploring the unsettling encounter of human actors with their artificial world of hermetic miniatures. But what has been so exciting about their work to date is the way it minimises the human factor, evoking a world of objects engaging autonomously, without any recognisable human intervention – 'bachelor machines', to use the Surrealist phrase, playing their own games in the dark. Their shorts, increasingly elusive stories of tremors set off by objects that have just vanished, attest to an apparent absence of manipulation that is in reality the very sign of that manipulation – the animator's invisible hand. (It wouldn't be difficult, if you were so inclined, to read the Quays' films as statements of theological anxiety.) The Quays sum it up best in their explanation of the brief *Stille Nacht III*, one of their more inscrutable shorts, in which a bullet rustles enigmatically among pine cones. 'It's what happens in the museum room at night.'

1996

Million-Dollar Graffiti: notes from the digital domain

Pigs have yet to fly on screen; cows already have, carried aloft by a computer-generated tornado in *Twister*. Over the short period covered by the reviews in this book, audiences have very quickly become used to miraculous imagery that less than a decade ago would have been unimaginable on film: melting men, sentient strands of water, stampedes of giant chicken-creatures through prehistoric landscapes, or of elephants through libraries. We've seen the human body wrenched out of shape, stretched and liquefied, and actors cloned into multiples of themselves. We've seen the Earth all but destroyed by spaceships a quarter of the size of the Moon, and then reprieved as if – in fantasy film's perennial get-out clause – it was *all a dream*. And, as yet, we haven't fully taken stock of how our eyes and imaginations are adapting to this onslaught of marvels – these fantasy objects laden with the irresistible gravity of the real, and at the same time with the elusive weightlessness of dream.

The rapid development of digital imaging technology, which had its first timid stirrings in the 1982 Disney experiment *Tron* and came of age in the late 1980s with *The Abyss* and *Terminator*

2, means that, social taboos apart, there are no longer many practical reasons why anything at all should not be represented on screen.[1] Computer-generated imagery (CGI) covers the whole material range, from the huge, numinous, unarguably solid presence of dinosaurs in *Jurassic Park* to the miniature, seemingly banal and, above all, weightless – like the feather that floats over the opening credits of *Forrest Gump*. It's the very immateriality and weightlessness of the digital image, its independence of either physical or imaginative gravity, that makes it so versatile.

The aspirations of digital imagery are nothing short of Promethean. CGI is not simply used for effects that would otherwise be too expensive or arduous to achieve – the traditional role of special-effects technology – but specialises in feats that are impossible, unnatural. George Lucas knew what he was doing when he called his effects company Industrial Light and *Magic*. CGI aspires to master all those aspects of nature that are traditionally beyond control. It tames the animal kingdom, which has always been notoriously intractable for film-makers, causing pigs to speak (*Babe*) or summoning up whole cavalcades of jungle beasts (*Jumanji*). It can harness the extremes of the weather, most grandiosely in *Twister*, although even a demurely naturalistic film like *Sense and Sensibility* has benefited from its rain effects. And in *Independence Day*, it can create a vision of the apocalyptic sublime, as clouds of fire billow over Earth's cities.

CGI can also recreate, transform, mutilate the human body, as in the extravagant perforation of Goldie Hawn's midriff in *Death Becomes Her*; the woman-into-monster transformation in *Species*; the blubbery metamorphoses of *The Nutty Professor*, in which two versions of Eddie Murphy slug it out within one body. Digitals already offer the possibility of recreating the dead: *The Crow* and *Wagons East!* were both completed after the untimely deaths of their respective stars, Brandon Lee and John Candy, whose living images were digitally integrated into the film. More

[1] So far, for example, we have not yet seen a digital erection, although director Paul Verhoeven claims he offered to provide one to a bashful Kyle MacLachlan in *Showgirls*.

radically, virtual versions of Marilyn Monroe, Bruce Lee and George Burns are in development – and may yet break the ultimate Promethean barrier by creating from scratch convincing simulacra of human life: James Cameron has announced a hundred-million-dollar film called *Avatar*, which will feature fully digitised actors, or, in *Variety*-speak, 'synthespians'.[2]

It's easy to see why imagery of such enormity and ambition has caught on with film-makers, despite the still considerable cost of the technology. It's not just that such images raise the stakes of what can be represented, but that they are, to use the cliché, more real than the real. They are certainly more dynamic than the real – in purely visual terms, at once more precise and more plastic than physical matter can be. Their hyper-real presence brings reality into question, and makes it look a little half-hearted. *Jumanji*'s rhinos seem not merely as good as real ones but better, enhanced for dramatic effect; one of them even turns and winks at the camera. They are certainly more charismatic than the film's nominal star Robin Williams, who plays second fiddle to their destructive energy. It's no accident that the big effects films (*Jurassic Park*, *Twister*, *Independence Day*, *Species*) tend to favour second-rank or faceless stars; actors look like disposable, in-animate attractions next to these dynamic marvels. (The only star whose charisma has actually benefited from CGI is Jim Carrey in *The Mask*, who successfully rides the phenomenon by using his body as a vehicle for its effects, thereby making CGI into his own personalised prosthesis.)

It's too early to say for sure whether, as its most fervent adepts might claim, digitisation really is bringing about a Copernican revolution in cinema. It's hard to imagine quite what that revolution might consist of – a radical change in the type of images we see on screen, a change in the very way we perceive them, or simply a constant upgrading of the technology by which film

[2] The term has been copyrighted by the effects company Kleiser-Walczak Construction Co; see 'H'wood cyber dweebs are raising the dead', *Variety*, 4–10 November 1996. See also Pat Kane, 'How to remake a star', *Guardian Friday Review*, 17 January 1997.

images are created? What is certain is that we have become used to CGI remarkably quickly. Cinema's capacity for representing the unrepresentable seemed to have turned a corner only a few years ago, when we were first dazzled, indeed mystified, by apparitions like the watery tentacle of *The Abyss* (1989), the protean, mercury-sleek android of *Terminator 2* (1991) and, above all, the dinosaurs of *Jurassic Park* (1993), those quintessential images of impossible life miraculously fished out of the stream of history. But already we are so used to these marvels that we tend to be disappointed by any new Hollywood blockbuster that doesn't feature digital manipulation to a spectacular degree. This process of domestication is already at work within *Jurassic Park* itself: it begins with the genuinely awe-inspiring sight of placid giants grazing in the hazy distance, and ends with the menacing velociraptors, which are no more than run-of-the-mill superlizards, crocodile-plated Freddy Kruegers.

We can't yet gauge what substantial effect this sudden glut of miracle is having on the film-goer's perception or imagination. But we can say that it represents a sudden and drastic change in the kind of illusion that film offers us. The tradition of cinematic *trompe-l'œil* since the work of silent pioneer Georges Méliès is based on the assumption that every illusion created on the screen has its ontological origins in some real event enacted in front of the camera – the magicianly stagecraft of Méliès's work, say, or the actual work of ink drawing in traditional cel animation. Méliès was one of the first to explore the possibilities of trickery within the camera, but, in the first instance, his films invoke and actually record a tradition of stage mechanics – of cardboard rockets, or actors cloaked in black to give the impression of disembodied heads and limbs. As late as the 1970s and early 1980s, the *Star Wars* trilogy, though it ushered in the age of digital illusion with the founding of effects house Industrial Light and Magic, was one of the last major projects to use the full array of traditional reality-based illusion, from matte painting to models.

In this tradition – let's call it 'analogue' filming, in parallel with the tape-and-vinyl technology that preceded digital sound recording – the act of filming disguises the original material nature of the event. It offers us a record of the event encoded in such a way that it provides a cue for our eyes and brain to participate in the work of illusion-making. Computer-generated imagery, on the other hand, may invoke the existence of a real object, but there is no guarantee that such an object ever existed; in fact, because CGI tends to specialise in the spectacular and fantastic, its use is practically a guarantee that the object *never* existed. The computer-generated image is purely the visual translation of a series of algorithms, by which the appearance of a solid object is conjured out of thin air – or rather, thin light – and then embedded in the texture of the film, compressed into the two-dimensional space of the celluloid frame.

Consider how far this takes us from the formulations of André Bazin, who in his 1945 essay 'The Ontology of the Photographic Image' argued that the power of photography, and therefore of film, was its ability to capture reality directly, with no other mediation than that of the photographic apparatus. Bazin locates photography in the tradition of art conceived as 'the preservation of life by a representation of life'[3]: 'For the first time, an image of the world is formed automatically, without the creative intervention of man.' He goes on to say, 'Photography affects us like a phenomenon of nature.'[4]

Bazin's arguments have been much contested, both theoretically and practically; whole schools of cinema exist that challenge the blithe assumption of cinema's realistic function. But digital imagery seems to shatter the primacy of the real entirely. No longer does a real object need to stand in front of a camera; in the digital world, we can sever as many attachments to the real as technology and our imaginations will allow. From a medium in which the human factor supposedly plays no part at all – or at least, takes a back seat to the laws of chemistry and optics that govern the photographic process – we arrive at one in which

---

[3] André Bazin, *What is Cinema?* trans. Hugh Gray (University of California Press, Berkeley, 1967) p. 10.
[4] Ibid., p. 13.

human creative invention is at its maximum, in which every aspect of the image is expressly fabricated.

Rather than being a simple 'preservation' of life, digital imagery aspires to be something more – its crystallisation, its liquefaction. It has the mystique of an alchemical process in which all matter, transmogrified through the medium of light, can become other matter: in which flesh becomes unstable, or passes through variously liquid, metallic or crystalline avatars. Digital imagery may as a rule incline to hyper-realism, but to hyper-realism at its most unstable. Any form, however complete, can morph into another; there's no reason why the most convincingly solid object, or indeed the whole screen, shouldn't suddenly dissolve into a shower of its constituent pixels (as it does in, say, *Super Mario Bros.* or the *Lawnmower Man* films, which explicitly if ineptly invoke the constructed, decorative nature of arcade-game or virtual-reality imagery). Little wonder that such images strike us as uncanny. Even more than Bazin's photography, CGI affects us as 'a force of nature' that can't easily be accounted for. In fact, one of the problems of CGI is that it unsettles the notion of authorship: we are no longer entirely sure where images come from. Should we attribute them to the director of a film (can we honestly talk about *Spielberg*'s dinosaurs or *Jan De Bont*'s twisters?), or are the real authors the effects houses that generated them – ILM, Digital Domain, Pixar? Or perhaps we should attribute them to the technology itself, as if to an invisible god, the ghost in the movie-machine?

Because these uncanny 'made objects' are so tightly integrated into the rest of the celluloid image as to be indivisible from it, there is no longer any firm distinction in the film frame between the real and the artificially generated – as there is, say, in *Who Framed Roger Rabbit*, where live action and animation coexist in the same space, interacting yet manifestly separate. In that film, we can easily read one set of images as being photographic and the other as simply graphic. But because hyper-realistic digital illusionism tends to level out all images to the same status within the frame, it does not invite us to play the same active part that earlier illusionism does. The trick is already performed for us. We can 'read' Méliès's beheadings as stage play, Mary Poppins's levitations as the wire-powered flight of Peter Pan panto, or Jessica Rabbit's sinuous sashaying as 'just the way she's drawn'. But with CGI at its most sophisticated, it's hard to read the digital object as anything *but* an object. We see the final sum but not the calculations, the product of the computing but not the computing itself; our eye can't read the programming, or even decompose the image into its original pixels, in the way that we might once have been able to decode a matte painting as painting.

Fred Raimondi, Visual Effects Supervisor at Digital Domain, makes the stakes perfectly clear: 'My goal is to do completely photo-real computer-generated scenes that are completely and totally believable – where the viewer would look at it and not be able to identify the technique, not be able to say, "Was that photographed, or was that computer-generated?"'[5] The aim, in other words, is to bypass the eye's critical faculty, so that the viewer will not only be unable to resolve the question of the distinction between reality and illusion, but will not even ask it in the first place.

Rather than engage in the making of the image, we're held spellbound by it, as in a car's headlights; the extreme precision of the object imposes on us a surfeit of data which our cognitive capacities, short-circuited, simply aren't up to analysing. Given enough information about the 'real' status of a dinosaur – the way it moves, the way its scales catch the light, the fact that its foot can apparently reduce a Land Rover to scrap metal – we are persuaded to ignore the obvious fact that such a monster cannot exist, and to accept it as 'perceptually realistic', to use Stephen Prince's term.[6]

Stunned, glutted and seduced into perceptual passivity, audiences are left with new appetites that constantly demand

[5] Interviewed in *Electric Passions*, Channel Four Television, 1996.
[6] Stephen Prince, 'True Lies: Perceptual Realism, Digital Images and Film Theory', *Film Quarterly*, Spring 1996, pp. 27–37.

stimulation. The sudden onslaught of the new imagery, and the speed with which the studios have latched onto digitals as the ultimate commercial weapon, recalls a similar explosion a century ago, the rapid world-wide proliferation of cinema in the years following the unveiling of the Lumière brothers' cinematograph. The history of Hollywood over the last five years is a rush towards constant improvement (you could say 're-armament'): towards bigger, more elaborately defined images; and towards more sophisticated technologies that can infiltrate the celluloid image more seamlessly. In fact, not to underrate audiences entirely, we are already learning to spot digital imagery, to detect it as a technique without necessarily ceasing to believe in the reality of what it shows us. There are some uses of CGI too coarsely integrated into a film to be plausible (*Eraser* and *Multiplicity* offer particularly rough examples); while the technique of morphing, the smooth slide from one form to another, is by nature too flagrant not to draw attention to itself. But seasoned film-goers are already attuned to sniffing out CGI even in its more subtle incarnations.

As CGI's shock effect wears off, it must be constantly renewed, leading to an inflation of imagery, to what has been called 'impact aesthetics', a visual culture in thrall to the shock of the new.[7] Occasionally, CGI does indeed come up with a spectacular novelty, and the shock waves duly hit the box-office. *Twister* – after *Independence Day*, the second most successful film in North America in 1996[8] – is a perfect emblem of the digital image at its most spectacular: its whirlwinds are nothing but swirling air, embodied in a two-dimensional construction of pure light, but they also remind us, against all expectation, how aggressively weighty such immateriality can be. Short of recapturing the awe evoked in those first few shots of *Jurassic Park*, CGI can at least

[7] Philip Hayward, quoted in Robin Baker, 'Computer Technology and Special Effects in Contemporary Cinema', *Future Visions: New Technologies of the Screen*, ed. Philip Hayward, Tana Wollen (BFI, London, 1993), p. 41.
[8] *Variety*, 13–19 January 1997.

find new ways to knock us off our feet; the digital arsenal is in the service of an increasingly warlike cinema of attrition.

As digitals rush towards ever more efficient magic, more dazzling apocalypses, the fabric of reality, as we're used to seeing it represented in cinema, is changing. It's hard to say what the overall change will have been over a decade of digital imagery, but already a diagnosis – admittedly, a somewhat alarmist one – is beginning to take shape. It seems as if the representable world were being invaded. We can trace three stages of digital encroachment into the cinematic image of the world; they are conceptual rather than strictly historical, since the types of imaging they represent overlap in different films, but taken together they provide a schema of the way in which the digital domain seems to be slowly becoming more like a digital dominion.

Let the first stage be represented by *Jurassic Park* – the first film to build its entire appeal on the shocking introduction of discrete digital entities into a recognisable real world, through the technique of compositing. The film's dinosaurs are fully integrated into the fictional world of the film as autonomous three-dimensional beings, but their existence does not threaten the coherence of that world. These digital beings are entirely believable creatures possessed of their own reality but, in a sense, safely contained within it; they are like marvels on display in a zoo or a theme park, *in* the world yet somehow suspended from it. It's this state that *Jurassic Park* explicitly dramatises: these creatures have come from an unimaginable elsewhere to make their logic-defying appearance in our world. In the film, the Park's dinosaurs have been created by technocrat-entrepreneur John Hammond (Richard Attenborough), who has had them cloned out of the minimal-unit material of DNA, just as the images of them have been generated by Industrial Light and Magic from the minimal unit of the pixel. In the story, the dinosaurs are contained in a theme-park environment; similarly, their terrifying image – a digital chimera with an amplified roar that is nevertheless capable of shaking rows of cinema seats – is safely contained within the narrow parameters of the two-dimensional film frame.

Arguably, this question of containment is the real theme of *Jurassic Park*. The film teases us with a speculation on what might happen if these apparently real images were to tear loose from the containing screen, just as Hammond's creatures threaten to break out of his Park.[9] What, *Jurassic Park* implicitly asks, would happen to the structure of visible reality if digital imagery were to break free from the bounds of the discrete object? The film has the familiar conservative thrust of much 'What if?' sci-fi; *Jurassic Park* glories in the computer's creations, only to conclude that information technology is ultimately an unpredictable ally, to be reined in to the maximum.

But what if the digital were to infiltrate reality, seep into it like a transforming virus? This is the possibility envisioned in the second stage of digitisation, embodied in *Forrest Gump*. The film's rewriting of the visible world is problematic, not so much in those virtuoso sequences that stitch Tom Hanks into period newsreel footage (simply a refinement of similar effects in Woody Allen's *Zelig*), but at those moments where the digital treatment is so discreet as to be clandestine, where it whittles away at represented reality, doctors it cosmetically. Most notoriously, digitals allow the film-makers to amputate the legs of actor Gary Sinise, playing a Vietnam war veteran – an assault on the body all the more devastating because it is undetectable. There is no dotted line at the knee, none of that fuzzy bordering we associate with traditional blue-screen work; and because most viewers are unfamiliar with Sinise as an actor, the incongruity of the effect can go unperceived in a way it would not have done if Tom Hanks had been the amputee.

This bloodless, scarless operation is one of the more drastic

[9] This is a scenario made even more concrete in the three-dimensional illusionism of the *Back to the Future* ride in the Universal Studios' theme parks in Hollywood and Florida; the public, 'flying' in a De Lorean car, experience the alarmingly vivid hallucination of being swallowed by a giant dinosaur. Digital Domain's *Terminator 2: 3D* show takes the audience's disorientation a stage further by mixing three-dimensional projection with live actors on stage, so that screen space and actual space merge unpredictably.

instances of digitals as an art not of creation but of erasure. The most common application of the digital cut-and-paste process is the 'painting-out' of safety wires in stunt scenes; it can also remove unwanted actors from shot, restore decorum to the cut of a swimsuit (*My Father The Hero*), or modify a bit of background product placement (*Demolition Man*).[10]

Forrest Gump doctors reality in more spectacular but equally imperceptible ways. The thousands of people that fill a baseball stadium in one of the film's more grandiose shots are in fact a crowd of extras photographed in one section of the stadium then digitally reproduced and re-applied to the image, pasted on like wallpaper. Unlike the obviously impossible images of *Jurassic Park*, nothing in this shot is impossible *per se* – there's no reason to think that a prestigious film-maker like Robert Zemeckis couldn't have afforded this many extras for the scene (or indeed, that he couldn't have managed some unusually complex airborne close-up tracking shots of the falling feather in the credit sequence). But digitals allow him to create all these images with unprecedented clarity and expediency, and, above all, to create them undetected.

In *Forrest Gump*, we can never entirely be sure what we're seeing. Where CGI's more ostentatious mirages flaunt their distance from familiar reality, the images of *Forrest Gump* seep into the real and merge with it. Clearly the film, as a comic-strip rewriting of recent American history, raises a new set of ethical questions about what aspects of visible reality it is appropriate for cinema to forge. These questions may be no different in kind to those that have always been asked about photography's power to falsify, but, at the very least, the stakes are raised immeasurably by the traceless nature of digital manipulation.

The third phase of digitisation might be legitimate cause for paranoia if it weren't, so far at least, a unique case. John Lasseter's *Toy Story* – made for Walt Disney by the digital production company Pixar – is the first feature film in which a digitally

[10] See *Premiere* (US), January 1996.

generated, convincingly three-dimensional world entirely supplants photographic reality. *Toy Story* was marketed simply as a de luxe upgrade of the traditional animation feature, perhaps for fear of the hi-tech angle scaring off the mainstream audience. But it represents rather more than that. In *Toy Story*, not only are the toy heroes digitally generated, but so are the backgrounds they move in; Lasseter and his team elaborate an entirely dynamic world in which objects and backgrounds are imbued with life, and the imaginary camera constantly shifts position, causing everything we see to somersault through a dizzying choreography of perspectives.

The eye so easily accepts *Toy Story* as being simply 'like' a cartoon, but more real, that once we start thinking about the film *as* a digital construction we become aware of something quite alarming – we realise it takes some considerable perceptual effort for the eye to read it consistently as such. The film's universe looks too perfect to be anything but autonomous, as if it had simply generated itself; it oppresses us with its plenitude, the suavity of its textures, its self-sufficiency – above all, with its coherence. Its objects both look real and obey real physical laws – they don't morph or dissolve, but interact as solids with the entirely con-structed universe they inhabit. This is no small matter: one of the great problems of such animation is to ensure that planes don't intersect where they shouldn't, that these mathematical abstrac-tions in the guise of solids actually behave like solids. The film's most extraordinary phenomenon is its simplest: the fact that when astronaut Buzz Lightyear lands on the floor he actually comes to a stop instead of passing through it like a ghost.

Toy Story presents us with a world designed from scratch, from its most basic physical laws up. It's a world indistinguishable from the real in one respect only: although it seems to obey the laws of the known universe, it is nevertheless stylised to resemble a two-dimensional cartoon miraculously pumped up to three dimensions, so that there is no chance of any viewer over five years old mistaking it for reality. After all, its inhabitants are toys. There's a simple, genre-driven reason for this: *Toy Story* is a

Disney film, and audiences need to be reassured they are still in the familiar corporate domain of Disney animation. But perhaps the film's benign nursery-idyll tone also serves to reassure us that there's nothing to fear, just yet – that the real is not yet being supplanted by this uncanny virtual universe. However, now that *Toy Story* has established a genre, it remains to be seen whether its successors will jettison the cartoon style and head towards more defined, and perhaps more alienating, simulacra. Viewer-friendly though it is, *Toy Story* already induces an uncanny malaise – the feeling of being shut inside a parallel, entirely hermetic reality.

Only the most paranoid speculation would suggest that *Toy Story*'s caricatural realism could ever supplant the real world photographed on film, but that's only because, for the foreseeable future, it will remain easier and cheaper to place real objects in front of a camera than to construct simulacra from scratch. And yet . . . Digital researchers continue to fine-tune existing technologies in the hope of conquering all those areas that CGI does not yet have a purchase on. In doing so, they close the gap between the real and the digital worlds.

Toy Story already unsettles the distinction between reality and artifice. It makes the world of toys more true to life than the world of humans: the geometric domain of the nursery is scrupulously mapped out, textured and finished; the toys themselves, their musculature, movements, expressions, the textures of their wood, plastic and paper surfaces, are minutely defined and calibrated. But the film's human universe is markedly less convincing, almost shoddy. The scrubby back garden looks half-formed, sketchy, like an afterthought; humans are bulbous, robotic, excessively cartoonish. It's only the natural universe that looks as if it was knocked up on a computer.

Here, the film is primarily making witty capital out of a specific limitation of computer imagery. Digitals still don't quite have the measure of organic material. Forms that can be reduced to geometric planes and curves are manageable: it's relatively easy to gather data about them, assemble composites of relevant shapes and then wrap textures around them. Organic forms (flesh, hair, vegetable matter) are much more complex and elusive than the inorganic (plastic or metal). Nevertheless CGI continues its assault on unconquered terrain. For the lion's mane alone in *Jumanji*, it took three months for ILM to create the appropriate software and then another five to generate the hair itself. Never mind that the result looks entirely unconvincing; what is impressive is its sheer tactile abstraction, like a mass of optical-fibre tentacles swaying underwater. Again, as with *Toy Story*, the film's narrative provides its own alibi for this artificial appearance. This doesn't look like a real lion, because it isn't: it is pure manifestation, a demon sprung fully formed out of a satanic board game. Still, it does suggest that the technology's limitations might supply a new strain of kitsch: if it can't always rival the real, digitisation might at least aim at the aesthetic of the lava lamp.

Such serendipitous misfires apart, CGI continues to colonise every field of visual expertise in which there remain objects to be quantified. It's as if everything needs to be duplicated and represented, as if no object will have taken its place in the visible universe until all its available data have been logged and its parameters reproduced. There's an encyclopaedic thrust here, as if the sum of objects in the world were gradually being inventoried and added to the digital repertoire. This emphasis on the replicable and the visible has its history; James Roberts points out that CGI is the latest stage in a project of visual research that began with Renaissance theory of perspective, and the culmination of a visual ideology in which 'the equation of what something is with what it means allows very little scope for any other reality than the optical'.[11]

The problem becomes apparent in the ontology of the digital as opposed to the photographic object. A traditional approach to the status of the object in film stresses the immediacy of its photographic capture, as if, to echo Bazin's terms, the object were simply embalmed in celluloid. The object appears to have soaked

[11] 'The Story of the Eye', *Frieze* 29, June–August 1996.

directly into the grain of the image, preserving its autonomy in the process. Consequently, the celluloid image always retains a degree of arbitrariness, each shot being obliged to cope with objects *as they are*. The film-maker's job is to control the extent of this arbitrariness, through framing, lighting, camera position, use of colour – all of which limit the object's tendency to be what it happens to be, and coerce it into being what the film-maker wants it to be.

But the object refuses to be brought to heel; once it is incorporated into the image, certain aspects of it will always be beyond the camera's control. A thing always carries an un-quantifiable surplus of meaning beyond the primary meaning for which it is destined. This surplus can include an actor's look and all the intangibles that comprise 'charisma', including associations carried over from his or her other films, which a viewer is free to read into the image. It can include the tendency of objects and people to be in not quite the right place at the right time, or con-tingencies such as the self-evident rubberiness of a rubber octopus; the films of Edward D. Wood Jr, in fact, provide a primer of the ways in which the intransigent object-ness of an object can eclipse the symbolic service into which a film-maker tries to press it.

Digitisation would seem to provide a foolproof method of disciplining the rebelliousness of things. The cut-and-paste func-tion can edit out accidents entirely. No more of those unpre-dictable passing dogs that enlivened Italian neo-realism, or strik-ing faces in crowds, as in *Les Enfants du Paradis*; in the new school of French costume drama, exemplified by Jean-Paul Rappeneau's *The Horseman on the Roof* (*Le Hussard sur le toit*), obtrusive extras are mercilessly excised. In this ruthless new world, only the strictly relevant objects are there for our attention. But by reducing the field of our attention, digitals also reduce the potential resonance of the image. In a film entirely controlled by the principle of relevance, it would be futile to look for the *some-thing extra* that viewers thrive on sniffing out; we'd find nothing except what we're given. What we see really would be what we get: no reality other than the optical.

Meaning is even more harshly constrained in those objects that are entirely digitally generated. Such an object can't get into the frame in the first place except as the result of a rigorously conceived set of calculations that determine its action and appearance down to the last detail. A digital image of the simplest natural object – a chunk of rock, say – is not simple at all, but a complex set of planes and curves that has had to be exhaustively analysed before it can have any objective existence, any 'perceptual reality'. For the rock to exist at all, digital artists have to use procedures such as ray tracing, reflection mapping, texture mapping; have to analyse its light properties, the way it would move, its degree of flexibility. The digital object is absolutely intended, determined; its only properties are those that are deemed essential. You could say that CGI implies a theological perspective, in which every object is the creation of a deity entirely in control of its faculties and which leaves nothing to chance – which mercilessly suppresses chance, in fact.

But what space do such creations leave for vagaries of the viewer's eye? Images that come to the screen charged with some degree of indeterminacy allow for idiosyncrasies of critical perception. When certain real objects in the frame distract our attention from others, or when an object's peripheral properties seem more striking than those that are supposedly its principal ones, we know that we have a certain scope for reading the image. We may choose to read the marginalia rather than the main text, or to ignore the distinction between text and marginalia altogether. We may be transfixed by the passer-by in the background rather than the star making the big speech; in fact, Robert Altman has developed a whole style out of our tendency to watch the 'wrong' person, listen to the 'wrong' conversation.

Within the limits determined by a film's discourse (narrative or non-narrative, realist or anti-realist), an object on screen is normally free to signify in whatever way the viewer is prepared to allow. In pre-digital representation (alarming but true: we can already talk about the 'pre-digital'), an object can literally represent itself, but it can also represent other things, depending on the rules of interpretation set by the context. The sea in Fellini's *Casanova* is clearly an expanse of plastic sheeting, but it is also a sea; the ambivalence does not have to be resolved.

But such ambivalence is foreign to the digital realm. A computer-generated object is caught within the strict bounds of its own appearance, simply because so much rigorous calculation has gone into constructing that appearance; the digital object is not perfected but *sur-fected*, saturated with its own tautological being. It is what it is; it can't be anything else. Except in such cases as *Jumanji*'s cartoonish lion, which make a virtue of their imperfection, the digital object cannot be anything other than literal and integral; its every aspect is required to cohere un-equivocally with the whole, and the whole to cohere with the larger picture it is incorporated into.

We are not required as viewers to take stock of such an object as potential material for metaphor; in fact, we're discouraged from doing so. We're simply asked to acknowledge the fact that the object has been made to exist. Any ambivalence, any symbolic or metaphoric potential in an object, is ruled out from the start. This goes side by side with another development: since there is no longer anything that technology cannot represent, there is no longer any need to allude to the unrepresentable, and so no need for symbolism, which developed in cinema both as a way of addressing the unspeakable and as a way round physical or financial restraints.

Hence the extraordinary lack of resonance that makes the new digital epics so frustrating. How is it, for example, that a film like *Twister* moves us so little? It is, after all, a classic example of what used to be called 'the cinema of wonder'; it does, after all, depict a series of extraordinary natural phenomena, the grandest of which is referred to by one character as 'the finger of God'. After such a metaphysical hard sell, how is it that *Twister*'s giant whirlwinds produce so little sublime awe? Certainly, there are obvious flaws in such films' economy – the technology is so expensive that the effects need to be cost-effective, that is, as visible as possible. Too bad if that means sidelining all the things that once might have been considered the backbone of such a film: plot, character, suspense. This is a comparatively new development – consider the extraordinarily slow-burning build-up of *Close Encounters of the Third Kind*, then compare the prosaic on-with-the-show pacing of *Jurassic Park*.

It might be said that the fault with the new spectacle lies in the way it is mobilised – *Independence Day* might conceivably have achieved some sense of holy terror if only the film hadn't been pitched at such a hysterical level of flag-waving crassness. But the deeper reason for the hollowness is in the nature of the images themselves. There is no longer any sense of trepidation in the prospect of seeing 'the finger of God', because we know that if Jan De Bont wants to show us that finger he can. The sublime comes pre-programmed, at a price, and that price is only partly financial; symbolic resonance is the first casualty. The very idea of representing a massive intergalactic nemesis seems to lead inexorably to transcendental bathos – *unless*, perhaps, we can be persuaded that some extraordinarily brazen feat of Mélièsesque gimcrackery is being pulled off before our eyes. I suspect it's in the nature of cinema that Moses parting the Red Sea with divine powers will always be less impressive than Cecil B. DeMille doing it with smoke and mirrors and a lot of audience goodwill.[12]

It's plausible to imagine that, over the next few years, the inflation of hyper-real illusion will result in audiences so jaded that there will be a massive backlash against digital fantasy;

[12] To be fair, *Independence Day* does indeed use such gimcrackery; it mixes CGI with more traditional forms of sci-fi special effect, including matte painting and models, and its technical aspects were publicised as being a return to the *Star Wars* tradition of artisanship. In fact, some reviewers, discerning an opaque creakiness to some of the effects, saw the film as an overtly camp pastiche of 1950s sci-fi B-movies. I personally couldn't see that any of the film's other effects fell short of CGI's standard of seamlessness, and felt that all its effects, digital or not, elicited that passive perceptual response I have described here. I'd argue that any film prominently featuring digital spectacle tends to put us into that passive mode of perception. CGI's effect is so persuasive that it engulfs a film; we see it even when it isn't there.

viewers will want guarantees that they are seeing reality itself, with a minimum of mediation and adulteration, and the more extreme the better. There are already signs that this is beginning to happen. The 1996 US box-office hit *Rumble in the Bronx*, a vehicle for Hong Kong's Jackie Chan, was prominently advertised as featuring 'the action star who does all his own stunts'. You can see the appeal of such a star when Hollywood's leading muscle-men increasingly palm off their audiences with feats that were clearly performed on computer consoles in Burbank.

If real action, why not real sex, and real pain too – no longer the contortions of digital morphing, but the body itself explored to its physical limits. Cases of actors putting on weight and taking the punches, like De Niro in *Raging Bull*, will no longer be Method anomalies but the norm; acting will become a form of brutal body art. It will no longer be enough to see an actor's legs digitally severed; he'll have to do it for real, or, at the very least, simulate amputation as torturously as Lon Chaney would have done in his day.

This new cult of the real will be pornographic, in fact – porno-graphy being the form of cinema that most fetishises the real, or at least the promise of it. Post-digital pornographic realism will value performance over simulation, insist on real taboo-breaking, real come-shots, or, in the case of that apocryphal *maudit* sub-genre the snuff movie, real death. There's no reason, indeed, why any of these extremes shouldn't eventually become mainstream, just as figures of physicality and mortality have begun to enter the mainstream of art debate from the performance margins – from the health-threatening, body-stretching art of performers like Stelarc, Ron Athey, Orlan, who respectively use prosthetics, blood-letting and surgery in ways we couldn't yet easily tolerate if we saw them on a cinema screen.

Such nightmare hyper-literalism would certainly provide that material weight that computer-generated imagery promises but so frustratingly denies us. Still, before we take that route of muscle and blood, perhaps there's room to salvage the immateriality of digitals for more fruitful use. At the risk of invoking some vaporous idealist code of aesthetics, I'd say there's still every possibility for CGI to be used in the service of poetry – by which I mean, simply, to create images that are not shackled to the sensationalist hyper-real but have some consciousness of their own texture and constructedness. Some directors working outside mainstream realism have tried, and it hasn't always worked: morphing has been used by Peter Jackson in his psychosexual drama *Heavenly Creatures* and by Terence Davies in *The Neon Bible*, and in both cases the effect was less to startle you with the images than to impress on you that the directors had suddenly acquired an effects budget.

A more successful 'invisible' use of digitals was the creation of snowfall in the Coen Brothers' *The Hudsucker Proxy* – it at once looked like real snow and at the same time tended to a Christmas-card abstraction in keeping with the film's stylisation. Another avenue was the densely unreal vision of Jeunet and Caro's *The City of Lost Children*, which uses the full range of digital effects – morphing, cloning, entirely created objects – to create an entirely self-enclosed picture-book universe. A residue of visual literalism may undermine the film's aspirations to the texture of dream, but nearly all its images are charged with some cultural allusion or other – Gustave Doré's engravings, Marcel Carné's films, *Tintin* comics and, above all, the Méliès tradition. What the film loses in being too concrete, it gains by placing CGI within a cultural history, and by drawing attention to itself as a performance of illusion-making, rather than just illusion provided ready-made.

There is also the option – practically unexplored in the mainstream, for obvious reasons – of using computer effects to loosen the hold of realism altogether and explode the economy of the film frame. In *Prospero's Books* and *The Pillow Book*, Peter Greenaway fragments the image, critically measuring the signifying power of the screen against other readable surfaces – painting, books, the human body. The latter film, in particular, consciously offers itself as a provocative if overly aesthetic manifesto for a new digital cinema, being as close as film has come to the multi-dimensional density of text and image offered by CD-ROM.

Such examples may seem to point towards a strain of art cinema that is becoming increasingly unfashionable, and which may soon be quite unfeasible in commercial terms, unless some massive change occurs in the cost of CGI, or some radically new funding system comes into effect world-wide. To be realistic, the signs are that digital research will continue to lead us into the questionable utopia of the theme-park ride. But even in the mainstream, there's scope for more imagination. In most respects, the Jim Carrey comic-book adaptation *The Mask* is commercial spectacle at its most pedestrian, yet there's a mercurial quality to its use of digitals that almost redeems the film. *The Mask* exceeds its entirely ordinary brief in the way that the colour green becomes its central fixation, almost its protagonist – the colour of the Mask's demonic face, and of the whirlwind he whips up in his transformation scenes. The film shamelessly recycles gags from old Tex Avery cartoons like *Red Hot Riding Hood* – the lolling tongue, the eyes popping out and remaining suspended in mid-air – and applies them in three dimensions to a human figure. In *Roger Rabbit*, cartoon was simply integrated into the real world; here it has escaped its restraints and formed a hybrid with the real, neither drawn nor photographic, but formed from the elasticity of light and colour.

A more thorough infiltration of the real by cartoonish CGI is accomplished by Tim Burton's *Mars Attacks!* Its hordes of little green men are ostentatiously impossible figures, whose cartoon nature is derived from a series of early 1960s trading cards. They belong neither on Planet Earth nor in the stable terrestrial reality that we expect from earth-invasion sci-fi, and which we find in the film's bullish counterpart, *Independence Day*. Inside their spacecraft, Burton's Martians inhabit a digital realm that is clearly made of sculpted light, the same material that comprises the nursery of *Toy Story*. But as soon as they arrive on Earth, the encroachment begins: their presence makes the known world and all the actors in it, from Jack Nicholson down, look like an extension of the cartoon universe. The recognisable real becomes simply a screen for Burton's little green vandals to deface: their zap-guns, erasing and redrawing human bodies as blazing green skeletons, are a joyously macabre figure of the explosive power of the pixel, which need show no respect for the real.

Anthony Lane once characterised CGI at its worst as 'million-dollar graffiti, scrawled across a crumbling film in the hope of keeping it upright'.[13] I'd argue that the state of graffiti is *exactly* what computer imagery should aspire to, and both *The Mask* and *Mars Attacks!* represent tentative mainstream moves in that direction. It's time we saw the realism of both CGI and analogue photography being flawed, scratched, riddled with graffiti – not just scrawled across a film's surface, but stitched into its workings, distressing it from the inside. The appeal of such a prospect is that you can't yet imagine quite where that aesthetic might eventually lead; you can only imagine something more vibrant and disorderly than we've yet seen, and, with any luck, closer to the reckless cartoonery of Tex Avery than to the technocratic dullness of *Twister* or *Independence Day*. In his famous challenge to what would become the French New Wave, Alexandre Astruc called for the *caméra-stylo*, the camera as the film-maker's pen for writing in a new visual language. Digital technology can take us far beyond the pen – it can be word processor, airbrush, spray gun, even a blowtorch to combust the real entirely. It's up to film-makers to invent new kinds of writing that meet the challenge of this new tool – or perhaps just reinvent the pleasures of the graffiti scrawl.

[13] *Independent on Sunday*, 21 September 1991, quoted by Baker 1993, p. 45.

Filmography

Films reviewed

The Age of Innocence (Martin Scorsese, USA 1993) Daniel Day-Lewis, Michelle Pfeiffer, Winona Ryder, Richard E. Grant, Alec McCowen. Screenplay (Scr): Jay Cocks, Martin Scorsese. Photography (Ph): Michael Ballhaus. 138 mins.

Apollo 13 (Ron Howard, USA 1995) Tom Hanks, Bill Paxton, Kevin Bacon, Gary Sinise, Ed Harris. Scr: William Broyles, J.R. & Al Reinert. Ph: Dean Cundey. 140 mins.

Bad Boys (Michael Bay, USA 1995) Martin Lawrence, Will Smith, Téa Leoni, Tcheky Karyo, Theresa Randle. Scr: Michael Barrie, Jim Mulholland, Doug Richardson. Ph: Howard Atherton. 118 mins.

Bad Lieutenant (Abel Ferrara, USA 1992) Harvey Keitel, Peggy Gormley, Victor Argo, Frankie Thorn, Zoe Lund. Scr: Abel Ferrara, Zoe Lund. Ph: Ken Kelsch. 96 mins.

Bandit Queen (Shekar Kapur, India/UK 1994) Seema Biswas, Nirmal Pandey, Manjoj Bajpai, Rajesh Vivek, Raghuvir Yadav. Scr: Mala Sen. Dialogue: Ranjit Kapoor. Ph: Ashok Mehta. 120 mins.

Batman Forever (Joel Schumacher, USA 1995) Val Kilmer, Tommy Lee Jones, Jim Carrey, Nicole Kidman, Chris O'Donnell. Scr: Lee Batchler, Janet Scott Batchler, Akiva Goldsman. Ph: Stephen Goldblatt. 120 mins.

Benny's Video (Michael Haneke, Austria/Switzerland 1992) Arno Frisch, Angela Winkler, Ulrich Mühe, Ingrid Stassner. Scr: Michael Haneke. Ph: Christian Berger. 110 mins.

The Big Sleep (Howard Hawks, USA 1946) Humphrey Bogart, Lauren Bacall, John Ridgley, Martha Vickers, Dorothy Malone. Scr: William Faulkner, Leigh Brackett, Jules Furthman. Ph: Sid Hickox. 114 mins.

Blade Runner (Ridley Scott, USA 1982; *The Director's Cut* 1992) Harrison Ford, Rutger Hauer, Sean Young, Edward James Olmos, Darryl Hannah. Scr: Hampton Fancher, David Peoples. Ph: Jordan Cronenweth. 117 mins.

Blue (Derek Jarman, UK 1993) Voices: John Quentin, Nigel Terry, Derek Jarman, Tilda Swinton. Scr: Derek Jarman. 76 mins.

Candyman (Bernard Rose, USA 1992) Virginia Madsen, Kasi Lemmons, Xander Berkeley, Tony Todd, Vanessa Williams. Scr: Bernard Rose. Ph: Anthony B. Richmond. 99 mins.

Casper (Brad Silberling, USA 1995) Christina Ricci, Bill Pullman, Cathy Moriarty, Eric Idle, Chauncey Leopardi. Scr: Sherri Stoner, Deanna Oliver. Ph: Dean Cundey. 100 mins.

Clerks (Kevin Smith, USA 1994) Brian O'Halloran, Jeff Anderson, Marilyn Ghigliotti, Lisa Spoonauer, Kevin Smith. Scr: Kevin Smith. Ph: David Klein. 92 mins.

The Conformist (Il Conformista) (Bernardo Bertolucci, Italy/France/Germany 1970) Jean-Louis Trintignant, Dominique Sanda, Stefania Sandrelli, Pierre Clémenti, Gastone Moschin. Scr: Bernardo Bertolucci. Ph: Vittorio Storaro. 113 mins.

Crimson Tide (Tony Scott, USA 1995) Denzel Washington, Gene Hackman, Matt Craven, George Dzundza, Viggo Mortensen. Scr: Michael Schiffer. Ph: Dariusz Wolski. 116 mins.

Damage (Louis Malle, UK/France 1992) Jeremy Irons, Juliette Binoche, Miranda Richardson, Rupert Graves, Leslie Caron. Scr: David Hare. Ph: Peter Biziou. 111 mins.

Dear Diary (*Caro Diario*) (Nanni Moretti, Italy/France 1994) Nanni Moretti, Jennifer Beals, Alexandre Rockwell, Renato Carpentieri, Antonio Neiwiller. Scr: Nanni Moretti. Ph: Giuseppe Lanci. 100 mins.

Dick Tracy (Warren Beatty, USA 1990) Warren Beatty, Glenne Headly, Madonna, Al Pacino, Dustin Hoffman. Scr: Jim Cash, Jack Epps Jr. Ph: Vittorio Storaro. 103 mins.

Eyes Without a Face (*Les Yeux sans visage*) (Georges Franju, France 1959) Pierre Brasseur, Alida Valli, Edith Scob, Juliette Mayniel, François Guérin. Scr: Jean Redon. Ph: Eugen Schüfftan. 90 mins.

Germinal (Claude Berri, France/Belgium/Italy 1993) Renaud, Gérard Depardieu, Miou-Miou, Judith Henry, Jean-Roger Milo. Scr: Claude Berri, Arlette Langmann. Ph: Yves Angelo. 158 mins.

Groundhog Day (Harold Ramis, USA 1993) Bill Murray, Andie MacDowell, Chris Elliott, Stephen Tobolowsky, Brian Doyle-Murray. Scr: Danny Rubin, Harold Ramis. Ph: John Bailey. 101 mins.

La Haine (*Hate*) (Mathieu Kassovitz, France 1995) Vincent Cassel, Hubert Kounde, Saïd Taghmaoui, Karim Belkhadra, Edouard Montoute. Scr: Mathieu Kassovitz. Ph: Pierre Aïm. 97 mins.

Heaven & Earth (Oliver Stone, USA 1993) Hiep Thi Le, Tommy Lee Jones, Joan Chen, Haing S. Ngor, Debbie Reynolds. Scr: Oliver Stone. Ph: Robert Richardson. 140 mins.

Indecent Proposal (Adrian Lyne, USA 1993) Robert Redford, Demi Moore, Woody Harrelson, Seymour Cassel, Oliver Platt. Scr: Amy Holden Jones. Ph: Howard Atherton. 117 mins.

Institute Benjamenta, or This Dream People Call Human Life (Brothers Quay, UK 1995) Mark Rylance, Alice Krige, Gottfried John, Daniel Smith. Scr: Alan Passes, Brothers Quay. Ph: Nic Knowland, Brothers Quay. 105 mins.

Jefferson in Paris (James Ivory, USA 1995) Nick Nolte, Greta Scacchi, Simon Callow, Gwyneth Paltrow, Thandie Newton. Scr: Ruth Prawer Jhabvala. Ph: Pierre Lhomme. 139 mins.

Junior (Ivan Reitman, USA 1994) Arnold Schwarzenegger, Danny DeVito, Emma Thompson, Frank Langella, Pamela Reed. Scr: Kevin Wade, Chris Conrad. Ph: Adam Greenberg. 110 mins.

Jurassic Park (Steven Spielberg, USA 1993) Sam Neill, Laura Dern, Jeff Goldblum, Richard Attenborough, Bob Peck. Scr: Michael Crichton, David Koepp. Ph: Dean Cundey. 127 mins.

Kika (Pedro Almodóvar, Spain 1993) Veronica Forqué, Peter Coyote, Victoria Abril, Alex Casanovas, Rossy de Palma. Scr: Pedro Almodóvar. Ph: Alfredo Mayo. 114 mins.

Last Action Hero (John McTiernan, USA 1993) Arnold Schwarzenegger, F. Murray Abraham, Charles Dance, Austin O'Brien, Robert Prosky. Scr: Shane Black, David Arnott. Ph: Dean Semler. 131 mins.

The Lion King (Roger Allers, Rob Minkoff, USA 1994) Voices: Rowan Atkinson, Matthew Broderick, Whoopi Goldberg, Jeremy Irons, James Earl Jones. Scr: Irene Mecchi, Jonathan Roberts, Linda Woolverton. 88 mins.

Man Bites Dog (*C'est arrivé près de chez vous*) (Rémy Belvaux, André Bonzel, Benoît Poelvoorde, Belgium 1992) Benoît Poelvoorde, Rémy Belvaux, André Bonzel, Jacqueline Poelvoorde-Pappaert, Nelly Pappaert. Scr: Rémy Belvaux, André Bonzel, Benoît Poelvoorde, Vincent Tavier. Ph: André Bonzel. 96 mins.

Mean Streets (Martin Scorsese, USA 1973) Harvey Keitel, Robert De Niro, David Proval, Amy Robinson, Richard Romanus. Scr: Martin Scorsese, Mardik Martin. Ph: Kent Wakeford. 110 mins.

Natural Born Killers (Oliver Stone, USA 1994) Woody Harrelson, Juliette Lewis, Robert Downey Jr, Tommy Lee Jones, Tom Sizemore. Scr: David Veloz, Richard Rutowski, Oliver Stone (story: Quentin Tarantino). Ph: Robert Richardson. 119 mins.

The Neon Bible (Terence Davies, UK 1995) Gena Rowlands, Diana Scarwid, Denis Leary, Jacob Tierney, Leo Burmester. Scr: Terence Davies. Ph: Mick Coulter. 91 mins.

Les Nuits fauves (*Savage Nights*) (Cyril Collard, France 1992) Cyril Collard, Romane Bohringer, Carlos Lopez, Corine Blue,

Claude Winter. Scr: Cyril Collard. Ph: Manuel Teran. 126
mins.

Orlando (Sally Potter, UK 1992) Tilda Swinton, Billy Zane, John
Wood, Lothaire Bluteau, Charlotte Valandrey. Scr: Sally
Potter. Ph: Alexei Rodionov. 93 mins.

Outbreak (Wolfgang Petersen, USA 1995) Dustin Hoffman, Rene
Russo, Morgan Freeman, Kevin Spacey, Donald Sutherland.
Scr: Laurence Dworet, Robert Roy Pool. Ph: Michael
Ballhaus. 128 mins.

Priit Pärn: Selected Films (Connoisseur Video, 1994) contains:
Breakfast on the Grass (1987) 27 mins; *Hotel E* (1991) 30
mins; *Time Out* (1984) 9 mins.

The Public Eye (Howard Franklin, USA 1992) Joe Pesci, Barbara
Hershey, Stanley Tucci, Jerry Adler, Jared Harris. Scr: Howard
Franklin. Ph: Peter Suschitsky. 99 mins.

The Quince Tree Sun (*El Sol de Membrillo*) (Victor Erice, Spain
1991) Antonio López, María Moreno, Enrique Gran, José
Carrtero. Ph: Javier Aguirresarobe, Angel Luis Fernández. 137
mins.

Reservoir Dogs (Quentin Tarantino, USA 1991) Harvey Keitel,
Tim Roth, Michael Madsen, Chris Penn, Steve Buscemi,
Lawrence Tierney, Eddie Bunker, Quentin Tarantino. Scr:
Quentin Tarantino. Ph: Andrej Sekula. 99 mins.

The Scent of Green Papaya (*L'Odeur de la papaye verte*/*Mui Du
Du Xanh*) (Tran Anh Hung, France 1993) Tran Nu Yên-Khê,
Lu Man San, Truong Thi Lôc, Nguyen Ahn Hoa, Vuong Hoa
Hôi. Scr: Tran Anh Hung. Ph: Benoît Delhomme. 104 mins.

Schindler's List (Steven Spielberg, USA 1993) Liam Neeson, Ben
Kingsley, Ralph Fiennes, Caroline Goodall, Embeth Davidtz.
Scr: Steven Zaillian. Ph: Janusz Kaminski. 195 mins.

The Secret Adventures of Tom Thumb (Dave Borthwick, UK
1993) Nick Upton, Deborah Collard, Frank Passingham, John
Schofield, Mike Gifford. Scr: Dave Borthwick. Ph: Dave
Borthwick, Frank Passingham. 60 mins.

Shadows and Fog (Woody Allen, USA 1991) Woody Allen, Kathy
Bates, John Cusack, Mia Farrow, Jodie Foster, Julie Kavner,

Madonna, John Malkovich, Kenneth Mars, Kate Nelligan, Donald Pleasence, Wallace Shawn, Lily Tomlin. Scr: Woody Allen. Ph: Carlo Di Palma. 85 mins.

Short Cuts (Robert Altman, USA 1993) Andie MacDowell, Bruce Davison, Jack Lemmon, Julianne Moore, Matthew Modine, Anne Archer, Fred Ward, Jennifer Jason Leigh, Chris Penn, Lili Taylor, Robert Downey Jr, Madeleine Stowe, Tim Robbins, Lily Tomlin, Tom Waits, Frances McDormand, Peter Gallagher, Annie Ross, Lori Singer, Lyle Lovett, Buck Henry, Huey Lewis. Scr: Robert Altman, Frank Barhydt. Ph: Walt Lloyd. 188 mins.

The Silences of the Palace (*Les Silences du palais/Saimt el qusur*) (Moufida Tlatli, France/Tunisia 1994) Ghalia Lacroix, Ahmel Hedhili, Hend Sabri, Najia Ouerghi, Sami Bouajila. Scr: Moufida Tlatli. Ph: Youssef Ben Youssef. 127 mins.

Sliver (Phillip Noyce, USA 1993) Sharon Stone, William Baldwin, Tom Berenger, Polly Walker, Colleen Camp. Scr: Joe Eszterhas. Ph: Vilmos Zsigmond. 108 mins.

The Tale of the Fox (*Le Roman de Renard*) (Wladyslaw Starewicz, France 1930–31) Voices: Claude Dauphin, Romain Bouquet, Sylvain Itkine, Léon Larive, Sylvia Bataille. Scr: Wladyslaw Starewicz, Irène Starewicz. Ph: Wladyslaw Starewicz. 65 mins.

Three Colours: Red (*Trois Couleurs: Rouge*) (Krzysztof Kieślowski, France/Switzerland/Poland 1994) Irène Jacob, Jean-Louis Trintignant, Frédérique Feder, Jean-Pierre Lorit. Scr: Krzysztof Kieślowski, Krzysztof Piesiewicz. Ph: Piotr Sobocinski. 99 mins.

Trespass (Walter Hill, USA 1992) Bill Paxton, Ice T, William Sadler, Ice Cube, Art Evans. Scr: Bob Gale, Robert Zemeckis. Ph: Lloyd Ahern. 101 mins.

Wes Craven's New Nightmare (Wes Craven, USA 1994) Robert Englund, Heather Langenkamp, John Saxon, Wes Craven, Miko Hughes. Scr: Wes Craven. Ph: Mark Irwin. 112 mins.

Wolf (Mike Nichols, USA 1994) Jack Nicholson, Michelle Pfeiffer, James Spader, Kate Nelligan, Christopher Plummer. Scr: Jim

Harrison, Wesley Strick. Ph: Giuseppe Rotunno. 125 mins.

Million-Dollar Graffiti

The Abyss (James Cameron, USA 1989; Special Edition 1992)

Babe (Chris Noonan, Australia 1995)

The City of Lost Children (*La Cité des enfants perdus*) (Jean-Pierre Jeunet, Marc Caro, France 1995)

Close Encounters of the Third Kind (Steven Spielberg, USA 1977)

The Crow (Alex Proyas, USA 1994)

Death Becomes Her (Robert Zemeckis, USA 1992)

Demolition Man (Marco Brambilla, USA 1993)

The Empire Strikes Back (Irvin Kershner, USA 1980; Special Edition 1997)

Eraser (Charles Russell, USA 1996)

Fellini's Casanova (*Il Casanova di Federico Fellini*) (Federico Fellini, Italy 1976)

Forrest Gump (Robert Zemeckis, USA 1994)

Heavenly Creatures (Peter Jackson, New Zealand 1994)

The Horseman on the Roof (*Le Hussard sur le toit*) (Jean-Paul Rappeneau, France 1995)

The Hudsucker Proxy (Joel Coen, USA 1994)

Independence Day (Roland Emmerich, USA 1996)

Jumanji (Joe Johnston, USA 1995)

The Lawnmower Man (Brett Leonard, UK/USA 1992)

Lawnmower Man 2: Beyond Cyberspace (Farhad Mann, USA 1995)

Mars Attacks! (Tim Burton, USA 1996)

The Mask (Chuck Russell, USA 1994)

Multiplicity (Harold Ramis, USA 1996)

My Father, The Hero (Steve Miner, USA 1994)

The Nutty Professor (Tom Shadyac, USA 1996)

The Pillow Book (Peter Greenaway, Netherlands/France/UK 1996)

Prospero's Books (Peter Greenaway, Netherlands/France/Italy 1991)

Return of the Jedi (Richard Marquand, USA 1983; Special
    Edition 1997)
Rumble in the Bronx (Stanley Tong, Hong Kong 1995)
Sense and Sensibility (Ang Lee, UK 1995)
Showgirls (Paul Verhoeven, USA 1995)
Species (Roger Donaldson, USA 1995)
Star Wars (George Lucas, USA 1977; Special Edition 1997)
Super Mario Bros. (Rocky Morton, Annabel Jankel, USA 1993)
Terminator 2: Judgment Day (James Cameron, USA 1991)
Toy Story (John Lasseter, USA 1995)
Tron (Steven Lisberger, USA 1982)
Twister (Jan de Bont, USA 1996)
Wagons East! (Peter Markle, USA 1994)
Who Framed Roger Rabbit (Robert Zemeckis, USA 1988)
Zelig (Woody Allen, USA 1983)

Other films mentioned
Aladdin (John Musker, Ron Clements, USA 1992)
Aliens (James Cameron, USA 1986)
Amadeus (Milos Forman, USA 1984)
Apocalypse Now (Francis Coppola, USA 1979)
Awakenings (Penny Marshall, USA 1990)
Bambi (David Hand, USA 1942)
Batman (Tim Burton, USA 1989)
Beauty and the Beast (Gary Trousdale, Kirk Wise, USA 1991)
Beetlejuice (Tim Burton, USA 1988)
Before Sunrise (Richard Linklater, USA 1995)
Being Human (Bill Forsyth, USA 1994)
La Belle Noiseuse (Jacques Rivette, France 1991)
Betty Blue (Jean-Jacques Beineix, France 1986)
Beverly Hills Cop (Martin Brest, USA 1984)
Blow-Up (Michelangelo Antonioni, UK 1966)
Blue Velvet (David Lynch, USA 1986)
Body of Evidence (Uli Edel, USA 1992)
The Bonfire of the Vanities (Brian de Palma, USA 1990)
Born on the Fourth of July (Oliver Stone, USA 1989)

Boyz N the Hood (John Singleton, USA 1991)

Bram Stoker's Dracula (Francis Ford Coppola, USA 1992)

Brazil (Terry Gilliam, UK 1985)

Cat People (Jacques Tourneur, USA 1942)

Cat People (Paul Schrader, USA 1982)

Un Chien andalou (Luis Buñuel, France 1928)

Child's Play 3 (Jack Bender, USA 1991)

A Clockwork Orange (Stanley Kubrick, UK 1971)

The Crazies (George A. Romero, USA 1973)

A Cry In The Dark (Fred Schepisi, Australia 1988)

Dances With Wolves (Kevin Costner, USA 1990)

Les Diaboliques (Henri-Georges Clouzot, France 1954)

Disclosure (Barry Levinson, USA 1994)

Do the Right Thing (Spike Lee, USA 1989)

The Doors (Oliver Stone, USA 1991)

The Double Life of Véronique (La Double Vie de Véronique)
    (Krzysztof Kieślowski, France 1991)

E.T. The Extra-Terrestrial (Steven Spielberg, USA 1982)

8½ (Otto e Mezzo) (Federico Fellini, Italy 1963)

Empire of the Sun (Steven Spielberg, USA 1987)

Les Enfants du Paradis (Marcel Carné, France 1945)

Europa (Lars von Trier, Denmark 1991)

The Exorcist (William Friedkin, USA 1973)

Falling Down (Joel Schumacher, USA 1992)

Fatal Attraction (Adrian Lyne, USA 1987)

Fearless (Peter Weir, USA 1993)

Female Trouble (John Waters, USA 1974)

Flashdance (Adrian Lyne, USA 1983)

The Flintstones (Brian Levant, USA 1994)

The Fly (David Cronenberg, USA 1986)

Frankenstein (James Whale, USA 1931)

The Good Earth (Sidney Franklin, USA 1937)

GoodFellas (Martin Scorsese, USA 1990)

Gremlins (Joe Dante, USA 1984)

Gremlins 2: The New Batch (Joe Dante, USA 1990)

Halloween (John Carpenter, USA 1978)

Hangin' With the Homeboys (Joseph B. Vasquez, USA 1991)

Hannah and her Sisters (Woody Allen, USA 1986)

Hard Times (Tempos Dificeis, Este Tempo) (João Botelho, Portugal/UK 1988)

The Heiress (William Wyler, USA 1949)

Hellraiser (Clive Barker, UK 1987)

Hellzapoppin' (H.C.Potter, USA 1941)

Henry: Portrait of a Serial Killer (John McNaughton, USA 1986)

Home Alone (Chris Columbus, USA 1990)

Home Alone 2: Lost in New York (Chris Columbus, USA 1992)

Hook (Steven Spielberg, USA 1991)

Housesitter (Frank Oz, USA 1992)

The Howling (Joe Dante, USA 1980)

Husbands and Wives (Woody Allen, USA 1992)

I Walked With a Zombie (Jacques Tourneur, USA 1943)

Invasion of the Body Snatchers (Don Siegel, USA 1956)

Invasion of the Body Snatchers (Philip Kaufman, USA 1978)

Jack (Frances Ford Coppola, USA 1996)

Jean de Florette (Claude Berri, France/Italy 1986)

JFK (Oliver Stone, USA 1991)

Juice (Ernest R. Dickerson, USA 1992)

The Jungle Book (Wolfgang Reitherman, USA 1967)

Kafka (Steven Soderbergh, USA/France 1991)

Killing Zoe (Roger Avary, USA 1994)

Kindergarten Cop (Ivan Reitman, USA 1990)

The King of Marvin Gardens (Bob Rafelson, USA 1972)

Last Tango in Paris (Bernardo Bertolucci, France/Italy/USA 1972)

Leap of Faith (Richard Pearce, USA 1992)

Lethal Weapon (Richard Donner, USA 1987)

Little Big Man (Arthur Penn, USA 1970)

Little Dorrit (Christine Edzard, UK 1987)

The Little Mermaid (John Musker, Ron Clements, USA 1989)

The Lover (L'Amant) (Jean-Jacques Annaud, France/UK 1992)

M (Fritz Lang, Germany 1931)

The Magnificent Ambersons (Orson Welles, USA 1942)
The Maltese Falcon (John Huston, USA 1941)
Marooned (John Sturges, USA 1969)
Mary Poppins (Robert Stevenson, USA 1964)
Menace II Society (Hughes Brothers, USA 1983)
Métisse (Mathieu Kassovitz, France/Belgium 1993)
Metropolis (Fritz Lang, Germany 1926)
Mrs Doubtfire (Chris Columbus, USA 1993)
Nashville (Robert Altman, USA 1975)
New Jack City (Mario Van Peebles, USA 1991)
Night and Fog (*Nuit et brouillard*) (Alain Resnais, France 1955)
Nightbreed (Clive Barker, USA 1990)
A Nightmare on Elm Street (Wes Craven, USA 1984)
Palombella Rossa (Nanni Moretti, Italy/France 1989)
Panic in the Streets (Elia Kazan, USA 1950)
Pink Flamingos (John Waters, USA 1972)
Platoon (Oliver Stone, USA 1986)
The Player (Robert Altman, USA 1992)
Poison (Todd Haynes, USA 1990)
Poltergeist (Tobe Hooper, USA 1982)
Popeye (Robert Altman, USA 1980)
Pulp Fiction (Quentin Tarantino, USA 1994)
Les Quatre Cents Coups (*The Four Hundred Blows*) (François
    Truffaut, France 1959)
Raging Bull (Martin Scorsese, USA 1980)
Raiders of the Lost Ark (Steven Spielberg, USA 1981)
Raise the Red Lantern (*Dahong Denglong Gaogao Gua*)
    (Zhang Yimou, Hong Kong 1991)
The Remains of the Day (James Ivory, UK/USA 1993)
RoboCop (Paul Verhoeven, USA 1987)
Scrooged (Richard Donner, USA 1988)
Serial Mom (John Waters, USA 1994)
The Serpent's Egg (*Das Schlangenei*) (Ingmar Bergman, West
    Germany/USA 1977)
sex, lies and videotape (Steven Soderbergh, USA 1989)
The Shining (Stanley Kubrick, UK 1980)

Shoah (Claude Lanzmann, France 1985)

Singin' in the Rain (Gene Kelly, Stanley Donen, USA 1952)

Sleep With Me (Rory Kelly, USA 1994)

Sophie's Choice (Alan J. Pakula, USA 1982)

The Spider's Stratagem (*La Strategia del Ragno*) (Bernardo Bertolucci, Italy 1970)

The Spirit of the Beehive (*El Espíritu de la Colmena*) (Victor Erice, Spain 1973)

Straight Out of Brooklyn (Matty Rich, USA 1991)

El Sur (*The South*) (Victor Erice, Spain/Italy 1983)

Taxi Driver (Martin Scorsese, USA 1976)

Tetsuo The Iron Man (*Tetsuo*) (Shinya Tsukamoto, Japan 1989)

Tetsuo II: Bodyhammer (Shinya Tsukamoto, Japan 1991)

The Thing (John Carpenter, USA 1982)

This is Spinal Tap (Rob Reiner, USA 1984)

Three Colours: Blue (*Trois Couleurs: Bleu*) (Krzysztof Kieślowski, France 1993)

Three Colours: White (*Trois Couleurs: Blanc*) (Krzysztof Kieślowski, France/Poland 1993)

Tie Me Up! Tie Me Down! (*¡Atame!*) (Pedro Almodóvar, Spain 1989)

Tirez sur le pianiste (*Shoot the Pianist*) (François Truffaut, France 1960)

Tootsie (Sydney Pollack, USA 1982)

Top Gun (Tony Scott, USA 1986)

Total Recall (Paul Verhoeven, USA 1990)

Tous les matins du monde (Alain Corneau, France 1992)

True Lies (James Cameron, USA 1994)

True Romance (Tony Scott, USA 1993)

Twins (Ivan Reitman, USA 1988)

Uranus (Claude Berri, France 1990)

La Vie est à nous (Jean Renoir, France 1936)

Wise Blood (John Huston, USA/Germany 1979)

Wittgenstein (Derek Jarman, UK 1993)

The Wizard of Oz (Victor Fleming, USA 1939)

Yellow Submarine (George Dunning, UK 1968)
A Zed and Two Noughts (Peter Greenaway, UK/Netherlands
   1985)